THE LAST LOOKOUT ON DUNN PEAK

Fire Spotting in Idaho's St. Joe National Forest

Nancy Sule Hammond

Basalt Books
Pullman, Washington

Basalt Books
PO Box 645910
Pullman, Washington 99164-5910
Phone: 800-354-7360
Email: basalt.books@wsu.edu
Website: basaltbooks.wsu.edu

All photographs are the property of the author unless otherwise indicated.

Library of Congress Cataloging-in-Publication Data
Names: Hammond, Nancy Sule, author.
Title: The last lookout on Dunn Peak : fire spotting in Idaho's St. Joe
    National Forest / Nancy Sule Hammond.
Description: Pullman, Washington : Basalt Books, 2023. | Includes
    bibliographical references.
Identifiers: LCCN 2023004281 | ISBN 9781638640080 (paperback)
Subjects: LCSH: Hammond, Nancy Sule. | Women fire lookouts—Idaho—Saint
    Joe National Forest—Biography. | Forest fires—Detection—Idaho—Saint
    Joe National Forest—Anecdotes. | Saint Joe National Forest
    (Idaho)--Biography. | BISAC: BIOGRAPHY & AUTOBIOGRAPHY /
    Personal Memoirs | HISTORY / United States / State & Local / West
    (AK, CA, CO, HI, ID, MT, NV, UT, WY)
Classification: LCC SD421.375 .H36 2023 | DDC
    634.9/618097969—dc23/eng/20230405
LC record available at https://lccn.loc.gov/2023004281

Basalt Books is an imprint of Washington State University Press.

The Washington State University Pullman campus is located on the homelands of the Niimíipuu (Nez Perce) Tribe and the Palus people. We acknowledge their presence here since time immemorial and recognize their continuing connection to the land, to the water, and to their ancestors. WSU Press is committed to publishing works that foster a deeper understanding of the Pacific Northwest and the contributions of its Native peoples.

On the cover: Don Hammond working on the Dunn Peak lookout tower, 1972. Image by Nancy Sule Hammond.
Cover design by Jeffry E. Hipp

For my parents, Jolan and Stephen Sule

Köszönöm, thank you.

CONTENTS

PREFACE

Don and I met because he failed ninth grade. In September 1964, he should have been on active duty with the U.S. Navy. Instead he was a high school senior dancing with me, a junior. His left arm held me tight around my waist. I snuggled my head against his shoulder. We bonded with an immediate chemistry. We'd been married for forty-nine years before we realized that if Don had been promoted from ninth grade the first time, we might have married different people.

Don had dreamed of becoming a fire lookout for the U.S. Forest Service in the Pacific Northwest since he was a boy. I studied hard to be the first in my family to earn a college degree. We both yearned to live a life spiced with adventures, a life far from our polluted steel mill hometown of Bethlehem, Pennsylvania. We'd do whatever it took to follow our dreams.

My dream came true first. I graduated from Kutztown University in 1970 with a degree in biology. Two months later Don and I danced at our wedding. Our one-bedroom apartment had been converted from an appliance store. Don worked full-time at the Bethlehem Steel and part-time as a grocery store clerk. I ran quality control tests on disposable medical syringes. We scrimped and saved every penny. I washed and reused aluminum foil and plastic wrap. It would take more money than either of us had ever seen in one place to chase after Don's dream to be a fire lookout.

Don's dream came true in 1972. He and I followed the fire control officer's pickup truck to Dunn Peak Lookout on the St. Joe National Forest in Idaho. We took in the vista of mountain ridges that stretched to the Montana border on the horizon. Instead of the tall, coniferous forests we'd expected, a scarred landscape covered in low scrub brush loomed before us. Don and I had arrived on the St. Joe unaware of the forest's significance in America's wildfire history.

The fire control officer pointed toward Setzer Creek running through a ravine below the lookout. He described how at suppertime on August 21, 1910, more than twenty-eight temporary firefighters had lined up at the camp's cook tent to fill their bowls with beef stew. The men were out-of-work, blacklisted union copper miners. They'd ridden a train from Butte, Montana, to fight fires for $2.50 a day because they needed the money. The exhausted men sat to eat. Gale force winds rose and fanned the flames they'd worked all day to control. A swirling firestorm raced up the ravine toward their camp. There was no escape. Every firefighter, the cook, and the cook's dog burned to death.

The Great Fire of 1910, our nation's largest wildfire, blazed across parts of Washington, Oregon, California, Nevada, Montana, and Idaho. On August 20–21, the Big Burn, the deadliest and most damaging of the fires, swept through the forests along the St. Joe River and crossed the Bitterroot Mountains into Montana. More than four million acres of valuable western white pine and every tree, bush, and blade of grass in the fire's path were reduced to charcoaled stumps and ashes. Hundreds of men, women, and children were burned, suffocated, crushed, or cooked to death.

The Big Burn's devastation caused the Forest Service to adopt a policy in 1935 to put out every forest fire by 10 AM the morning after it was spotted. More than 8,000 fire lookout towers were constructed across America to support this policy. Most of the 992 towers erected in Idaho were concentrated on the St. Joe and Coeur d'Alene National Forests to protect the regenerating woodlands destroyed by the Big Burn. Dunn Peak's first permanent lookout tower had been erected in 1932. It was replaced in 1958 by the tower Don worked on.

Don had expected to be rehired for a second fire season as a lookout. But budget cuts and technology favoring air patrol over lookouts had forced the fire control officer to close three towers, including Dunn Peak. After 1972 the Forest Service only stationed temporary observers in the tower during storms or emergencies. Donald Thomas Hammond was the last lookout on Dunn Peak.

Don and I spent two more amazing summers working on the St. Joe National Forest on Middle Sister Peak Lookout in 1973 and 2010. These recollections of our lookout life and our other experiences span more than fifty years. They relate how the St. Joe Forest (now a part of the Panhandle National Forests), the U.S. Forest Service, and Don and I have changed.

Now journey back through time with Don and me. Drive primitive fireroads to the rocky summits of Dunn Peak and Middle Sister Peak. Climb the lookout towers' ladder-like see-through stairs, pace narrow catwalks cantilevered over open air thirty feet above the ground, and admire the panoramas of mountain peaks and forests spread out below. But beware, storm clouds are building and the forest is dry. Any lightning strike could ignite a raging wildfire...

Note: The fires of August 20–21, 1910, have several names. Ruby El Hult called them Fire Blitz in the Bitter Roots in *Northwest Disaster: Avalanche and Fire*, published in 1960. In 1978 Stan Cohen and Don Miller published *The Big Burn, The Northwest's Forest Fire of 1910*. Timothy Egan titled his 2010 bestseller *The Big Burn: Teddy Roosevelt and the Fire that Saved America*. Sandra A. Crowell and David O. Asleson named the fire The Devil's Broom in *Up the Swiftwater, A Pictorial History of the Colorful Upper St. Joe River Country*. Another name for the August fires is the Big Blowup. I chose the Big Burn because that was the name people in Avery, Idaho used in 1972 when Don and I first learned of the fires.

PART I

DUNN PEAK
LOOKOUT, 1972

1

WHEN YOU WISH UPON A STAR

One Saturday night a determined seventeen-year-old boy, possessed by an impossible dream, danced into my life. He recognized that he had to be at exactly the right place at precisely the right time to make his dream come true. No wishing star had enough power to overcome such astronomical odds. He had to achieve this wish himself, and he never quit trying. I was fifteen that night in 1964. My heart ached with loneliness. I'd prayed for months to find someone to love. I knew other boys who were smarter and richer and just as nice. But unlike them, this boy understood that I, too, had my own impossible dream.

Avery District's fire control officer found himself in a bind. Idaho's St. Joe National Forest was unusually dry for so early in the 1972 fire season. Thunderstorms were predicted for Monday night. The college student Wade had hired to be the fire lookout on Dunn Peak telephoned Friday morning to say sorry, he wouldn't be coming. Wade slammed down the receiver. Everyone in the office braced for the explosion. His face blazed crimson. Spit flew from his mouth. Somebody, he yelled, had better find him a new lookout by the end of the day, or else!

The thinning crew chief jumped at the chance to score points with his boss. He had the perfect candidate, a new guy on his crew. A city kid from Pennsylvania, as green as grass, but a hard worker. Every day for two weeks he'd bent the chief's ear about being a lookout. "And he's married," the crew chief enticed, because he knew that Wade preferred married couples on his lookouts.

Wade stabbed his finger toward the crew chief's face. "Then he's our lookout for Dunn Peak. You make damn sure he takes the job."

Thinning brush is blisteringly hot, dust-clogged, bug-infested drudgery. It was the only work Don could get with the Forest Service that summer. He muscled a chainsaw spewing gasoline fumes to chop down clumps of bushes and tree saplings taller than his head. He hauled the cuttings to a cleared area and piled them to be burned when the fire season was over. That Friday the crew broke for lunch under the shade of a tall fir, except for one guy who strapped a .44 magnum revolver to his hip and went off to scout for black bears. The crew chief drove up, strode toward the crew, and hollered, "Hey, Hammond, were you serious or bullshitting me about working on a lookout? 'Cause if you're serious I need to know right now."

On Sunday morning our compact 1970 Opel Kadett station wagon was loaded up through its roof rack. Don and I had squeezed in everything we imagined that two people and our Dalmatian, Misty, might need to survive the summer in a fire-lookout tower isolated in the forests of Idaho. I hooked the back-porch screen door, locked and bolted the kitchen door, closed and latched all the windows, and switched on a table lamp in the living room. I was a born worrier. I was nervous about coming back to our empty house in Moscow, a town in Latah County, in the Idaho Panhandle. I would be there alone, all by myself, for the first time in my life. I'd be on the lookout only on weekends because I had to keep my job at the University of Idaho. And we'd decided that Misty was better off on the lookout than alone in the house while I was at work. I trusted our next-door neighbor's promise to keep an eye out and make sure our cozy bungalow with pillars on the front porch stayed safe until I returned.

I unzipped my keyring from the inside pocket of my purse. I remembered how grown up I'd felt the day my mother entrusted me with my very own key to our back door. She warned me not to lose it. She waggled her finger at my nose to emphasize that she was serious. I understood without her telling me that if I lost my key and a homicidal maniac found it, unlocked the back door, and murdered us all in our beds, it would be my fault. I turned my key to engage the front door lock, twisted the doorknob, and pushed hard to double-check that the door was secure.

I lowered myself into our green wagon's black Naugahyde bucket seat, buckled my lap belt, opened the window just enough to let in a cooling breeze, unfolded an Idaho map on my lap, put on my sunglasses, and assumed my usual position as trip navigator. Don liked to drive, and I liked to let him. He asked if I was finally ready. I nodded yes. He turned the key in the ignition and steered our wagon toward the job that he'd dreamed of since he was a boy, a fire lookout for the United States Forest Service.

Our bungalow in Moscow, Idaho, 1972

We drove north on State Route 95 from Moscow. Moscow sits on the northern edge of a fertile geographical area called the Palouse. Rolling hillsides carpeted in summer-green stalks of unripe wheat soon merged with sun-dappled stands of pine and fir. We'd explored this area when we'd moved from Twin Falls ten months earlier. But Don's classes at the University of Idaho plus my two jobs had kept us too busy to venture east of the highway. I directed Don to turn right on Route 6 toward Potlatch. From there on we entered new territory.

Potlatch reminded us of a derelict Pennsylvania coal mining town. The bungalows on Nob Hill and the smaller houses downtown all had a sad facade of neglect. Charles Weyerhaeuser, the first president of the Potlatch Lumber

Company, had opened this company-owned community in 1907. Weyerhaeuser had expected that the benefits of two boarding houses, two schools, two churches, a hotel, store, bank, post office, and an opera house would encourage his employees to work hard. Saloons were prohibited. Potlatch was dissolved as a company town in 1950.

The lumber company's massive, decaying mill sat a short distance down the road. Built in 1903, the mill was said to have been the world's largest, powered by steam. It processed trees cut from the company's one hundred thousand acres of virgin western white pine, trees more than one hundred years old and up to two hundred feet tall. Fire, disease, and the post–World War II demand for houses had diminished Potlatch's supply of white pine. We drove past the mill's log yard. Long straight piles of timber, precisely stacked two stories high, occupied a fraction of the open space. Pulsating arcs of water kept the wood wet to make the bark easier to remove, the wood easier to saw, prevent fungus and mold from developing, and keep insects out. Some logs would be chipped to bits, hauled to Potlatch's pulp mill in Lewiston, and processed into toilet paper. (The Potlatch Lumber Mill would close in 1981 and be razed to the ground in 1983.)

I was thrilled to be starting our lookout adventure, the reason we'd come to Idaho. But I always imagined the worst. I pressed my finger hard on the razor-thin red line we followed on the map, certain that if I lost touch with our route we'd be cast adrift into the wilds of Idaho. Route 6 paralleled railroad tracks lined with empty cars designed to haul timber. Potlatch Lumber had completed the Washington, Idaho, and Montana Railway (WI&M) in 1906. The Milwaukee Road had purchased the line in the 1960s. Don and I thought it odd that in the middle of rural Idaho we were driving past towns and rail sidings named Princeton, Harvard, Yale, Stanford, Vassar, and Cornell. In 1860 an enterprising teamster had established Princeton, a pack train camp to haul supplies to gold prospectors in the mountains. He'd named the camp for his hometown of Princeton, Minnesota. The WI&M had named the post office in their depot Harvard to complement Princeton. An engineer had named a rail siding Cornell after his alma mater. College-aged sons of the company's managers who worked summers on the railroad had named other sidings Yale, Purdue, and Wellesley. It's said that two nearby sidings derived their names not from colleges but from settlers: Inman A. Stanford and James R. Vassar.

Don and I crossed the bridge over the Palouse River. Route 6 stretched ahead, arrow straight. Dense stands of tall, thin, regrowth western white pine, erect as soldiers, crowded in, consumed the edge of the road, and left no room for a car to pull over. I felt like we'd driven into a natural work of art. A stripe of cobalt blue sky topped the line of black macadam. Green needles crowned the perpendicular brown tree trunks that filled in both sides of the road. The entire composition receded in geometric precision to the vanishing point on the horizon. Sunlight strobed between the trunks on my right and stung my eyes.

Lumber mill and town of Potlatch Idaho, circa 1913
(University of Idaho Digital Initiatives, 457_202_2_444, MG 457,
Box 202, Folder 2. Donated by John D. Cress)

An Idaho log yard

In the thirty-five miles since leaving Potlatch, we'd passed the tiny town of Emida with its two rusting gas pumps, a lot of trees, and no other vehicle. Route 6 dead-ended at Route 3. I directed Don to turn left, north toward St. Maries. I cautioned myself to memorize these turns because I'd be my own navigator when I drove home alone. We crossed the St. Maries River at Mashburn. Several miles beyond, the fireplace aroma of burning pine rose from a small, independent lumber yard that occupied a flat clearing next to the road. The pleasing scent emanated from a conical steel teepee burner about thirty feet tall. The burner converted the lumberyard's scrap wood and sawdust to ash. At night North Idaho's teepee burners glowed like red hot mini-volcanoes and discharged blinking firefly embers high into the cool night air.

At lunchtime Don pulled into a gas station in St. Maries. We didn't know where we'd find the next station, so he topped off the tank while I used the restroom. We ate wrinkled hot dogs that had rolled on a grill all morning, washed them down with icy cans of cola, and let Misty stretch her legs. I spread out the map on the hood. A blue line even skinnier than the red one we'd been following turned east along the St. Joe River toward Avery, a town so small the mapmaker didn't fill in its dot. Don traced the blue line with his finger, checking to be sure I was steering him in the right direction.

Our path agreed on, we backtracked onto Route 3. We crossed the St. Joe, claimed to be the world's highest navigable river at 2,128 feet in elevation. Tugboats moored along the shoreline trailed what looked like massive brown lily pads. These brails were constructed from logs fastened end to end to form a boom that corralled sawn timber. The timber would be loaded onto log-carrying railroad cars and transported to the mill at Potlatch.

Don turned right onto the river road. Tall cottonwoods lined both riverbanks and shaded the deep water to ebony. The river here is called the "Shadowy St. Joe." Boats, from canoes to cabin cruisers, were moored to ramshackle docks in front of homey vacation cottages. Dirt tracks led back to red-stained barns made of logs that sagged next to weather-worn, cedar-shingled farmhouses. Further ahead, massive logs formed an arch to protect a bridge from logging trucks hauling timber piled high enough to damage its superstructure. Across the bridge the river ran shallower and faster and ceased to be navigable. Campgrounds and resorts dotted this stretch of the St. Joe, called "up the swiftwater."

Miles on, near Calder, the paved road ended in a wide lane of rough gravel. Even farther on, the gravel ended in a narrow dirt road that squeezed between a vertical cliff and a drop-off into the racing river. There were no

Log arch preceding bridge on the St. Joe River Road

The "shadowy St. Joe" River. This area of the river is called "up the swiftwater."

guardrails. Maintenance crews had dumped truckloads of boulders to fill in voids the river had washed away. Don swished the windshield wipers to clear off the dust our tires kicked up from the road. Despite the hot afternoon we closed the windows to keep the grit out of our eyes and from grinding between our teeth. Our first close encounter with a speeding logging truck taught Don to honk three sharp warning toots as we approached every blind curve. It had never occurred to me that driving to Don's dream job in a national forest would be dangerous.

Pennsylvania's only national forest, the Allegheny, is located in the state's northwest corner, far from our hometown of Bethlehem. Don and I had never been there. With no example to guide us, we'd equated national forests with wilderness areas, like those we'd seen Sunday nights on *The Magical World of Disney*. When we'd moved from Pennsylvania to Twin Falls, we discovered a national forest twenty-five miles south of town. We bought a backpack, canteens, and a compass to immerse ourselves in a rugged wilderness hike devoid of human intrusion. We arrived at the sign welcoming us to the Sawtooth National Forest and gaped in disbelief. Nothing blocked us from driving through. Two lanes of striped macadam continued past the sign into the scenic grandeur of the southern Sawtooth Mountains. Campgrounds, picnic areas, corrals for hunters who rode horses into the backcountry, parking lots for snowmobilers, and a small ski run with a cabin for equipment rental lined the road. We passed appealing trailheads, but we only got out of the car to use the restrooms. We'd counted on a wilderness experience. We felt disappointed.

In 1964 President Johnson signed the Wilderness Act, which protected 9.1 million acres from development by placing the land in the National Wilderness Preservation System. As a result, wilderness areas must remain free of roads and structures, and motorized equipment and mechanical transport aren't permitted. In 1972 Idaho's Selway Bitterroot Wilderness covered 1.1 million acres, the Craters of the Moon National Wilderness Area covered more than 43,000 acres, and the Sawtooth Wilderness more than 217,000 acres.

In 1972 Idaho's national forests were the Boise, Caribou-Targhee, Clearwater, Coeur d'Alene, Kaniksu, St. Joe, Nez Perce, Payette, Salmon-Challis, and Sawtooth. Recreation facilities in national forests and grasslands employ thousands of people. Recreation fees provide as much as half of the Forest Service's annual fee receipts. Fees for land use, timber, power, grazing, and minerals comprise the other half. The service also grants permits to commercially graze, log, mine, or trap animals. In Idaho, state game wardens enforce regulations to fish or hunt in national forests, including issuing licenses to kill big game species of moose, mountain goats, bighorn sheep, deer, elk, pronghorns, black bears, mountain lions, and wolves.

One slow-driving hour after we'd left St. Maries we crossed back to the north side of the river. The Avery District ranger station at Hoyt Flat was the first building we'd seen for miles. The drive in a sweltering car, our shoulders soaked with streams of Misty's drool, had worn the edge off our excitement. We opened the windows and took a few minutes to compose ourselves. We kissed for luck, then walked into the one-story cinder block building. Forest Service workers in pressed uniforms talked on push-button phones and typed on electric typewriters. Their break room had a refrigerator and a commercial coffee maker. It looked so normal. It gave me a glimmer of hope that living in a lookout might not be as primitive as I'd seen on TV. Wanda, the dispatcher, told us we could buy dinner at The Beanery in Avery, and we had a room for the night in the bunkhouse. Wade would meet us there the next day at 7:00 AM sharp to guide us to the lookout.

"We're driving, in our car?" I asked to confirm what Wanda had meant. I'd seen on TV where lookouts had to ride to their tower on horses with their suitcases tied onto a string of pack mules. With that worry relieved, my sense of adventure began to bubble back up.

Don drove east along the narrow V-shaped St. Joe River valley. Thick coniferous forests shaded the south side. We wondered why the mountainsides on the north were sun-drenched, covered only with scrub brush and a few scattered tall conifers. Avery squeezed onto the mud flats where the North Fork of the St. Joe flows into the river. It surprised us that the town wasn't built around a lumber mill, like Potlatch. Avery had been built by a railroad. Creosoted poles lined deserted tracks and supported a canopy of wires that connected to an abandoned roundhouse, a brick building where locomotives had been repaired. Most of Avery's other buildings were constructed of wood siding, all painted the same shade of brown. The paint peeled from neglect. We guessed an empty building with two plate-glass front windows could have been a general store; a multistory building, we surmised, a railroad dormitory. The train station and post office, still in use, anchored the downtown. On the river's south bank, modest homes clustered around a schoolhouse next to a playground.

Don and I both liked to learn the facts and stories behind what we were looking at. Don was a history major, and my mother often accused me of being too nosey. We wondered how a railroad town had come to exist inside a national forest. We'd explored the entire town and still had time before dinner. It was Sunday. The visitor center was open. It seemed a likely place to have our questions answered. The town historian was happy for a fresh audience. He pointed out old photographs hung on the walls and artifacts displayed in glass cases. He said the bunkhouse where we'd be spending the night had been built in 1928. The North Fork ranger station, next to the bunkhouse, had become a private residence in 1967, after the new ranger station had been built at Hoyt Flat. Then he explained why Avery is a railroad town.

In 1901 the directors of the Chicago, Milwaukee, and St. Paul Railroad had decided to build a 1,400-mile western extension to supply transportation to America's underserved northwest intermountain states. They incorporated the subsidiary Chicago, Milwaukee, and Puget Sound Railway to build an almost perfectly straight road that would extend from Evarts, South Dakota and cross the Missouri River at Mobridge. The line would continue through Montana and Idaho lands rich in agriculture, forest, and mineral wealth, and terminate at the lucrative ports of Seattle and Tacoma on Washington's Puget Sound.

In 1905 President Theodore Roosevelt had transferred America's forest reserves from the Interior Department to the Department of Agriculture. Gifford Pinchot, head of Agriculture's Department of Forestry, named his new organization the United States Forest Service. He wanted to emphasize his philosophy that America's forest reserves existed to serve the people and were not to be reserved from use. In Idaho's Coeur d'Alene Forest Reserve, Ranger Ralph N. Debitt had moved into the ranger station at Rocky Riffle, three miles downriver from the confluence of the St. Joe River with its North Fork. Debitt's wife Jessie managed the post office named in honor of Pinchot.

That year the St. Paul embarked on a record-setting schedule to lay the last rail on its mainline extension by April 1, 1909. Three sections would be worked simultaneously: Mobridge, South Dakota to Butte, Montana; Butte to Pinchot, Idaho; and Pinchot to Seattle and Tacoma, Washington. By the line's completion workers would excavate 60 million cubic yards of material, drive 360,000 yards of tunnel, erect 20 miles of bridges, and lay 200,000 tons of 85 pound rails at a total estimated cost of $85 million. The chairman of St. Paul's Board of Directors declared that this expenditure contemplated a strictly first-class road in all respects.

The once peaceful forests around Pinchot overflowed with railroad surveyors, engineers, accountants, and payroll clerks. Local sawyers cleared a right-of-way for the rails and space for the roundhouse. Teamsters hauled timber to lumber mills. Carpenters erected a commissary, a beanery, bunkhouses, and office buildings. Families from as far away as West Virginia found work and lived in boxcars or wood-framed canvas tents. No saloons were permitted in federal forests, but cheap liquor flowed under the counter in sporting houses on the edge of town. Surveyors discovered that the railway's planned route ran right through the Rocky Riffle ranger station. The new North Fork station was completed clear of the tracks. The railway drove home its final spike on May 19, 1909.

Newly inaugurated President Taft did not see eye-to-eye with Pinchot and dismissed him as head of the Forest Service. William Rockefeller had been a major financer of the Chicago, Milwaukee, and St. Paul. He was also no fan of Pinchot. On February 14, 1910, six weeks after Taft had fired Pinchot, Pinchot, Idaho was renamed Avery, for Rockefeller's grandson. A rail siding was named Ethelton for his daughter. Avery, Idaho, boasted a growing population of about 250 residents. In 1912 the Puget Sound Railway conveyed its franchises and properties back to its parent company.

Between 1917 and 1920 the Milwaukee Road had electrified 656 miles of its main line from Harlowton, Montana, through Avery, to Seattle and Tacoma, the longest electrified rail lines in the world. The railroad brought prosperity to Avery. The town boasted two tennis courts, a new school with a gymnasium, and a peak population of 1,100 people. The Milwaukee Road's famed transcontinental Olympian and Columbian passenger trains stopped in town long enough to change engines. In the 1930s the Civilian Conservation Corps constructed the first roads into Avery. In the 1940s, powerful diesel locomotives began to overtake the Milwaukee's less efficient electrified technology. Avery began to decline. By the 1960s Avery's economy survived on recreation, the Forest Service, the remnants of the Milwaukee Road, and diminished timber cutting. The town historian told us that the Milwaukee Road planned to phase out its remaining electrified operations in the coming summer.

A few locals walked in to chat. The historian concluded our lesson with a wave of his arm that took in the whole town. "And most interesting of all," he said, "Avery survived the Big Burn in 1910." Don and I thanked him for the information and promised to return. An event called the Big Burn sounded exciting and dangerous. We wanted to learn more about it.

After the history lesson Don and I were hungry. We walked across the street hoping to find The Beanery. Don braced his feet on the wood-plank sidewalk and pulled open a heavy door covered with tar paper. A 5x7 note card tacked at eye level warned in thick black marker, "No Calks or Knives!" Don explained without my asking that calks are heavy, laced leather boots with metal spikes sticking out from the soles. The spikes give loggers traction as they scramble over fallen timber. I didn't need an explanation for the knives.

I'd grown up going to steelworker bars with my parents. Workers sometimes drank too much, itched for a fight, and reached for the knife tucked in their black leather engineer boots. Savvy bartenders knew how to cool things off. I never saw anyone pull out their blade. Don assured me that he'd packed his big fishing knife. Better safe than sorry, I agreed. The bartender said he only served grilled hot dogs and directed us to The Beanery.

Don and I walked into the knotty pine-paneled dining room. Dressed in our Pennsylvania-preppy chinos and button-down shirts, the locals knew right away that we didn't belong. The waitress spread the word that we were the new lookouts for Dunn Peak and the diners turned back to their meals. Don and I savored each mouthful of tender chicken-fried steak with a side of crispy hash browns, all smothered in a velvety dark brown gravy. Dessert was vanilla ice cream melting over apple pie warm from the oven. We ordered three plain hamburgers to go, two for Misty's dinner and one for her breakfast, because neither of us wanted to dig her kibble out of the crammed back end of our station wagon. Our last stop before the bunkhouse was Sheffy's store for gasoline. We gulped at the inflated price but filled the tank because Sheffy's had the only public gas pumps in town.

Wanda had directed us where to turn north off the river road to find the bunkhouse. The short steep climb dead-ended in trees on the side of the mountain. We parked in front of an imposing two-story structure built from thick logs. We untied our suitcases from the roof rack, knocked off the road dust, let Misty out, walked in through the door, and hollered hello. The fire crew paused their nickel-and-dime poker game at the kitchen table, said hello back, scratched Misty's ears, and directed us upstairs to our room. Don noticed that the door didn't have a lock. Like a scene from a scary movie, he wedged the wooden desk chair under the doorknob even though no one on the fire crew looked dangerous to me. Misty would bark if anyone tried to break in. Besides, we were in the middle of a huge forest. Despite my anxiety, even I doubted that Jack the Ripper lurked about. I thought it was sweet that Don was so protective. He scrambled onto the top bunk. Misty curled up on the braided rug next to my bunk. The beds had only scratchy grey wool Army blankets for warmth against the chilly night, but the cotton sheets tucked around the thin mattresses were soft and clean. Sleep came fast and hard our first night in the St. Joe Forest.

Eighteen months earlier Don and I had followed his wishing star into the unknown. Our families were sad when we left Pennsylvania, but no one had told us not to go. I think they all recognized that one day Don and I would turn our dreams into action and head for the horizon. We'd struck out for Idaho completely on our own, or so we thought. We didn't realize when we left that we carried our support system with us. When we ran into problems, help from the people who loved us was quick, unquestioning, and steadfast.

Avery District Bunkhouse and Old North Fork Ranger Station

Every few weeks my mother sent us a care package. Don and I smoothed out the crumpled newspaper she'd used for cushioning and saved it to read the local news later. My mother had wrapped each treat in layers of aluminum foil and plastic wrap, wound it with yards of Scotch tape until it looked like a mummy, and twist-tied it in a plastic bag. We guessed at what might be hidden inside. It could be Don's favorite Oreos, Reese's Peanut Butter Cups for me, Wrigley's Spearmint gum to share, or a Christmas surprise like her homemade Hungarian poppy seed or walnut rolls. My mother spent time and effort to put our care packages together. Then she carried the heavy boxes five city blocks to mail them at the post office. She could have put an eight-cent stamp on an envelope with a $20 bill inside and dropped it in the mailbox half a block from her house. Twenty dollars would buy us groceries for a week. But that would have felt like charity. What my mother sent us was a gift.

2

WHERE ARE THE TREES?

The previous Friday Don had been at exactly the right place, at precisely the right time. That Monday morning in June 1972, Don began his job as an official fire lookout for the U.S. Forest Service because he'd never quit trying.

Monday's sun rose bright in a cloudless blue sky. Don and I waited in our room until the noisy fire crew cleared out of the bunkhouse. Then we helped ourselves to lukewarm coffee and two donuts they'd left in the kitchen. We wondered what we'd find on Dunn Peak. Neither of us had ever seen an actual lookout before, only ones on TV. How would we cook? Where would we go to the bathroom? Would bears be a problem? We'd soon find out.

We loaded our suitcases onto the roof rack, put Misty in the back seat, and waited outside for Wade. Our breath condensed in the cold mountain air. I was telling Don again how happy I was that we didn't have to pack in on mules when Wade arrived in his Forest Service pickup precisely at 7:00 AM. He yelled out his window to follow him. Wade drove his truck straight into the mountain, veered right, and disappeared. Don followed with blind trust. I held my breath.

Hidden behind the trees, Fireroad 1934 zig-zagged up the steep mountainside. Wade maneuvered the hairpin switchbacks with familiar ease. We'd never seen such a road. Don gripped the steering wheel with his left hand, grabbed the gearshift with his right, and downshifted to keep our overloaded wagon moving forward. Powder-dry dirt lay thick on the road. On every turn Wade's tires threw out billowing clouds of yellow dust that engulfed our wagon. Don couldn't see Wade's truck ahead or the edge of the road. He leaned in close to the windshield. He groaned with worry that his first day as a fire lookout might be his last. My worry was that I'd have to drive down this death spiral by myself on my way home.

The tight turns straightened out on the level saddle along the ridge leading to Dunn Peak's summit. The air cleared in front of us. Don shifted to third gear. We relaxed enough to pry our gaze from the precipitous unguarded road edge. We took in the mountain panorama that had opened before us. I was stunned.

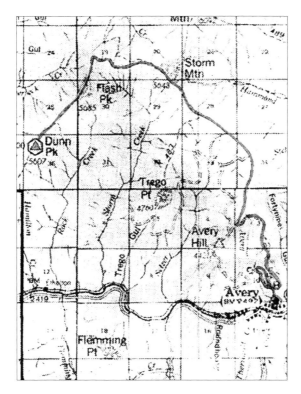

The route from Avery, Idaho, to the Dunn Peak Lookout on a U.S. Forest Service map, 1972

"Where are the trees?" I asked, puzzled by what I saw. We were in a national forest. I'd expected to find majestic conifers—lots of them. But every mountain for miles around was covered in stubby scrub brush and weeds. Now

Dunn Peak Lookout, 1972

I understood why that other lookout had quit—he was embarrassed to work in a forest without trees. A lookout wouldn't have much to do with no trees to protect. I thought a fire might even improve this scruffy scenery. Don sat up straight and replied to my question using his serious tone. He didn't care if there weren't any trees. As of today he was a paid fire lookout for the United States Forest Service and to him nothing else mattered.

Wade pumped his brakes to negotiate the final curve. Filtered through the dust on our windshield, Dunn Peak Lookout appeared on the mountaintop like an airy white cloud perched on a two-story foundation of thick timbers.

Wade parked on the flattened summit and jumped out. He swept his arm over the vista of mountain ridges lined in perfect order one behind the other to the horizon. "Welcome to your new home sweet home. What do you think?"

"I'm so excited I can hardly catch my breath," Don gasped.

"You're more than a mile high," Wade said. "Dunn Peak is 5,604 feet above sea level. You'll adjust. In a few days you'll climb these stairs like they're nothing."

I didn't want to insult Don's new boss, but he had asked what we thought. I asked why the lookout was so short compared to the towers I'd seen on TV. Wade didn't seem to mind my question. In fact it opened a floodgate of information that he'd obviously given to many lookouts before us. Wade explained that Dunn Peak's catwalk only needed to be twenty feet off the ground to have visibility to the forest's boundary on the Montana border and clear sight lines that overlapped with those of the other lookouts. Crystal Peak Lookout was forty-one feet tall and Conrad Lookout stood at fifty-three feet for visibility over their coverage zones. The living area at the top, called the cab, was fifteen by fifteen feet square with windows on all four sides. The cubicle underneath had been added to store equipment. Wade emphasized that the cubicle was locked. Everything we'd brought from home had to go into the cab.

Wade paused for a breath. Don jumped in and asked why there weren't any trees. Wade cleared his throat. He began to tell us the astounding history of the St. Joe Forest, a history Don and I knew nothing about. "The worst of it happened right there on Setzer Creek," Wade said. He pointed toward a deep ravine below Dunn Peak.

In 1910 the Avery District had been part of the Coeur d'Alene National Forest. By August so many fires burned in the district that the ranger couldn't find enough men to hire to control them. A howling windstorm rose on August 20 and fanned the fires into one giant unstoppable conflagration called the

Big Burn. In two days of hell that monstrous blaze destroyed every tree on millions of acres and wiped out more than one-third of the town of Wallace, killing townspeople asleep in their beds and gruesomely ending the lives of homesteaders, miners, soldiers, and firefighters. Gale-force winds pushed a firestorm along Setzer Creek that incinerated more than twenty-eight temporary firefighters camped in the ravine. The next day rescuers rushed from Avery to search for survivors. They mistook the firefighters' charred remains for burned trees and trampled parts of the men's broken bodies into the ground.

The aftermath of a wildfire "hurricane" in a heavy stand of Idaho white pine on the North Fork of the St. Joe River, near Coeur d'Alene, Idaho, 1910.
(Library of Congress: https://lccn.loc.gov/90715255)

I was confused, and a little afraid. I'd expected to have a summer filled with happy, exciting adventures in a peaceful green forest. Instead Wade had introduced us to the stark reality of uncontrolled wildfires. The catastrophic Big Burn had reduced these forests to ash right where we stood on Dunn Peak and burned firefighters alive. This was 1972, I reasoned to calm myself. Surely wildfires like that couldn't happen again. The Forest Service uses parachuting smoke jumpers and hot shots and huge bombers that dump tons of retardant to put out every forest fire. I'd seen it all on TV. Yet, in the short time I'd been around Wade, I'd judged him to be a thoughtful man who didn't exaggerate. Could a forest fire still become so destructive and deadly that firefighters or even lookouts might die doing their job? What had Don signed up for? Nobody before Wade had warned us that this job could be dangerous.

Wallace, Idaho, destroyed by forest fires, 1910
(Library of Congress: https://lccn.loc.gov/90715594)

Before 1910, Wade continued to explain, fast growing western white pine had been the dominant species in the Coeur d'Alene forest. The wood's straight grain, ease of shaping, and resistance to warping made it highly valued for flooring, trim, and moldings. White pines that grew on Dunn Peak would have lived 250 to 400 years or more. A 300-year-old specimen could have been 60 inches thick and still grow to surpass 200 feet in height. Western white pine had contributed so abundantly to Idaho's history and economy that it had been named the state tree in 1935.

Wade stood silent while Don and I surveyed the St. Joe's ruined expanses still struggling to rise from its ashes. Then he explained that, if left untouched after a wildfire, a forest of western white pine could be reborn within fifty years with thousands of trees per acre. But the 1910 Big Burn had raged so hot it eradicated every seed waiting to germinate in the forest floor duff, sterilized the soil of its beneficial microorganisms, and melted and fused the soil's nutritional minerals. Through the 1930s the Forest Service had replanted the St. Joe with species unsuitable for the environment. The weak specimens found few nutrients in the depleted soil, developed diseases, and died. In 1934 a spark from a coal-burning locomotive ignited another fire on Setzer Creek that burned thirty-seven thousand acres between Dunn Peak and Avery. That fire wiped out many of the replanted trees that had managed to survive.

In 1910 a lumberman in British Columbia, Canada, had imported western white pine seedlings from France that were infected with white pine blister rust. The deadly disease soon spread through Idaho's forests. In 1943 blister rust was designated a universal epidemic. Native bark beetles, white pine pole blight, and clear-cut logging to supply the post–World War II housing boom accelerated the species' decline. Once known as King Pine, western white pine barely survives on approximately 5 percent of its former domain.

I understood why I saw little else but scrub brush on the mountains for miles around. It had taken more than sixty years for much of the St. Joe Forest to begin its recovery. With cheer in his voice, Wade called our attention to tall, young lodgepole pines growing close to the lookout. Lodgepoles are one of the first species to repopulate a burned-over forest because their cones require heat from a fire to open and release their seeds. He pointed toward healthy stands of conifers growing in protected stream-fed draws. These were species suited to the climate and conditions of the St. Joe Forest. Trees that had been planted on the hillsides and ridges more recently had just grown tall enough to break out above the scrub. Wade turned and spoke straight to Don. As the lookout on Dunn Peak, Wade expected him to make damn certain that these mountains didn't burn again. In just a few minutes, Wade had impressed Don with the unexpected gravity of his new job.

My empty stomach set off its lunchtime alarm. I didn't care how anxious Don might be to get into the tower. If he expected me to help him cart our stuff twenty feet straight up, I needed to eat. I pulled three lemon-lime sodas and some packages of deli ham and cheese out of the cooler in the back of the wagon. I couldn't find where we'd crammed the bread, mayonnaise, pickles, chips, or napkins. I wiped off my dusty hands on my already dusty chinos and made three plain meat and cheese rolls. Wade had brown-bagged his lunch, but he took the cold soda. Don and I shared the extra roll.

I had to pee. Ordinarily that wasn't a problem for me out in the woods. (Idaho had proved stingy in providing roadside rest stops compared to Pennsylvania.) I kept tissues in the glove compartment and a small shovel under my seat. I'd learned to plant my feet far apart and point them downhill for better balance and drainage. But here I stood next to a man I'd just met, and no tree nearby was big enough for me to squat behind. So, I asked, "Uh, Wade ... is there a bathroom somewhere?" He pointed to a rocky, downhill path.

I used the outhouse and hiked the length of a city block back to the summit. Don had unpacked everything from our wagon into a huge pile on the ground. Wade announced that he was going to unload the water cans from his truck, just in case we'd entertained any thought of him helping us. Don and I turned our attention away from the awe-inspiring surround of open sky and shifted our focus onto the cab. All our stuff had to be inside that miniscule 225 square feet of space before the thunderstorms hit.

I squared my shoulders to attack the two steepest flights of stairs I'd ever encountered. One step at a time, I hauled a stuffed suitcase or an overloaded cardboard box up the first flight. I leaned hard against the cubicle on the landing to catch my breath. The second flight was so steep that I couldn't see my feet under me. I propped my elbow against the rail to steady myself in case I missed my footing. When my head cleared the hatch, I hefted my load up and plopped it onto the catwalk. I hung my head between my outstretched arms to catch my breath again. I climbed the final steps to the cantilevered wood-slat catwalk and lugged my load fifteen feet into the cab. At least the catwalk was flat. I deposited my load on the worn wood floor and exhaled a "hurray." I rested on the lookout's only bench for six seconds, then started back down so Don didn't think I was slacking. In the nearly two years we'd been married we'd agreed that if one worked, the other worked. I washed the dishes. Don dried and put them away. Friday nights we cleaned house. Don worked Saturday and Sunday at a grocery store. I did the laundry and ironing. That way neither of us felt slighted that the other one pulled an easier load.

The afternoon sun colored the huge, building thunderheads into shades of pink and orange. We'd carried everything from our wagon into the cab except Misty's fifty pound bag of kibble. Don grabbed one end of the bag and I grabbed the other. He walked backward up the stairs and I lifted from underneath. Misty guarded her precious cargo the entire length of its perilous journey. Wade helped Don carry our water cans onto the catwalk. He informed us that his crew would fill the cans every week at the bunkhouse and drop them off. But after today, Don would have to lift them by himself.

Finally, we were done. Don and I were exhausted. We rested on the bench, looked around the cab, and wondered where in this tiny see-through box we could store all of our stuff mounded on the floor. A single bed with two deep drawers underneath sat against one wall. I was surprised to see that someone had made the bed with military precision. A rectangular dinette table, a two-shelf bookcase, and a long cabinet with several doors occupied the other walls. I noticed that none of the furniture was tall enough to block the windows. I looked around again. There was nowhere for me to sleep. Would I be the first wife in this lookout? Don and I had dated for more than five years and agreed that an engagement ring was a frivolous expense. But we'd splurged on one luxury item before our wedding, a top-of-the-line king size bed. For us, sleeping comfortably far outweighed a piece of jewelry. No way was I going to bump butts and knock knees all summer squished into a single bed with my husband. I required my own sleeping accommodations, with elbow room.

Wade walked into the cab. He announced that his crew had stacked enough firewood for the stove to see us through the week. We had to cook on a wood stove? I'd never done that. I'd been so occupied carrying in boxes that I'd missed the misshapen hulk of black cast iron hidden behind our mound of stuff. A groan escaped my throat. Wade apologized with a half-smile. If he found extra money in next month's budget maybe he'd install a propane stove. Wade spent the next half hour showing Don how to operate the radio and the Osborne Firefinder (see the next chapter for more on this device) and fill in the logbook. He said he'd rather have a lookout call in a cloud than not call in a smoke. He wanted every fire doused as soon as possible. By then I'd forgotten to complain about my missing bed.

The thunderheads had piled thousands of feet into the air and blocked the sun. The sky turned dark gray. Wade was anxious to get back to Avery before the storm hit. He was sorry that my first night on the lookout wouldn't be more romantic. He wished me a safe drive home. Don and I followed him out the door, happy to wave goodbye to him. Wade turned back at the hatch. He'd thought of a few more things Don and I needed to know. If lightning hit the tower, the charge would strike one of five grounded lightning rods on the roof, follow the half-inch thick copper wire along a corner timber, and discharge deep into the earth. If electrical charges built up close to the lookout and the copper grounding cables glowed, Misty and I should stay on the bed until the threat of lightning passed. The Firefinder, the two-way radio, and the wood stove were also grounded. Each leg of the bench sat in a glass insulator for extra protection. Steel cables that angled out from each corner of the lookout were attached to stakes anchored deep in the ground. In fourteen years no storm had been strong enough to blow the tower over. Wade promised we'd survive this storm, too.

Dunn Peak Lookout's grounding cables and tie-down wires

Learning the territory

Wade walked down three steps, then turned back again. We had to close the hatch's trap door at night. Nothing prevented an inattentive person from falling through. And we needed to slide a thick bolt through the hasp to secure the hatch. That would keep out unwanted visitors and critters, especially bears. Black bears liked to snack on the trash in the lookout's garbage pit. Wade's crew had piled boulders on top to discourage their digging, but the bears had tossed the boulders aside. Unless we were sure no bears prowled nearby, we should keep Misty on a leash when she was on the ground. The bears could toss her around like the boulders.

When I was a teenager, I'd spent two weeks at a camp in Pennsylvania's Pocono Mountains. I slept in a comfy bunkbed in a cabin with electric lights. The toilets flushed and the showers had hot water. I thought that camp experience had qualified me to deal with whatever dangers the St. Joe Forest could throw at us. Wade's warnings made me realize that I knew nothing at all about an up-close and personal interaction with Mother Nature in the raw. I began to wonder if I should take Misty home tomorrow and stay there for the summer. Don could have this mountain and its dangers all to himself. Being a lookout was his dream job, not mine. No bear was going to eat my dog.

Wade finally drove off to Avery. Don and I were on our own. We needed a hot meal to face the storm. Don carried in wood and lit a fire. I dug out a pot, plastic forks and paper plates, a can of Dinty Moore beef stew, and sourdough rolls from the grocery store bakery. While I heated the stew, Don cleared our stuff away from the rectangular wooden podium in the center of the lookout. He'd need to align the lightning strikes in the Osborne Firefinder attached to its top. I cleaned up after dinner. Misty laid on her quilt for the first time all day. Don studied the Osborne's map to learn the names of the mountains and creeks surrounding the lookout. Wind rattled the windows.

Each window was more than five feet tall and divided into four stacked rectangular panes. Seven windows lined each of three walls of the lookout. The fourth wall had the door and six windows, for a total of twenty-seven. Only the middle window on each wall opened out. There were no screens to impair visibility. At the end of the fire season, white painted wood panels stored in the cubicle would be screwed over the windows for protection from winter storms. The lookout set at an angle from true north to face the prevailing southwest direction of incoming weather more directly. The cab's door opened to the north, the leeward side, away from the weather. The cab set on four thick square creosote-treated timbers. A pair of crossed timbers spanned each level and braced each side of the tower. The wind blew harder. The tower shook.

It would be dark soon. Don checked the level of white gasoline in the reservoirs on the base of the two red camp lanterns to make sure they held enough fuel to last through the storm. He pumped air into the reservoirs to pressurize the gas. He installed mantels, ignited them, and let them burn to a delicate ashy web. He opened the valve on the reservoir to let out a slow stream of vapor through the mantel. He used a long wooden match to carefully ignite the vapor. If the match bumped the ashy mantle it would collapse into nothingness. If Don's fingers were too close when the vapor ignited, they'd get singed. He lowered the lantern's glass globe and adjusted the gas flow to give us a steady light. The lantern's pleasant murmur filled every corner of the lookout. The gaslight's silvery glow seemed to hold back the growing storm's deep blackness that pushed against the bare windows.

Around 10:30 Don turned off the lanterns and knocked down the fire in the stove. The lookout had to be dark for him to see through the windows. A small battery-powered lamp hung over the Firefinder. Its tiny bulb gave off enough light that he could mark lightning strikes on the map, but it was dim enough to not interfere with his night vision. The first bolt of lightning split the sky at 11 o'clock. If Don said "cloud-to-cloud," he ignored the flash. But when he shouted, "ground strike," he aligned the bolt with the Osborne to record its position. He'd monitor those areas for any glow from a fire. At first light he'd be out on the catwalk searching for smokes. That night Don got to be the fire lookout he'd dreamed of since he was a boy.

The storm stalled over our heads. I jumped at each lightning strike. I wrapped my arms around Misty and explained to her in my calmest voice that we'd be safe. I prayed to God that Wade had told us the truth. Lightning bolts split into a hundred tentacles in front of my eyes and seared across the pitch-black sky with the intensity of a blue-white sun. Each instantaneous thunderclap bounced around inside my body. My adrenaline surged like I was on a roller coaster. After a few strikes my fear turned to excitement. I waited for the thrill of the next explosion. The storm moved off slowly. The temperature tumbled into the thirties. Don restoked a cozy fire. Exhausted from the day's excitement we fell asleep snuggled in the single bed, not minding the close quarters.

I'd drunk two cans of cola to keep awake for the storm. I woke Don with the unwelcome news that I needed to use the outhouse. I wished I'd packed an emergency bucket to use on the catwalk instead. Soft firelight leaked from the wood stove and brightened the lookout enough for me to zip my goose down parka over my flannel pajamas, pull on socks, tie my sneakers, and hook on Misty's leash. Don handed me the lantern he'd lit. I waited on the catwalk while he put on his coat and shoes. I could see my breath. I shivered so hard that I had to pee even more.

Don shined his flashlight across the ground in wide arcs to make sure no critters waited to pounce. I told Misty to bark loudly and meanly to scare them off. All seemed safe. Don lifted the trap door. Unafraid, Misty pulled me down the stairs, hit the ground, and squatted to pee. I had to hold it in. A lookout before us had lined the steep, rock-studded, dirt path with white painted rocks so we didn't stray off. I shifted the hissing lantern across the path like a Catholic priest swinging prayers from a smoking censer. No wild beasts marred our journey.

Don and Misty guarded the outhouse. I set my lantern on the splintered wood box that dared to call itself a toilet. I guessed the previous lookouts had all been outdoorsmen because the Forest Service had never deemed it necessary to put a toilet seat on the hole sawed in the middle. No flies buzzed about in the cold—only the smell rose to assault my nose. Heat from my lantern warmed the air in the tiny shack, but not the wood. Wow, it was cold! I adjusted myself back to reach the hole that every Dunn Peak lookout had used since 1958. My sneakers dangled inches above the concrete floor. I counted off one-thousand-one, one-thousand-two. My pee hit the bottom after "two," landing on whatever was piled at the bottom of that black pit. I shook the mouse-chewed bits off the roll of toilet paper and dropped the used tissue between my legs. No need to flush. Rustling noises in the vault encouraged me to move on. Don had taken care of his business in the bushes. Back in our warm lookout we fell asleep, satisfied that we'd overcome every challenge Mother Nature had thrown our way. Wade was right. We'd survived our first storm in the wild Idaho forest.

At first light Don was on the catwalk searching the forest with his binoculars. Every lookout radioed in good news to Avery. No one had spotted a smoke from last night's ground strikes. Don and I spent the rest of the morning organizing our stuff. I'd head off Dunn Peak right after lunch. Yesterday I'd been ready to pack my suitcase and never come back to the lookout. Today it hurt my heart to think about leaving. But I had to go home. If I lost my job, Don might need to drop out of college. I couldn't let that happen. We'd both worked too hard to get this far. Maybe I was too concerned about our separation. After all, I'd be back at the lookout on Friday.

Don closed and locked my car door. He reminded me to stop at Hoyt Flat to have the dispatcher radio him that I'd gotten off the mountain okay.

We shared a parting kiss. I told Misty to be a good girl and drove off. I kept my eyes peeled ahead on the fireroad's unguarded drop-off and forgot to look back. I knew, without needing to see, that Don and Misty watched my dust cloud until I drove around the curve that took me out of their view.

I stopped at Hoyt Flat and filled the gas tank in St. Maries. I rehearsed my path home; back onto Route 3, right on Route 6 after Mashburn, and left on 95 after Potlatch. I'd be in Moscow after just two turns. I couldn't get lost. I relaxed and took in the clean, green Idaho mountains, forests, and farms. I reached White Pine Drive. Its long stretch of macadam ran straight to the horizon. My little green wagon was the only car on the road. A new sensation gripped me. I wanted another adrenaline rush like I'd felt in last night's storm. I stomped the wagon's gas pedal to the floor and pushed her as fast as she could go. The speedometer read ninety when its cable broke. For the rest of the summer I had to guess how fast I was driving.

I turned left on Route 95 into familiar territory. I didn't want to cook or dirty the kitchen when I got home, but I was too grimy to sit in a restaurant. Fried chicken and coleslaw from the grocery store sounded perfect. I knew the house would be okay, but I'd be there alone. No Don to kiss me hello. No Misty to push her head in to share our hug. First I'd go next door to thank Mike and Shirley for keeping an eye out. I'd watch the news while I ate, then take a bubble bath. I needed to buy a cot, a sturdy bucket, two sleeping bags, and two powerful flashlights. Damn, why had I quit my cashier job so soon? Wish I still had my employee discount. I shouldn't have wine tonight. Tomorrow I'll check the growth on my fungus samples. Doc will have fresh specimens for me to catalogue and prep for inoculation. I hoped the grocery store had chicken wings left.

When Don and I had first arrived in Moscow from Twin Falls, I had a hard time finding a job. In that small college town, I'd competed with students and students' spouses also looking for work. I'd called my parents from the pay phone at the grocery store when I'd landed a job. My dad's voice couldn't hide his disappointment that his college graduate daughter would be working as a cashier in a discount store. Weeks later I phoned with the news that, because I had a biology degree, I'd gotten a second job in the College of Forestry's pathology lab assisting with research on forest diseases. From two thousand miles away I heard my father smile.

3

WHAT IF I SPOT A SMOKE?

If Don was an official Forest Service lookout for only one summer, he'd have a story to tell for the rest of his life. If fate allowed him to return to the St. Joe Forest after fifty years, he hoped to find the mountains around Dunn Peak covered in tall sturdy trees that he helped to protect from fire.

On Don's first morning alone in the lookout, without me there to distract him, he buckled down to master the important aspects of his job. Avery District provided their lookouts with high-magnification binoculars. Lookouts were required to conduct binocular searches of the terrain from the catwalk for at least twenty minutes of every hour when on duty, except on rainy or foggy days. Wildfires can begin in locations hidden from a lookout's view—under a canopy of trees, in a gulley, on the opposite side of a peak, or too far away to spot the flames. In most cases the ignited forest sends up a smoke plume, a locator beacon for an observant fire lookout. On some mornings cool air flowed off the mountains and condensed the moisture rising from the St. Joe River. The ground fog settled into the ravines and valleys around Dunn Peak. The rising sun broke the fog apart and smoke-like wisps floated toward the sky. Don called in a few false sightings until he learned to distinguish between fog and smoke. The fire crew taught him that fog is white and smoke is blue.

Elers Koch graduated from the Yale Forest School in 1903 and went to work in Montana's Lolo Forest Reserve. Elers glued a map of the Lolo Forest onto a board. He cut two slits in the ends of a narrow strip of tin and bent the ends up at a ninety-degree angle to make a simple surveyor's alidade, a sighting device for determining direction or measuring angles. When Elers spotted a smoke, he'd set his alidade on the map board and align the smoke in the two slits. He'd measure the horizontal angle of the smoke in a clockwise direction from true north. He'd use this azimuth heading to direct firefighters to the smoke's location.

William Bushnell Osborne, Jr., graduated from the Yale Forest School in 1909. His firsthand experiences during the Great Fires of 1910 had influenced him to develop a more accurate instrument to determine a smoke's location. Osborne etched 360-degree marks onto the edge of a circular steel base. He secured the base to a tree stump on top of a lookout mountain. He attached a scaled map of the area visible from the centered mountain onto the base. He pivoted an alidade with a taut vertical horsehair on the front sight and vertical slit on the rear sight over the center of the map. Forest guards circled the alidade over the map, aligned a smoke in the view finders, and determined the azimuth heading from the degree marks on the rim. Osborne named the instrument the Firefinder. They went into commercial production in 1913 and proved so accurate that most lookout towers contained modified Firefinders by 1934. It's said that Osborne never took payment for his invention.

Art Halvorson on Baptiste Lookout, circa 1915–1920,
Hungry Horse Ranger District. US Forest Service—Flathead National Forest

Centered in Dunn Peak's cab, an adjustable metal mounting on tracks attached an Osborne Firefinder to the top of a wooden podium. An accurate azimuth reading, precise to one sixtieth of one degree, depended on the Osborne's proper alignment. Every morning lookouts were to adjust the Firefinder to level, the sights to plumb, and the rotating sight ring and scaled distance tape to a specific bearing posted on the podium.

The edge of the Firefinder's upper metal plate was scribed in 360 degrees, and each degree was marked in half, or 30 minutes. A scaled map of the St. Joe Forest, with Dunn Peak Lookout at its center, was attached to the plate. The map was divided into a numbered grid based on the Bureau of Land Management's township and range system. Townships are 6 miles on a side, or 36 square miles. Each township is subdivided into 36 numbered sections that are 1 mile square and contain 640 acres. Each section is further divided into quarter sections of 160 acres. Quarter sections are designated based on the compass: NE, SE, SW, and NW. Townships are bounded by numbered range lines on the east and west and by numbered township lines on the north and south.

Don used "permanent" smokes from the Avery dump, cabin fireplaces, and restaurant exhausts to hone his ability to take an azimuth reading. If a window frame blocked his sight line, he'd adjust the Firefinder on its tracks to get a clear view. He used the handle on the sight ring to revolve the alidade between the edge of the map and the upper plate. The alidade's taller rear sight had a narrow, scaled vertical slit and a sliding peep hole. Don peered through the rear sight and turned the alidade to exactly center the smoke on the front sight's taut vertical horsehair, crossed by two horizontal hairs. The slit in the rear sight was aligned to a zero mark on the Vernier scale attached to the edge of the sight ring. Don read where the zero mark aligned with a degree or minute mark on the upper plate. If the zero mark fell between, he read left to the next alignment on the Vernier scale. He added that number to the minutes.

A scaled metal tape connected the front and rear sights. The tape's zero point was set over the map's center pin. Don used a red grease pencil to mark the approximate location of lightning strikes on the erasable laminated map. He used the tape's scale to estimate the distance to a ground strike or a smoke.

For accuracy, Don recorded a smoke's location and nearby landmarks in the logbook before he radioed Avery. The entry might read: N.F. Clearwater, Spotted Louis, T43N, R6E, Sec. 35, SE of NW. Azimuth 186°30'. Don radioed in the smoke located between the North Fork of the Clearwater River and Spotted Louis Creek at Township 43 North, Range 6 East, in the southeast of the northwest corner of Section 35, at azimuth 186 degrees and 30 minutes.

Using Dunn Peak lookout's Osborne Firefinder

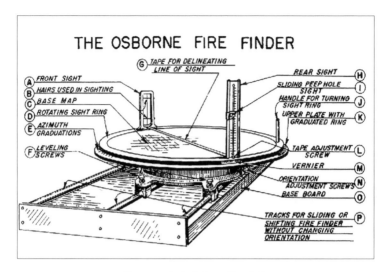

Diagram of the Osborne Firefinder

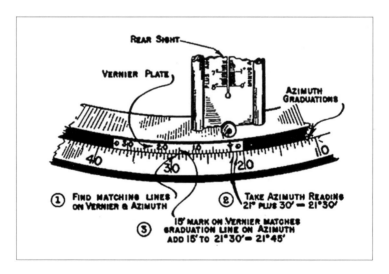

Vernier plate on the Osborne Firefinder

The lookout's two-way Motorola battery-powered radio was the only connection St. Joe lookouts had with the outside world. Their radios were tuned to a dedicated frequency. Fire crews and other personnel used separate frequencies for their communications. Forest Service regulations required lookouts' radios to be operational at all times and used only for official business. If the radio's transmission showed any sign of deterioration, lookouts immediately replaced the one large battery. Avery might not receive a weak signal. In the time it took to change the battery, a fire could spread out of control.

The Motorola's simple push-the-button-on-the-microphone operation presented no challenge for Don. He'd been a radioman in the Navy. Every morning at 8:00 and every evening at 5:00, Don competed with the lookouts on Middle Sister, Snow Peak, Crystal, Simmons, Huckleberry, Bald Mountain, Roundtop, and Conrad to be the first to rid themselves of the tedious but necessary chore of check-in.

Don lifted the microphone close to his mouth and depressed the button. "Avery, this is Dunn Peak."

"Dunn Peak, Avery," the dispatcher radioed back.

"My morning check-in, Wanda. Dunn Peak clear."

"Avery clear."

Another lookout immediately grabbed the airwave. The conversation repeated itself until all the lookouts checked in. Small things entertain isolated lookouts. The sole female lookout that summer staffed Crystal Peak. She possessed an expressive voice fit for commercial radio. We smiled every time we heard her distinctive warble of, "Crystal clear!"

The lookout's radio resonated with the pulse of the St. Joe Forest. On foggy or rainy days, hardly a crackle emanated from its speaker. A lookout might take advantage of the Low fire danger rating and ask Wanda for permission to come to town for a shower, do laundry, or go grocery shopping. When rain settled in for days, bored anonymous fire crew pranksters took to the radio to entertain us with contraband jokes and limericks, although none were even slightly naughty because Wanda recognized every voice on the radio.

When thunderstorms approached, the fire control officer radioed the lookouts for real-time weather observations. He used the information to deploy his spotters and fire crews. Lightning generated a frenzy of transmissions. The fire control officer repositioned his crews based on the locations of reported ground strikes.

The first lookout who radioed in a smoke reigned as king of the frequency. His transmission alerted the other lookouts to break radio silence only to call in their coordinating azimuths or a new smoke. Avery plotted each azimuth on a wall-sized map of the forest. The fire should be located where the lines intersected. But azimuth readings alone didn't always pinpoint a fire. In the St. Joe's rugged terrain, sometimes only one or two lookouts could spot a smoke. The fire control officer depended on the lookouts' familiarity with their territory to narrow the smoke's location to within one-quarter of a numbered square mile section on the Osborne map, such as the northeast corner of section 24. Lookouts were also expected to report whether they could see the fire's base and how fast the flames and/or the smoke were growing. The fire control officer used that data to estimate how many firefighters and what equipment to deploy, and whether or not to fly air patrol.

The more accurate a lookout's location report, the quicker a spotter arrived on the scene. He deposed the lookout as king of the frequency. The fire control officer further refined his response based on the spotter's on-site report and updates from the lookouts. Then the spotter switched to the firefighting frequency. That cleared the lookouts' frequency for reports of new smokes or lightning strikes. Lookouts heard updates on the fire when Avery or headquarters at St. Maries radioed out a report. Or we'd overhear bits of information when a firefighter, out of range to contact Avery directly, relayed a message through Middle Sister Peak Lookout's radio repeater.

Since he was a boy, Don had struggled to concentrate long enough to finish a book or even a magazine article. But he lost all sense of time poring over colorful maps in an atlas. Or he'd unfold a gas station roadmap and let his imagination carry him from town to town. Don spent hours studying the Osborne's map. He paced the catwalk every morning with the binoculars pressed to his face. He scrutinized the territory spread out before him until the name of every distinguishing feature and its relative position to other features formed a hardwired connection in his brain. He memorized the name, numbered section, and quarter-square location of each prominent St. Joe landmark. Mastodon Mountain, Foolhen Mountain, Moon Peak, Cedar Mountain, Storm Mountain, Stevens Peak, Arid Peak, Tanglefoot Point, Triangle Peak, Big Dick Point, Shefoot Mountain, and Turner Peak all rise higher than one mile in elevation to crown the St. Joe's ridges. Don noted that from west to east, Big Creek, Black Prince Creek, Slate Creek, Storm Creek, Setzer Creek, Skookum Creek, and Bird Creek run between the ridges and drain into the St. Joe River. He wondered if Hammond Point along the North Fork had been named for an unknown relative.

Despite Don's dedication, Mother Nature sometimes seduced him to abandon his binoculars and take in the widescreen wonders of her creation. He observed how the mist rising from the river fractured the rays of the morning sun into fleeting rainbow kaleidoscopes. The afternoon sun projected exaggerated cloud shadows that coursed over the ridges and discolored the forest from green to gray. Sunsets in cloudless skies produced nothing to recommend them. But when the rays of the sinking sun filtered through layers of clouds, the rainbow's seven wavelengths fluctuated in startling variations to create a brilliant display.

One calm sunny afternoon the lookout's radio sprang to life. "Dunn Peak, this is the fire control officer. Over."

"This is Dunn Peak. Over."

"Do you see any smokes, Don?"

Don made a cursory check. "No, Wade, I don't spot anything. Over."

"Well look harder, Dunn Peak!" Wade yelled. He'd set off a smoke bomb to test the new lookout on the district. Don missed spotting the smoke for a few more minutes.

"Okay, Wade, I see it now." Don relayed the correct azimuth reading, section number, quarter section, and nearby place names.

"That's better, Dunn Peak. Keep a sharper eye out in the future. Wade clear."

Every lookout on the forest heard Don's embarrassing miss of the test smoke. Don had failed so often in school. It pained him to fail again so early in his dream job. It implied to others that he might not have the aptitude to succeed as a lookout. He was determined to not disappoint again.

4

LASSIE *SAVED HIM*

Donald Thomas Hammond grew up through the 1950s and '60s in the gritty steel town of Bethlehem, Pennsylvania. Gray, rancid smoke and fumes bellowed from the Bethlehem Steel Company's blast furnaces that lined the fish-killing Lehigh River. When Don looked out his bedroom window toward the forest of maples and oaks on South Mountain, the grime-filled air so blurred his view that he couldn't distinguish one individual tree from another.

Sixth-grader Don stood out as an easy target for schoolyard bullies. He was a poor student and painfully thin. Tommy, Don's best friend who lived on the same street, would tease him, "If you stand sideways and stick out your tongue you look like a zipper."

Don never doubted that older, stronger, fearless Tommy always had his back. Once, when the bullies threatened him, fast-talking Don baited them to meet him by his house after school. Don stood alone as the menacing wannabe thugs marched up the sidewalk toward him. He spat out insults in their direction as his only defense. The bullies laughed at the skinny kid's fat mouth and overblown sense of confidence. Then Tommy stepped out from behind the bushes, flexed his well-muscled arms, and calmly lit a cigarette. The bullies turned tail and ran. After Tommy's father fell ill, he left school to get a job to help his family. Don lost his protector.

In junior high Don was assigned to special classes with other slow learners. His former tormenters took Latin or German and forgot about skinny, dumb Don. But nature abhors a vacuum. Built like a linebacker, her friends called her Popeye. She wore her bleached hair teased and twisted into a sprayed-stiff beehive. Her white lipstick contrasted starkly beneath thick, pointed curves of black eyeliner. "Meet me out back after school, Hammond," she threatened. "I'm gonna beatchew to a pulp."

"You and who's army?" Don smart-mouthed back with false bravado. He knew that Popeye really did have an army, a gang of tough hoods uniformed in studded, black leather motorcycle jackets, pegged pants, and slicked back D.A. haircuts.

Classes had finished for the day. Don stood in the lobby next to the gym. He nervously surveyed the students lingering outside. He had to face Popeye and her gang alone. There was no Tommy to protect him this time. Coach Sylvester tromped by. His practiced eye recognized a kid in need. "Hey, you wanna sign up to wrestle?" he called out to Don.

Don sized up the coach, built like a locomotive. He weighed his options and decided. "You bet, Coach. I could use some fast moves, and more muscle."

On Saturday nights during the early 1960s, not yet famous rock and roll groups drove seventy miles north from Philadelphia to the Lehigh Valley. They honed their acts performing live at school dances, including Don's junior high. The lean crooners advertised their well-groomed appeal wearing sports jackets with narrow lapels and brass buttons, white shirts with tab collars, skinny ties, and pompadour haircuts. Girls at school noticed that, with his toned wrestler's physique and American Bandstand style, ninth-grader Don could pass for one of those rock and roll singers. Out of the blue Don was cool.

But being popular and on the wrestling team didn't improve Don's grades. He couldn't spell or sit still to read a book. In the 1960s educators debated whether dyslexia was a valid concept. Don had failed seventh grade, went to summer school, and passed. He'd failed eighth grade, went to summer school, and passed. He failed ninth grade, went to summer school, and failed again. Don believed he had to repeat ninth grade because he was dumb. The thing he wished for most was to be an average student. Aiming for average became his scholastic goal.

Don's parents had been drawn into the Eisenhower-era expansion of technologically advanced consumer goods. Before 1960 they owned an automatic washer and dryer, a frost-free refrigerator-freezer, and an RCA color television set. TV programs broadcast "in living color" transported Don to the majestic mountains and deserts of the American West. Hard-working cattle ranchers, a black caped crusader, and a coonskin-capped trailblazer became his role models; adventurous heroes who always lent a helping hand. But it was *Lassie* that saved him.

When Don was in high school, he and Tom cruised Hamilton Street to pick up girls. Tom had left his car running out front. He walked into Don's living room and couldn't believe his eyes. "Donboy! Why in the hell're you watchin' *Lassie*? You comin' to cruise or not?"

Don in ninth grade
(Don Hammond family photo; used with permission)

Don jabbed his finger at the TV. A careless smoker had thrown a cigarette out of his car and started a forest fire. Lookouts on two fire towers had spotted the smoke and radioed in their azimuth readings. Ranger Corey Stuart ordered out crews and equipment to battle the blaze. "They saved the forest, Tom. I'm gonna be a lookout someday. You'll see."

When I was a junior in high school, my dad drove me to the Hi-Spot dances at the YMCA on Saturday nights. My friends and I paired up on the fast dances. On slow dances we huddled and waited for a boy. My friend Joni had set her cap for Don. One Saturday night, every time the DJ had announced a ladies' choice, she'd trekked across the gym floor and asked Don to dance. I slouched in a metal folding chair parked against the wall and studied the way Don led her around the floor. He was a good dancer, a sharp dresser, and cute, too. Taller than me. Joni could be persistent. I felt sorry for him.

The following Saturday the DJ announced the first slow song of the night. Joni hadn't arrived yet. I was surprised to see Don walking across the floor toward my group of friends. He looked me straight in the eye and asked me to dance. I put great stock in being a good friend, but something about this boy drew me in. I said yes. Don asked about Joni while we danced. I politely answered each question. Most boys I slow danced with walked away at the end of the song and left me alone in the middle of the floor. I felt rejected and exposed. Don escorted me back to my group. It took me three steps across the hardwood floor to feel the soft pressure of his warm hand still on my back. Joni had arrived while we were dancing. She gave Don a seductive smile and apologized for being late. I regretted that this one dance might be all that Don and I ever shared. Joni grilled me through the next three fast songs. I told her not to worry. Don had spent the entire dance asking about her.

The DJ announced the next slow song. Don started across the floor. Joni turned toward him, lifted her chin, and pulled back her shoulders to fluff up her chest. Don focused his eyes on his chosen partner and extended his hand in silent invitation, to me. Joni's eyes shot me daggers, but I didn't care. I accepted Don's hand.

Don pulled me in close. This boy and I fit together. From the way he held me, I had no doubt he knew it, too. Not one word passed between us as we danced. I closed my eyes and focused on how my cheek rested in a hollow on his muscular shoulder. I breathed in his English Leather aftershave mixed with my Ambush cologne. And I worried. Would we have another dance? Don's hand at my back guided me off the floor to the sitting area out front. We found two chairs and discovered it was easy to talk. Kids started flowing out the doors. My dad was waiting out front to drive me home. I asked Don if he needed a ride, hoping he'd say no. I wasn't prepared for a boy meets dad encounter.

Don smoothly sidestepped my offer. He didn't explain that he depended on his thumb and the kindness of strangers for transportation. And he didn't explain that if his older sister, Jean, hadn't given him two quarters, he wouldn't have had money to get into the dance that night. Small kindnesses given can sometimes multiply to change a person's life.

My dad sensed my distraction as we drove home. "You're quiet. Anything go wrong at the dance?" he asked.

"No. The dance was fine. I'm just tired," I deflected. I didn't want to answer his questions. I needed to think, not talk.

Dad parked in front of the house. I ran to let myself in the back door. Mom waited at her usual spot at the kitchen table. I kissed her cheek and spoke next to her ear. She had a hearing impairment. I didn't want to waste time repeating my message. "The dance was fun, Mom. I'm going right to bed. Goodnight."

If I woke my grandparents, I'd catch holy hell. The location of every creak on the staircase was burned into my brain for self-protection. I sprinted over two steps at a time, swung around the newel post at the top, ducked into the narrow hallway behind my parents' front bedroom, then pivoted a sharp right onto the steep enclosed staircase to my bedroom sanctuary in the attic. Shoes and all, I threw myself onto my chenille bedspread in a haze of confusion. My dammed-up emotions gushed out. I wiped away my useless tears and closed my eyes. I focused inside my chest to recapture that bewildering sense of absolute rightness I'd experienced the second time I danced with that boy.

I hadn't expected Don to be waiting outside my homeroom when the dismissal bell rang. It was my sixteenth birthday. Classmates rushed past and wished me happy birthday. Don gave me a quick kiss. He complained that I hadn't let him know it was my birthday. His voice softened as he got to what he'd come for. His Naval Reserve Surface Division was having a Navy Day dinner dance at Hotel Bethlehem. Would I go with him? I told him that was the best birthday gift ever. I kissed him back, long and slow.

Don knew that his record of failing grades wouldn't get him into college. He wanted more than a predictable job in a polluted steel town. He longed for adventure. He hoped that by joining the Navy, he could get out of town with honor and train for a higher skilled job than a common laborer. In 1945 Don's father had served as gunner's mate on a ship in the Battle of Okinawa, the bloodiest battle of the Pacific War. In October 1962, American schoolkids practiced duck-and-cover drills in fear of a nuclear attack by the Soviet Union. The USS *Kankakee*, with Don's older brother on board, had refueled Navy war ships surrounding Cuba to block Soviet trawlers from landing ballistic missiles on the island. Don followed in his family's footsteps. The summer before Don's senior year in high school, the summer before we met, he'd completed the Navy's experimental boot camp for Naval Reserve recruits at the Philadelphia Naval Base.

Don sure knew how to impress a girl on their first official date. The Navy Day dance would be a formal event in the upstairs ballroom of the ritziest hotel in town. I told my mother I needed a special dress. She grabbed her pocketbook out of the dining room buffet. I gritted my teeth for our shopping excursion. Commissioned salesclerks in Bethlehem's formal dress departments were accustomed to waiting on Moravian College coeds headed for fraternity dances at Lehigh University, and the country club wives and daughters of Bethlehem Steel executives. My mother had fashionable outfits and high heels in her closet, but she wore a house dress and scuffed Oxfords to go shopping. If it was cold, she'd put on her knockabout coat and tie a flowery babushka on her head. My mother was a second-generation American—her parents had immigrated to the United States from Hungary before she was born. She spoke English and Hungarian with equal fluency. Inside a store's dressing room she'd talk to me in English. But when the clerk came to check on us, she'd proclaim in Hungarian that the dress was a poorly sewn rag or a grossly overpriced piece of chintz. I'd swallow my embarrassment and politely tell the clerk that the dress wasn't quite what I was looking for. The clerks looked down their noses at my mother like she was an immigrant fresh off the boat. I couldn't wait to get out of the store. I never understood why she behaved that way. Maybe my grandmother had made her translate, too, when they'd gone shopping.

Our last stop was the classiest dress shop in town. My mother and I examined every inch of me reflected in the three-way mirror and nodded our mutual assent. This was *my* dress. The well-tailored matte-black crepe molded perfectly onto my 5-foot, 6-inch, 115-pound frame. The dress featured a knee-length pencil skirt with a kick pleat perfect for dancing, a bateau neckline, no sleeves, no back, and a spicy flared bolero top. A shiny, pleated, black satin cummerbund, accented at the back with a large rectangular rhinestone buckle, left no doubt that this black crepe was formal, not funereal. Out of character, my mother reached for her pocketbook before I read her the price tag.

I'd wondered if Don would arrive for our date wearing the same green, wool sports jacket he wore to the Saturday dances. I'd daydreamed of him decked out in a new charcoal grey flannel suit as he twirled me around the ballroom floor. He rang the doorbell. I chastised myself for my incorrect expectations. All 5 feet and 11 inches of Don's 120-pound, toned wrestler's body stood at my door, handsomely packaged in his blue bell-bottomed Navy uniform. He held a pink corsage box in his right hand and had tucked his white sailor hat under his left arm. I realized that I loved a man in uniform. This boy was something special meant just for me.

Don graduated from Liberty High school in 1965 by the skin of his teeth. A few weeks later he left for two years of active duty as a radioman on the USS *Amphion* AR-13 docked in Norfolk, Virginia. We faced our first separation. I'd soon be a high school senior with football games, Saturday night dances, and college in my future. Don's ship could sail to the far corners of the earth, or he could be transferred to a river boat in Vietnam's Mekong Delta. We returned our going-steady class rings to their original owner and vowed to date other people to test the validity of our feelings. We also agreed to keep seeing each other. I went to dances, but it felt wrong to be in the arms of someone other than Don. I wrote him long letters on pastel yellow stationery so he could spot them in the stack at mail call. Don employed his trusty thumb and hitchhiked home from Norfolk across the Chesapeake Bay Bridge Tunnel. Friday nights I paced in front of our living room window watching for him to arrive. If he didn't pull up to the curb by 10 o'clock, I knew he hadn't gotten liberty, or no one had stopped to give my sailor a ride. I stomped on every creaky step to the attic and cried myself to sleep. I never met any boys I liked better. Except for brief excursions to Jamaica and Martinique to qualify her crew for sea pay, Don's repair ship stayed docked in Norfolk. We exchanged our class rings again.

Don separated from active duty on Bastille Day, 1967. No self-respecting twenty-year-old Navy veteran with discharge money burning a hole in his pocket wanted to squire his girlfriend around in his parents' worn out four-door Ford. So, when Don returned, he parked his own 1961 powder blue Ford Fairlane in front of my house and leaped out to ask me for a drive.

That afternoon we burned a lot of gasoline cruising the Pennsylvania countryside. We sat so close together on the front bench seat that a piece of paper couldn't slip between us. "Nancy, we need to talk," Don began in a serious tone. He said that while he was on the ship he'd had a lot of time to think about his future. He shared his hopes and dreams with love and sincerity. He needed to know if my plans could fit with his. I struggled to absorb his unexpected revelation.

"You're called to be a minister?!" I had a problem imagining Don as a minister, standing behind a pulpit on Sunday morning. He was sexy, he liked to drink beer and play poker, and he could talk like a sailor. I had never, ever, thought I'd marry a minister. Being royalty had appealed to me. I thought I might marry Prince Charles. Or the ruggedly handsome TV actor who played Paladin on *Have Gun—Will Travel*. And I swore I'd never marry an undertaker. That pretty much was it for my wedding plans. But I had a problem imagining myself as a minister's wife. They wore print dresses, white gloves, and hats with veils. They taught Sunday school and hosted bridge parties. That wasn't me. I wore slacks to church, sat in the back pew, and doodled on the bulletin. I stank at cards. And *I* could talk like a sailor, too. Everybody expected Don and me to get married. We did, too. But Don had to find a job. I had three years of college to finish. Anything could happen in three years. We knew it was too soon to get engaged. Don hadn't actually asked me to marry him. He'd asked me if I could be his wife, a minister's wife—someday.

Don and his 1961 Ford Fairlane

I was almost three weeks old when I was baptized on Halloween in the Hungarian Reformed Church on the south side of Bethlehem. It was where my Kery grandparents had raised my mother and her siblings. This Protestant denomination dates from the Debrecen Synod of 1567. The denomination suffered two hundred years of repression under the ruling Roman Catholic Hapsburgs, until the end of the monarchy in World War I. Some Hungarian immigrants, beginning with the end of serfdom in 1848, had carried their Protestant beliefs and their desire to worship in the Hungarian language with them to the United States.

Don onboard the USS Amphion
(Don Hammond family photo; used with permission)

My mother had changed her membership to an English-speaking Evangelical and Reformed church a half-block down the alley behind our house. Since before I could remember, she had sent me to Sunday school every week. She'd iron my starched Sunday dress, rub a dab of Vaseline over my black patent leather Mary Jane shoes to polish them to a high shine, and place a dime next to my glass of chocolate milk for me to put in the offering plate. Large posters of Jesus surrounded by adoring children of every color decorated the tidy classrooms. I sat in the back row on a small wooden chair to hear the day's lesson. When it was time to sing, I turned my chair around to be in the front row next to the piano. After class I'd march upstairs for worship and sit next to my mother in the second pew from the back of the sanctuary.

My church taught us children to be religious, to abide by the tenets of our denomination. But in my late teens I sensed a tantalizing faith beyond these bounds. Two songs and one lesson from my early Sunday school classes led me to identify myself as spiritual rather than religious. We'd sung "Jesus Loves the Little Children." I wanted to be like Jesus. If I loved like Jesus, I had to treat people of different races, backgrounds, and lifestyles who lived in my hometown and beyond as equals. When I'd sing "This Little Light of Mine," I loved to shout, "No!" I wouldn't hide my shining light under a bushel. I believed God was on my side when I stood up to people who shamed me for being a girl and for being too damn smart for my own good. I came to believe that everyone on this planet is born with the light of humanity shining within them. I chose to believe that this light is a touch of the divine.

In the lesson, the boy Samuel thought he heard his mentor Eli call to him in the night. Samuel woke Eli three times. Eli told the child it was God's voice he heard and instructed Samuel to listen the next time he heard God call. I'd never heard voices as a child. But when I was in grade school I had a vivid dream of touring the inside of a tree. Elements of the dream had a fairy tale quality. The tree rose without end into the sky, like Jack's beanstalk. The small creatures who guided me looked like Santa's elves. I moved through the bark into the tree's interior like Alice through the looking glass. Sap flowed through vessels in the trunk and out into its sturdy branches. As I rose higher, rooms behind ornate silver grills filled each level. A warm blue-white glow emanated through the grillwork and lit the tree's interior. I woke with a feeling of confidence. As I grew older, questions or understandings or ideas popped unbidden into my brain from nowhere, for no reason. Like Samuel, I learned to listen. Like Jesus' mother Mary, I pondered these things in my heart. Sometimes what I pondered caused me to change what I believed. Sometimes it caused me to change how I treated people. Sometimes it caused me to take action. I believe because I listened and changed and acted, and still do, that life has taken me to places I never imagined possible.

Don blazed ahead with his next question, as though he already knew my answer. Would I go west with him? He wanted to be a fire lookout with the Forest Service. I shook my head in confusion. How could he be a minister and a fire lookout? Where would he find people to preach to in the middle of a forest? How could I go west? I was in college. My mother would kill me if I didn't get married in Bethlehem. How could our plans possibly fit together?

Don had it all worked out. I'd graduate, we'd get married, he'd get accepted to a college in the west, and then we'd move. The Forest Service was more likely to hire a lookout who was a local rather than someone who had to drive from Pennsylvania. He'd use his GI Bill for college expenses and work as a lookout in the summer. He'd graduate from college then go to seminary. This was a side of Don I'd never seen before. He'd matured into a man in the Navy. His plan included me and my dreams. I loved him more. Maybe this could work. But where in the hell had he gotten the harebrained idea to be a fire lookout? "Watching *Lassie*," Don admitted.

Don maneuvered his Ford next to the curb in front of my house. We sealed the deal for our future with a long embrace. "Holy smoke," Don exhaled.

5

A MOUTHFUL OF SPAGHETTI

Back in Moscow I bought a folding cot and two goose down mummy-style sleeping bags for the lookout. Don had decided that without me in his bed, he'd need more than a thin woolen blanket to stay warm. I packed long wooden matches and old newspapers to use for kindling in the stove, rags and spray cleaner for the windows, first-aid supplies, a broom and a dustpan, disinfectant spray and fly tape for the outhouse, a coffee can to protect the toilet paper from mice, and a sturdy emergency bucket. Friday night, back on the lookout, I plumped my pillow, snuggled into my sleeping bag on my folding cot, and slept soundly in the luxury of my personal space with elbow room.

There was no need for an alarm clock on Dunn Peak. The June sun rises on the St. Joe before 5:00 AM. Regulations required that the lookout's windows be unobstructed at all times. I turned away from the uncomfortable brightness and drifted in and out of sleep. Thoughts churned in my head. How many people get to do this? I'm lying on a cot twenty feet off the ground in a fire lookout on top of a mile-high mountain. I'm surrounded by a national forest that burned in the nation's largest forest fire. Don is living his dream job. I'm happy for him. We worked hard to get here. But I'd never put myself in Don's dream. It was always Don on the lookout, not Don and Nancy. Yet here I was, dozing in a sun-warmed, glass-walled cab in the sky.

My mind slipped back to stories my dad had told me about when he'd been a lookout on top of a mountain, searching the sky with binoculars. His mountain had been in Hawaii. He'd been a military police officer who protected

Army installations from Japanese war planes. He said that even though his feet froze standing in the snow, he'd been proud to do his duty, despite the pain. My dad had it hard growing up. He was the third oldest of six boys and one girl born to Hungarian immigrants. His father had developed coal worker's pneumoconiosis, or black lung disease. The family moved from Michigan to Bethlehem so his father could work aboveground in the steel mills. My dad left school in seventh grade and went to work when his father died. Maybe that's when my dad started drinking. He'd been smoking cigarettes since he was nine years old.

When Don and I phoned my parents with the news that Don had been hired as a lookout, my dad got choked up. I think he was proud that Don had achieved his dream. My dad never achieved his. I was about twelve when I found an old photograph of him wearing an auxiliary police uniform. I asked him why he'd become a volunteer after the war instead of joining the Bethlehem police force. He avoided my question. I had to guess at the answer. My dad never carried one extra ounce of weight on his wiry, average build. A narrow fringe of wispy brown hair curved around his otherwise bald head. He was soft-spoken and didn't waste words. His family were his only friends. One of my mother's younger brothers stood a strapping six feet, three inches tall and had a full head of thick dark hair. He'd been a star football player on Bethlehem High's team the year they won a state co-championship. My uncle had no experience in police work, yet after the war he'd been hired by the Bethlehem police force. He and my dad rarely spoke.

My dad had often disappointed me. I'd wanted him to move us into our own home, like my cousins had. I wanted a dad who worked nine-to-five in an office, like my friends' fathers on the block. I wanted a dad who came home sober. But my dad had resigned himself to his lot in life. He carried his burdens inside with no complaint. He swallowed my mother's criticisms and my grandfather's insults. My dad didn't yell or curse. He didn't laugh. He never changed.

My Kery grandparents had also emigrated from Hungary. My mother was the eldest of her six surviving siblings. My grandmother had suffered one still birth and several miscarriages. My grandparents operated a butcher shop that adjoined their house near the steel mills. My mother left school after sixth grade. I think mostly because of her hearing impairment, but maybe also to take care of her four brothers and two sisters while my grandmother worked in their shop and cooked and cleaned and did the washing. My mother never spoke of it and I never asked.

My grandfather Kery was a handsome, dapper, shrewd businessman. Thick silver hair crowned his tall, robust frame. He employed his expressive baritone voice to manipulate customers into buying his merchandise or to reinforce that he alone made the decisions for his family. Papa sold the butcher shop and bought a prosperous confectionary store, still close to the steel mills. Regular customers called my grandmother Mom. They called my grandfather Mr. Kery. To show off his self-made prosperity, Papa purchased a house on the northwest side of Bethlehem, on the same street where some of the top steel company executives lived. My mother never left home. When she married, my dad moved into Papa's house. I never thought it was any of my business to ask why. I arrived two years later. I was mostly obedient growing up. It was hard to be disobedient as an only child under the scrutiny of four adults.

When I was eleven all my friends had transistor radios. I begged my parents for a red, plastic handheld model with a chrome speaker. It cost $29.95, a fortune in those days. My dad told me I could have it, but I had to buy it myself. Suddenly I had money coming in from everywhere. My mother let me keep the change when I walked two blocks to the grocery store to buy milk and bread. Relatives gave me cash for my birthday and Christmas instead of clothes. My mother's friend came from New York City for a visit, said she'd heard I was saving for a transistor, and handed me $5.00. It took months, but I finally had enough money. I handed my mother $30.00. She opened the door on her side of the dining room buffet, pushed aside her pocketbook, lifted out my radio, and handed it to me without ceremony. I grabbed it, raced upstairs to my bedroom, threw myself on my bed, and tuned it to the pop music station, WAEB.

A door adjoined my bedroom to my grandparents' bedroom. My grandfather's alarm rang at 5:00 AM every morning. He had his store open and ready at 6:30 to catch workers walking past it to and from the 7:00 AM shift change at the Steel. At night I'd turn my transistor's volume to a whisper so he wouldn't hear it. But he did. My mother told me I'd have to quit listening to my radio at night or move to the bedroom in the attic. I worried that the goblins who lived in the cubbyholes under the eaves would come for me in the dark. But I wouldn't give up my radio. I moved to the attic.

The summer I was twelve, my next-door neighbor felt it necessary to take me on as her special project. Mrs. Stein had been raised wealthy. Her father had founded the local Neuweiler Brewery. She belonged to the best clubs. She played bridge with manicured nails and had a housekeeper and a yard man. She was a bit younger than my grandmother and had no children. Mrs. Stein and I sat at her kitchen table and pretended we were at one of her clubs. We sipped Chinese tea from bone china cups. She served me department store petit fours on a silver platter monogrammed with her husband's initials. She mentioned that she'd been observing me and my family. She said I needed to wear a bra. At first I was angry. I thought she had a lot of nerve meddling in my life. But my mother seemed relieved when I told her to take me bra shopping.

Bertha Stein, nee Neuweiler, circa 1967

One afternoon over iced tea and strawberry shortcake, Mrs. Stein told me she'd never met a man as proud of his child as my father. She said he'd pushed me in my carriage when I was a baby, then in my stroller. When I could walk he'd hold my hand to make sure I didn't tumble. When I got tired he'd carry me home. "Nancy," she said, "no other father on this block ever walked with his child."

My dad had no friends among the men in our neighborhood. Papa and the man on the corner owned their own businesses. The rest had offices at the Lehigh Valley Railroad or the Bethlehem Steel. My dad was a common laborer. He brought home work pants so saturated with his salty sweat that my mother stood them upright on the basement floor to wait to be laundered. Mrs. Stein helped me to understand that despite my father's lack of education, despite his lack of a high-paying job, despite his demons, he was a man of character. She helped me to recognize how important I was to him, how he stood up for me, how he struggled to give me everything I wanted.

Because of Mrs. Stein's guidance, I paid attention to the ways my dad exerted the steel in his backbone—with strength, but without threat. He told my mother to let me go to my friend's birthday party. I'd never been to a movie theater before. He told her it wasn't charity to let the Steins give me a scholarship to summer camp. Dad bought the TV I'd begged for and installed it in Papa's living room without asking for his approval. My grandparents never disciplined me. Papa always tattled on my misbehavior to my father, not to my mother. I came to believe that my dad had insisted that my grandparents not interfere.

My dad taught me to stand up for myself. He showed me how to hammer a nail and saw a board. He warned me that I'd break my thumb if I tucked it in my fist to hit someone. Then he made me punch his palm, hard. He taught me how to use my knee if a boy got fresh. He made me apologize when I hurt my mother's feelings. I took my dad's expectations for me to heart. I used them to challenge my vision of who I wanted to become. When my mother got really mad at me, she'd yell that I was just like my father. I valued those words as her highest compliment.

The five of us shared Papa's house in relative harmony until I was thirteen and my mother was forty-nine. A seismic shift occurred when I entered womanhood with my mother in the throes of menopause. Every conversation between us ended in shouts and tears. My grandmother gave up her role as our mediator. My dad came home smelling of whiskey with beer chasers. I retreated to my sanctuary in the attic to keep the peace.

The summer I was fifteen, the tension in our household escalated with the outside temperature. My friend Liz had asked if I wanted to volunteer with her as a hospital candy striper. I was an honor roll student, biology was my favorite subject, I'd considered nursing as a career, and I needed to get out of the house. Papa hounded my parents. What did they mean I wouldn't get paid? I was old enough to earn my own money. Why did I need more school? I'd just get married!

At the end of August, my parents sat me down for a rare face-to-face discussion. I told them I'd learned that nursing wasn't for me. I promised my parents I'd get a degree I could use to get a good job. They promised to do everything they could to help. We agreed it made financial sense for me to live at home and attend college in town. In my heart I wanted to challenge myself with the hard science curriculum at Lehigh University, but the school only accepted boys. I would apply to Moravian College.

Until that discussion I'd had doubts about my mother's hierarchy of family allegiances. I'd often wondered whether she was more my father's wife or my grandfather's daughter. I thought she judged me a poor fourth behind my grandmother. Now, at least on the subject of my education, I knew I could count on a solid three against two majority. My mother informed Papa that I'd been accepted to Moravian. Papa didn't tolerate challenges to his authority. After that day he never said a civil word to me again. In fact he said nothing to me at all. If he couldn't bend me to his will, then for him I didn't exist, even though we shared space in the same house. The longer he shunned me the more respect I lost for him, and the more respect I gained for myself. I mourned the loss of our relationship, but I refused to allow Papa to decide what happened with my life.

I was the first in my family to go to college. I'd never planned to be a groundbreaker. It went against my nature as an introvert. I struggled to adjust to college life. It embarrassed me (more than it should have) to wear the college's freshman beanie. Tensions spiraled at home. Papa complained that my typing kept him awake. He called my dad a weakling with no control over his child. At Christmas Dad gave me the bad news that he couldn't afford my next tuition payment. I'd have to transfer to a less expensive college. But first I'd have to get a job to earn money to help pay for my tuition. I sold men's underwear, pajamas, and ties at a strip mall discount store for seven months. My mother went to work, too. She cleaned a funeral home. Papa eased up on my dad because he liked that I had a paying job. When I transferred to Kutztown State College, twenty-six miles from home, any hope of a reconciliation with my grandfather evaporated. My grandfather didn't speak another word to me for fourteen years, until he was eighty-nine.

After the Navy Don attended a preparatory school to hone his study skills. He was accepted to Kutztown. I was excited to see him every day, but he wanted a lot of my time. I had ecology papers to write and chemistry exams to study for. Don still hadn't mastered how to take notes or study. He struggled with his classes. His grade point average fell below 2.0. The dean of students called Don into his office and advised him to find a good factory job. Don was crushed to fail again. Soon after leaving college, he was hired by the Bethlehem

Steel as a timekeeper. It didn't take him long to get over being disappointed with himself. The men he worked with didn't care that he'd flunked out of college. They liked to listen to his Navy stories and his plans to be a lookout. They told him their own dreams. These men had worked at the Steel for ten or fifteen years and hadn't made a move. Don realized their dreams were all talk. He vowed to be different. He'd use the Steel as his means to earn enough money to break away. He kept these plans to himself, in case he failed again.

It was December 1968. Don hadn't mentioned going back to college or becoming a minister or a fire lookout for a while. He seemed to be settling in at the Steel. I loved Don. I loved his dreams. I was worried that he'd abandoned them. I was determined to go west, like we'd planned. I didn't want to go by myself, but I would if I had to. I worried that Don had turned into a quitter. I worried I might not love him if he had.

My grandparents had gone to bed after our traditional Christmas Day buffet for the entire family. Don had lost money playing poker at the kitchen table with my Dad, aunts, and uncles. He and I had dated for so long that my relatives all thought of him as a member of the family. My parents loved Don, too. He could do no wrong in their eyes. My mother and I had put away the last of the food and dishes. I'd hung my apron inside the basement door and headed into the living room where Don waited. Dad walked past and gave me a quick smile. I wondered why? The only light in the room glowed from the tree lights and the electric candelabra in the front window. I thought it odd that Don sat perched on the arm of the sofa. I was tired from the day's hubbub. I settled next to him and kicked off my heels. Don told me he loved me. I yawned and said I loved him too. My eyes grew heavy. I started to doze. Don started a speech. Nothing, he said, would stop him from becoming a minister. I nodded. He would finish college and seminary. I was glad to hear that. He'd started an extra job, part-time in the produce department at the Acme. I paid attention. He asked if I could take extra credits to graduate on time. A feeling prickled in my brain. Had Don asked my dad for my hand? I sat up straight and looked him in the eye. He smiled. This was it. The answers I'd wanted. The proposal I'd waited for. My man was no quitter.

Don got down on one knee and took my hand. "Nancy Ann Sule, will you marry me? You said you didn't need a ring."

"Yes, I want to marry you. I don't need a ring to prove we're engaged." It was the best Christmas gift ever.

Don and I walked into the kitchen. My parents sat at the table drinking beer.

"Well, what did you say?" my mother asked. I turned and gave Don a long kiss. "That's what I thought," she smiled.

"It's about time," my dad said, and took a swig of his beer.

Don and I planned to get married on June 27, 1970. We'd rent a cheap apartment. I'd get a job. We'd scrimp and save every spare penny. We had no doubt we'd leave Bethlehem for the clean, green, pine-forested west as soon as possible. We just didn't yet know where exactly we'd be going.

"You know the kind of wedding I want you to have," my dad said. He handed me a pile of cash and emphasized there'd be no more. Dad didn't need to explain his expectations for my wedding. Traditional Hungarian weddings were the only kind I knew. There'd be an afternoon ceremony in my home church. Don's parents and mine would each host a small reception at their homes for close family and friends. There'd be a sit-down dinner in a hall big enough to seat seventy. Don and I would cut the cake. The band on stage would play polkas and rock and roll. There'd be an open bar and a bride dance. People would pay for a short spin with me around the dance floor. One of my uncles or cousins would tuck me under his arm and run off with me. We'd hide until Don collected my ransom money from our guests. I'd throw my bouquet. Don would throw my garter. We'd leave to start our honeymoon, cash in hand.

My mother and I bought my sample wedding gown on sale for $100. It was a sleek A-line with an empire waist, scoop neck, short sleeves, and a long detachable train that hung from the shoulders. Appliqued flowers and bows accented the gown and the train. Crystal beading highlighted the bows. It fit me like it had been custom-tailored. It was my something new. Then my parents bowed out. It surprised me that they expected Don and me to do everything ourselves. But it turned out to be less complicated that way.

I bought a McCall's sewing pattern that matched the style of my gown and yards of yellow cotton embroidered with tiny yellow rosebuds. I sewed my maid of honor's gown using my grandmother's treadle Singer sewing machine in my attic bedroom. My two bridesmaids sewed their gowns. The men rented black tuxedos, bow ties, and ruffled shirts. Don and I negotiated deals for a photographer, flowers, beer and whiskey, and our cake. We had to move our wedding one week later because the Masonic Temple had double-booked the day. We had to move our wedding one more week because the band and the minister refused to work on the Fourth of July. And Don refused to get married on Independence Day. Thankfully, we'd waited until the last minute to order our invitations, just in case we had to change the date.

My grandparents had left the house before I woke up on my wedding day. I sneaked a handkerchief from my grandmother's dresser and tucked it in my bouquet. It was my something old. I'd asked my married bridesmaid if I could wear her veil. It was my something borrowed. I slipped the garter my mother had worn on her wedding day onto my leg. It was my something blue. I put a sixpence in my shoe. It hurt my foot. I took it out. A rain squall showered good luck onto our special day. The skies cleared just in time for my bridesmaids and me to walk the one block to my church. Friends and family had crowded into the Gothic sanctuary with its exquisite stained glass windows. My dad had drowned his nerves in whiskey. I had to poke him to answer the second time the minister asked, "Who gives this woman?" Don and I shuttled the ten blocks between the gatherings at our parents' houses, then headed to our reception. This was the only wedding either of us planned to have. We'd decided to enjoy our reception to the very end. My husband held me close as we danced. I breathed in my Ambush mixed with his English Leather. We were still dancing when the band played, "Goodnight, Irene." We waved goodbye to our parents and the other stragglers. We drove off to our long awaited honeymoon, still dressed in our wedding clothes.

Our wedding day with our parents, 1970

Don and I settled into our one-bedroom apartment. It was a converted appliance store in the middle of a stretch of row homes that spanned the entire block. I mailed out my resume to job openings in the west. Don applied to western colleges. We'd agreed that wherever I got my best job offer or wherever the best college was located that accepted Don was where we would go. We received a single reply. Idaho State University in Pocatello accepted Don on the condition that he complete a semester at a junior college. ISU seemed leery of a twenty-three-year-old Vietnam-era veteran who worked in a Pennsylvania steel mill, had graduated 972nd in his high school class of 1,016 students, and had failed in his first attempt at college.

Don, however, had no doubt that he could prove himself worthy of ISU. He decided to attend a junior college in Idaho so he could knock on the ISU registrar's door the very next day after he'd completed his conditional semester—and so he could find a summer job as a fire lookout in the wonder-filled wilds of Idaho. The College of Southern Idaho in Twin Falls accepted Don. We were giddy that our road west would take us to live where not one, but two waterfalls flowed from forested, green mountains. We hoped our dream had found a home.

Our trusty Opel packed and ready to go to Idaho

Five months married on the cold cloudy morning of December 26, 1970, all things seemed possible. Don and I waved goodbye to our families gathered on the icy sidewalk to see us off. We left Pennsylvania with most of our worldly belongings crammed inside our little green Opel. We drove off toward our future in Idaho so enthused that neither of us looked back, not that we could have seen out the cluttered back window.

We arrived in Twin Falls early on New Year's Eve. There were no mountains, no forests, and nothing was green. The waterfalls flowed through a deep canyon gouged out eons before into the flat, arid Snake River Plateau. Our prearranged apartment was in a moldy basement with an illicit past. Total strangers invited us into their home for a New Year's Eve party. Until we found jobs, we survived on the russet potatoes the previous tenants had left in a straw-lined pit dug in the back yard of our new apartment. I worked three jobs. Don drove to Mountain Home and bought a Dalmatian puppy. We discovered that we loved the Idaho desert.

Don made the dean's list at CSI. The morning after he received his grades we drove two hours east to Pocatello. The Idaho State registrar examined a folder with Don's name on the tab. She looked perplexed and asked to see Don's acceptance letter and his grades from CSI. She exhaled a snort. "Your grades don't meet our standards. You were accepted by mistake. I'll allow you to register, though, on probation, of course." Don was stunned and embarrassed. He took in a deep breath and looked the registrar in the eye. He made it clear he didn't want ISU to lower its standards on his account. The registrar called after us as we walked out. "Try the University of Idaho. They might take you, even with your grades."

Don phoned the Idaho registrar, explained his conversation with Idaho State, and sent in his transcripts. The registrar called back and, without a heartbeat of hesitation, told Don to pack his belongings and move to Moscow. And, the registrar added, the University of Idaho was proud to have him as a student. By Thanksgiving we lived in a rented two-bedroom bungalow and had three jobs between us. We cheered for the U of I Vandals. We played Risk and drank wine on Friday nights with our new friends Ron and Amy. Don settled into his classwork and proved himself a solid student.

Winter thawed. Don's hope of working as a fire lookout reemerged with full force. He was in the perfect place to turn his dream into reality. We knew Dale from church. He worked for the Potlatch District of the St. Joe National Forest. Don asked for his help to get hired as a lookout. Dale said he was sorry.

All the lookouts were already staffed with the people who had worked there the summer before. The only jobs open were on thinning crews. Don said he'd take any job in the forest. He wanted to be available, just in case a lookout didn't show up.

When we'd first arrived in Moscow, Amy had advised us to put our money into the First Bank of Troy, located in a small town east of Moscow. She said Frank Brocke would shake our hands when we walked in and ask us what we needed. I thought it strange for a bank teller to greet people at the door. Amy surprised me. She said Frank wasn't a teller, it was his bank. All the stores in Moscow accepted the bank's counter checks because Frank never bounced a check. When the man who had robbed his bank got out of jail, Frank gave him a job.

Don walked into the First Bank of Troy. President Frank Otto Brocke shook his hand and asked him what he needed. Don said he had to buy steel-toed Red Wing boots before he could start his job with the Forest Service. The boots cost $87.50 at David's department store. Don didn't have the money. Frank asked if Don had borrowed from him before. Our car's differential had conked out going over Lost Trail Pass a few months earlier. Don had called the bank from the Buick dealership in Pocatello to get a loan to pay for the repairs. Frank told Don to write the check because the money was already in his account. The car dealer called Don a liar. Don reminded Frank that he had to talk to the dealer himself to prove that Don's check was good. Frank Brocke nodded in remembrance. Then he wrote $100 on a sheet of the bank's letterhead and handed it to Don. "Give this to the teller," he directed. "You'll need heavy socks and there's tax. Pay me back when you're able. Good luck."

I thought Don would be starving after thinning brush all day, but he wasn't eating his spaghetti. He leaned forward, folded his arms onto the dinner table and looked me in the eye. He asked if I could manage being alone for part of the summer. He'd been offered a job as a lookout. With overtime he should earn enough so I could quit cashiering at the discount store and come up on weekends. But I'd have to keep my job at the university to pay the rent. Don raised his eyebrows and tilted his head. "How about it?" he asked with a smile.

Of course I could manage. This was why we'd come to Idaho. This could be Don's only chance to be a Forest Service lookout, the job he'd dreamed of since he was a boy. I'd adjust my hours at the lab and drive to the lookout on Friday and back on Sunday. Weekends on the lookout could be a second honeymoon. I was so excited for Don. I told him I'd drive to the lookout with him. There was no way I'd miss out on the beginning of this adventure. It was Friday night. We had to leave Sunday morning. I needed to do laundry and buy groceries. What should we pack? Don mumbled a reply. I couldn't understand what he said. He finally had a mouthful of spaghetti.

Misty and me at Shoshone Falls, spring 1971

Christmas tree cutting
at Big Boulder campground

Decorating done, Moscow, 1971

6

LIVIN' LA VIDA LOOKOUT

I looked forward to my trips on White Pine Drive. A sense of protected ease settled over me. I didn't understand until my gray-haired years that this forested corridor transported me back to Bethlehem, back to the street that runs in front of my childhood home. In my youth branches of tall Norway maples interlaced to form an arched canopy that spanned the street for blocks. I noticed the squirrels and birds and bugs that lived in this urban woodland. I observed their behavior. I marveled at the mystery of the trees changing with the seasons. I developed a thirst to educate myself about nature. I began to wonder where I fit into nature's scheme.

I wandered my street alone until I met Don. When we dated in high school Don walked out his back door and turned left into the alley. In a few steps the alley merged into my street. In ten blocks Don arrived at my front door. We'd stroll the neighborhood between our houses in the privacy of darkness. In winter we'd peek into lamp-lit living rooms and comment on the décor and Christmas decorations. In summer we'd discuss landscaping, outdoor furniture, and what we'd cook on the grill. We'd pause in front of my church and talk about our beliefs. We began to learn each other's likes and dislikes. We began to decide if we wanted to stay together. When we ran out of words I'd snuggle my shoulder under Don's arm, tilt my head against his neck, and lift my chin so our lips could meet in a kiss. It was important to learn if we liked each other in that way, too.

St. Maries was jammed with vacationers. It was the weekend before the Fourth of July. I waited in line to get gas. Traffic clogged the river road and kicked up a dust storm. Campgrounds were filled to capacity. RVs and pickups with campers on the back squeezed onto every wide spot on the road. A haze of pine-scented smoke from their campfires hung low over the river. I stopped at Hoyt Flat and asked Wanda to radio Don that I was on my way.

Wanda said the lookouts were on overtime because the forest was dry, and campers could be careless. They threw away lit cigarettes, left campfires unattended, and set off illegal fireworks. The specter of the 1910 Big Burn still loomed large in the minds of the workers of the St. Joe Forest. Many had grown up hearing stories of the death and destruction witnessed by friends and relatives. People in Avery feared that the recovering forest could be reduced to ashes again. I'd thought ahead and brought binoculars from home to help Don look for smokes.

Past the bunkhouse I downshifted to second gear to climb the switchbacks. Our wagon shimmied in the deep dust. The engine struggled. My heart raced at the thought of tipping over the crumbling road edge. At least Don knew I was on my way. He'd radio Wanda if I didn't arrive on time. I told myself I could handle this predicament. I shifted to first gear and told our wagon to pretend it was a Jeep. At the top of the hairpin spiral I opened my window, pulled in a deep breath of clean mountain air, smiled at my success, and shifted to third gear along the ridge.

My mother had never learned to drive, but she could steer if she had to. Some Sunday nights when my dad had a long weekend off, he'd drink too much at the Amvets club. My mother drank her fair share, but she held her liquor better. I never saw her drunk. We three had perfected the drive home. Mom and I steadied dad as he stumbled from the bar stool to the car. Dad arranged himself in the driver's seat while mom and I climbed in. Mom dug the car keys out of her pocketbook, slid across the bench seat, put the key in the ignition, and grabbed the steering wheel with both hands. Dad turned the key, worked the gas and the clutch, and shifted. When a traffic light turned red, Mom directed, "Slow down, Steve."

I learned to trust in the power of prayer watching from the back seat as my parents drove in tandem. We never got stopped by the police and we always made it home safe. I hated when the car got parked with one wheel on the curb. Mrs. Stein could be critical. "I see your father drove home drunk last night," she'd jab at me. I never explained how it really happened. It was none of her business.

When I was fifteen my mother rejected my request for a learner's permit. She said I didn't have anywhere to go that I needed the car. She had a point. I couldn't muster one reason to counter her argument. I just wanted to keep up with my friends. Dad negotiated that I would wait until I was seventeen. That suited me, because I hated the thought of driving our dented Plymouth with a three-speed shift on the steering column. I hoped by then my parents would spring for a newer car.

One Saturday morning, just before I turned seventeen, I walked into the kitchen. Dad set his coffee cup on the table, stubbed out his cigarette, and quizzed me. "So, do you like it?" I had no idea what he meant. "It's parked out front. Try the driver's seat."

I raced to the street and screeched my penny loafers to a halt in front of a 1961 aqua blue Mercury Comet with fins and chrome. It was only four years old. It was an automatic. "Is it really ours?" I asked in thrilled disbelief. My dad just smiled, lit another cigarette, and handed me the key. I didn't get the car often. My dad needed it to get to work. My lack of experience made me a cautious driver.

A few months before our wedding, Don had bought a brand new 1970 Opel Kadett station wagon for our drive west. He instructed me from the passenger seat how to shift the four-on-the floor transmission. I ground the gears. Don winced. I searched for the balance between the gas and the clutch. The wagon lurched down the street and stalled. Don grunted. I cried in frustration, worried that I'd ruined the transmission. Don consoled and encouraged me. I did better on my next try. It took days until I shifted without a grind or a jerk. I was proud of myself. I complimented Don for being a patient teacher. We'd made the best of a bad situation.

The hours I'd driven alone on Idaho's back roads had increased my confidence and self-reliance. I'd come to believe I could handle a challenge on my own. I didn't want to be alone, without Don and Misty, but I was learning that I could manage. I steered around the ninety-degree curve onto the cliffside that drops into Storm Creek. A golden eagle sat perched on the road with her talons curved over the edge. Annoyed by my intrusion, the skilled aerialist unfolded her wings full width, released her grip, and pushed off without a single flap. She soared away on the updrafts rising from the valley and shrank to a black speck against the Idaho-blue sky. It was over in seconds. That eagle knew when she let go and spread her wings, the air would hold her up, and she could soar. Years later I'd remember her flight when I faced a major decision.

Don waved hello from the catwalk. When we'd first arrived on Dunn Peak, I'd worried that Misty might be afraid to climb the lookout's steep, open-sided stairs. Silly me. Misty spotted one of the golden-mantled ground squirrels that lived in the rock pile below the lookout. She charged down from the catwalk at breakneck speed, barely negotiated the turns on the landings, and flew straight past me. No matter how fast she ran, the squirrels always skittered into their burrow before she arrived. I had to wait for my hug until Misty sniffed and pawed at the rock pile to show that she knew exactly where those critters were hiding. Misty and the squirrels spent hours playing hide and seek until either she or the squirrels decided they had something better to do.

I turned to climb the stairs and yelped in happy surprise. A fat propane tank sat strapped to the landing. Now we could cook with gas. The fire crew still supplied us with logs chain-sawed to fit the wood stove's fire box. Don had to split the logs down to firewood. He aimed his axe blade at cracks in the log and swung hard. With two or three chops, he broke the log in two. Then he'd split the halves into smaller pieces easy to burn. If the log had knots where a branch had grown out, Don pounded in a steel wedge with a sledgehammer to split it. An adage teaches that firewood warms you twice, once when you chop it and once when you burn it. Don decided that on a lookout firewood warms you a third time—when you haul it up two flights of stairs. As happy as I was to have propane to cook with, I'd come to enjoy that ugly hulk of a wood stove. Its fires kept the lookout toasty and romantic.

Lookout towers have no plumbing, so the fire crew also supplied our water. They filled six 10-gallon steel milk cans at the bunkhouse, then trucked them 12 miles to the lookout. True to what Wade had told us, his crew unloaded the cans onto the ground. Don lugged them up the two flights of stairs by himself. It was hard work. Ten gallons of water weigh 83.5 pounds. Each steel can weighed about 15 pounds. Don hefted nearly 100 pounds up four steps from the ground to the first landing, up twelve steps at a 50-degree angle to the second landing, up steeper steps to the hatch, through the hatch, across the catwalk, and into the cab. A pounding, rhythmic *ka-thunk, ka-thunk, ka-thunk* vibrated the lookout as he stopped to catch his breath after each lift. Those precious 60 gallons had to last us one week, longer if the crew became busy with fire control duties. Don had arranged the water runs for Thursday or early Friday so he could hitch a ride to shower at the bunkhouse. He usually smelled fresh when I arrived on Friday afternoon.

Don and I washed dishes and ourselves the old-fashioned way. We heated water in a pot on the stove, poured just enough into a plastic basin to get everything clean, washed with soapy water, rinsed with clean water in another basin, and then dried. We hung wet towels over the railing and laid heavy flat rocks on top to keep them from blowing off into the trees.

Misty watching for ground squirrels

Watching for smokes

Chopping firewood

Lifting our water cans

Water became my gauge for how personal standards can slip away on a lookout. If I arrived to find empty water cans lined on the ground, I knew the fire crew had been busy that week. That meant Don hadn't had a shower, and it meant we needed to conserve what water we had left to cook and wash dishes. Our personal hygiene shifted to a low priority. I discovered that if we both smelled bad, neither of us minded. Every Sunday night back in Moscow, I sank into our clawfoot tub for a long, hot bubble bath, whether we'd had plenty of water on the lookout or not.

White painted rocks formed the perimeter of the helispot on Dunn Peak's flattened summit and spelled out its location on Dunn. By the 1970s helicopters had proven a valuable tool in fighting large forest fires. Pilots who had ferried soldiers to Vietnam's combat fields now transported firefighters to battle blazes. Or they lowered a huge bucket slung below the helicopter's belly into a river or a lake, filled it with water, and dumped the water onto a blaze. I'd have been thrilled to watch a pilot maneuver a pinpoint landing on Dunn Peak's summit, but I knew if that happened, the St. Joe Forest, or Don and I, faced danger.

Prominent signs featuring Smokey Bear stood along the St. Joe's main roads. They informed forest users of the fire danger and reminded the users that they served as the first line of defense against forest fires. The Forest Service had held conferences in 1940 and 1954 to emphasize the need for a uniform, nationwide, scientifically based fire danger rating system. Versions of a fire danger system outlined in 1961 had been field-tested up until 1971 at nearly 150 unique locations. The National Fire Danger Rating System (NFDRS) was officially implemented in the summer of 1972. The NFDRS tracks the effects of previous weather on live and dead fuels and adjusts the effects based on predicted weather conditions. Seven data points, objective and subjective estimates, fire behavior components, and the fire danger index were combined into a complex set of equations to derive a scaled occurrence number.

The calculated fire danger is expressed in five class levels that can be understood by the general public:

- Low (Green)—Fires are not easily started,
- Moderate (Blue)—Fires start easily and spread at a moderate rate,
- High (Yellow)—Fires start easily and spread at a fast rate,
- Very High (Orange)—Fires start easily, spread rapidly, and quickly increase in intensity, and
- Extreme (Red)—The fire situation is explosive and can result in extensive property damage.

Dunn Peak's helispot

US Forest Service fire danger sign

When the fire crew had installed our propane stove, Wade walked Don down the hill to two wooden, ventilated boxes on tall legs that housed a Forest Service manual weather station. Don became the St. Joe's official weatherman. The smaller shelter housed a calibrated half-inch thick rod of Ponderosa pine attached to a scale that measured the moisture content of the forest's fuels. In the larger shelter two thermometers measured minimum and maximum air temperatures, a battery-operated fan psychrometer and disc recorded relative humidity, and an anemometer with a mechanical counter gave the wind speed in miles per hour. On its exterior the larger shelter also supported a wind direction system and a precipitation gauge. Don radioed in his readings every day. Wade plugged the data into the NFDRS equations and used the results to decide how best to deploy his fire control resources. His crew adjusted the fire danger levels on the Smokey Bear signs to inform the public of current conditions.

That Saturday night the lookouts' overtime ended at 7:00 PM with no smokes reported. Don, Misty, and I escaped the tower for a walk. Locals had warned us it was dangerous to surprise a foraging bear. Don had his fishing knife laced onto his belt, Misty had a bell tied onto her collar, and we blew referee whistles hung on our necks to alert bears that we were coming. We'd hoped the noisy holiday crowds had chased the bears into the back country. But just to be safe, we drove out to the fireroad to walk where Misty could run loose.

Overall, I'm a no-nonsense daughter of a steel mill laborer and a funeral home cleaning lady. But when I was young and my dad took us on Sunday drives, I'd sometimes get queasy feelings in the pit of my stomach. I knew what I'd see ahead, even though I'd never been there before. As an adult, Don noticed that in public places strangers sometimes did a double take upon seeing me. They'd stare at me perplexed about why I looked familiar to them. Often, when I'd been introduced to people from Maine to Hawaii, they'd ask if we'd met before. Not in this life, I sometimes thought.

We reached the drop-off into Setzer Creek. The setting sun cast long shadows into the deep ravine. Misty skidded to a dead stop and let out a low growl. The hair rose along her spine. I swear I saw the shadows move. Some nights I thought I heard screams on the wind. Don read my troubled expression and asked what was wrong. I admitted that being so close to a deathtrap where firefighters had been burned alive gave me the creeps. I wondered if the spirits of those burned firefighters still gathered at their cook tent for dinner. Had anyone warned them to run for their lives? Could history repeat itself? Could

Forest Service manual weather station

Don and I become victims of a raging wildfire? Don said I worried too much about things that would never happen. Maybe he was right. I wanted to know how such deadly events had come to happen at this very spot, just sixty-two years earlier.

On New Year's Day, 1910, a tempest near Seattle smashed boats and ships moored in Washington's Puget Sound into piles of kindling. Less than two weeks later, off the coast of Coos Bay, Oregon, towering waves swamped the coal-carrying steamer Czarina and claimed twenty-four lives of her twenty-five man crew. Through the month a series of frigid storms moved inland off the north Pacific and saturated the mountain ranges in Washington, Idaho, and Montana with snow so constant and so deep that railroads struggled to keep traffic moving along their lines.

Then January's weather shifted abruptly. Temperatures reached above freezing on mountains with up to seven thousand feet elevation. Crystalline arms on snowflakes interlock to form a strong, supportive mesh that helps to stabilize snowpacks on steep mountains. The warm temperatures melted the snow's supportive mesh. Trees in the snow act like rebar embedded in concrete and help to secure the snow from sliding down the mountain. Coal-burning locomotives had ignited fires that had burned off most of the trees growing on the slopes along the tracks. When the stress on a snowpack exceeds the strength within it, an avalanche plunges with force equivalent to a tidal wave.

Frigid temperatures returned to the mountains early in February and froze thick icy crusts over the compressed snow. More storms from the north Pacific carried in more snow that fell in the cold temperatures with a fleecy or granular consistency. Persistent winds pushed the airy powder into huge drifts in the canyons. On high ridges, immense, cantilevered, snowy platforms perched on top of unstable slabs of compressed, frozen snow. Weighty snow drifts lay at the ready to descend on railroad tracks and small towns situated below steep, deforested mountainsides. The first avalanches fell in accustomed locations and did little damage. But in the last week of February, avalanches swept away houses in the north Idaho towns of Adair, Mace, Dorsey, and Burke. At least twenty-six people—miners, their wives, and their children—were killed as they slept. Avalanches in Washington and Oregon smothered five railroad workers.

High in Washington's Cascade Range, two Great Northern trains had been trapped for days in towering drifts at the depot in Wellington. In the pre-dawn darkness on March 1, 1910, exploding thunder discharged the deadliest avalanche in U.S. history. A quarter-mile wide white wall of death detached from the burned-over mountain slope above Wellington. The avalanche descended without warning on the trains filled with sleeping passengers and railroad crewmen, rammed the trains into the depths of Tye Canyon, and entombed them and their occupants under 480 inches of suffocating, crushing snow. The catastrophe extinguished at least 96 lives.

Later in March the weather shifted dramatically again. Abnormally high temperatures thawed the snow-glutted mountains. Torrents of meltwater sluiced down and flooded the valleys. But no moisture fell from the sky. The U.S. Weather Bureau reported the month as the driest March in Idaho since the Bureau began keeping records in 1894.

No April showers relieved the bone-dry weather pattern. Idaho and Montana recorded their hottest April temperatures ever. Mountain snow drifts melted six weeks earlier than usual. Vegetation flourished on the damp forest floors watered by the moisture from the melting snowbanks. By the end of the month the plentiful sunshine, warm temperatures, and constant dry winds had sucked up the winter's abundant moisture. The lush vegetation seared in the lethal dryness. Forest floors transformed into tinderboxes crammed full of kindling needing just one spark to ignite an inferno.

In 1908 Gifford Pinchot had organized the national forests into six autonomous regional districts. District Forester William Buckhout Greeley supervised District One, headquartered in Missoula, Montana. The non-smoking, non-drinking, wiry six-footer was the son and grandson of New England Congregational ministers. Greeley had graduated Phi Beta Kappa from the University of California at Berkley in 1901 and graduated at the top of the Yale Forest School class of 1904. In 1905 Greeley went to work for Pinchot. He was put in charge of southern California's Sierra Forest Reserve and adopted as his own the cooperative firefighting system developed there between private lumbermen and the government.

In 1909 District One included 22 national forests and spanned 41 million acres across northeast Washington, north Idaho, Montana, North Dakota, northwest South Dakota, Minnesota, and Michigan. A single forest guard, armed with axes, picks, shovels, and buckets, patrolled an average of 59 thousand acres on horseback. In 1910 District One's Coeur d'Alene National Forest comprised more than 2.2 million acres. In 1911 the Forest Service would cede more than 1 million acres from the Coeur d'Alene and Clearwater forests to form the St. Joe National Forest.

The U.S. Congress had slashed District One's 1909 appropriations by more than 60 percent. Greeley complained that because of the reduced budget his men could patrol only one-quarter of the district's forests, leaving the rest at risk. Greeley's most experienced rangers sat tied to their desks filling out forms for agricultural land claims, timber sales, and grazing allocations instead of managing patrols and firefighters out in the field.

The first 1910 fire in District One large enough to be recorded ignited on April 29 in northwest Montana's Blackfeet Forest. April lightning storms rarely occur in the intermountain west. Careless campers, loggers, or homesteaders started some of these early fires. But the overwhelming majority originated near railroad construction sites and along tracks traveled by coal-powered locomotives, widely scorned as the arsonists of the forest.

Temperatures soared in June. The lack of rain broke records. Forest floors crackled underfoot with explosive tinder earlier in the season than anyone had ever experienced. More than one hundred northwest weather stations reported no measurable rain in July. It was the fifth consecutive month with below-normal precipitation. Rivers ran lower than ever recorded. Lumber operations halted because streams were too dry to float logs to the mills. Temperatures in usually cool mountain towns climbed to one hundred degrees. Parching winds blew like bellows and revived smoldering fires that had been sparked back in April. Jagged forks of dry lightning ignited new blazes near Flathead, Montana; Colville, Washington; the Idaho Coeur d'Alenes; and in eastern Oregon. The uncontrolled conflagrations consumed thousands of acres of valuable timber, destroyed lumber mills and mining facilities, and incinerated homesteads. The intermountain west's clear air filled with so much smoke that it blocked the sunshine.

The fifty unseasonably early and large fires that burned across District One threatened both national and private forests. Timber company owners strong-armed the Secretary of Agriculture to allow Greeley to exceed his meager emergency budget. Greeley hired three hundred temporary firefighters and dispatched them into the forests equipped with new axes, mattocks, shovels, crosscut saws, boilers, washtubs, coffee pots, and frying pans purchased at local hardware stores. Instead of wearing his standard office uniform, Greeley came to work armored in heavy logging boots and a sturdy work shirt prominently pinned with his bronze Forest Service badge. He personally supervised the worst battles out in the forest.

In past fire seasons Greeley had restricted District One's losses to less than one percent of its total area. But in 1910 he warned that any fire begun under such treacherous conditions could almost instantaneously flare beyond the influence of human endeavor. Heavy smoke clouded the interior forests. Greeley withdrew his lookout and patrol system because the men could no longer distinguish smoke coming off a new fire from the smoke hanging in the air.

At the end of July, welcome showers put out or checked scores of the blazes in District One. But in District Six, Forester C.S. Chapman fought to control wildfires raging along both slopes of Washington's Cascades and in the Blue Mountains of Wallowa County, Oregon. Washington's *Spokane Daily Chronicle* raised the alarm that the forest fires had altered from destructive to deadly and killed five people.

The size and number of wildfires increased in August under record-breaking drought, unparalleled high temperatures, and prevailing westerly winds. The ill-equipped and underfunded five-year-old Forest Service was hard-pressed to control, let alone extinguish, the expanding multitude of blazes in Idaho, Montana, Washington, Oregon, Nevada, and northern California. Greeley strategically placed his regular employees in charge of firefighting crews. He assigned patrol duties to inexperienced temporary employees or abandoned patrols altogether.

Thirteen wildfires burned beyond control in Idaho's Coeur d'Alene National Forest. Ranger Debitt managed 650 temporary firefighters who battled the four largest blazes. Mining and timber companies, railroads, and the state of Idaho employed nearly as many firefighters to protect state- and privately-owned land and buildings. The unleashed fury and destructive potential of the wildfires were contained, only to a small degree, by the combined determined efforts of Forest Service rangers and forest guards, temporary firefighters, Native American reservation agents and crews, private timber protection associations, U.S. Army troops, state militias, railroad and lumber men, miners, city firefighters, and ordinary townspeople and homesteaders who battled together to overcome the common threat.

Special Puget Sound trains loaded with supplies and newly hired firefighters made frequent runs into Avery. Pack trains sixty to eighty horses in length waited at the depot to load the thousands of pounds of provisions. The unpredictable wind-driven flames and caustic ash-filled skies made for hazardous conditions to transport supplies out to remote camps. Many of the temporary firefighters soon tired of the dangerous work and the deprivation, called for their time, and caught a train back home.

Greeley became desperate to find enough firefighters to control the raging blazes. The employment agencies he'd contracted with in nearby large cities had already drained their supply of men looking for work. He'd arranged with local constabularies to offer firefighting as an alternative to jail sentences for convicted criminals. Greeley knew that a lot of copper miners in Butte, Montana had been unemployed for months. Bitter, and sometimes violent, labor disputes had raged between the mine owners and members of the International Workers of the World union, or the IWW, whose members were known as Wobblies. On August 4, a sweltering day, a Puget Sound train Greeley had appropriated steamed into Butte from Avery. Heat waves twisted out from the engine's black underbelly. The locomotive seemed to swell and heave on the rails. An employment agent swore that any man, union member or not, blacklisted or not, who boarded the train would have a job fighting fires at 25 cents an hour plus board and a train ride home. As a bonus, the agent enticed, the Forest Service would pay the $1.00 job fee owed the employment agency. Harry C. Schick, Deer Lodge Forest's Assistant Superintendent, stood near the train and verified that the employment agent spoke the truth. News of paying jobs raced through Butte's neighborhoods. Copper miners filled the passenger cars and traveled 242 miles for a paying job.

The miners detrained at Avery with only the clothes they were wearing— dark wool suits, street shoes, and felt fedoras or wool caps. The men feared losing their personal belongings in the confusion of the fires. Groups were assigned to field camps and fed bacon, potatoes, beans, and onions cooked together in washtubs, sourdough bread to sop up the stew, and coffee to wash it down. The Forest Service supplied each man with a cheap, thin trail blanket called a sougan to ward off the nighttime chill. The men set to work. They hacked away trees and brush with axes and mattocks to clear-cut a firebreak to control a wildfire's forward progress. Or they scooped dirt and needles with shovels or their bare hands and threw it back on the front edge of the blaze. Or they beat the flames down with wet blankets. Greeley complained that a lot of the temporaries were the weakest link in his chain, bums and hoboes who loafed on the job or soon quit. But, Greeley asserted, he had wonderful assistance from men who had worked in logging camps and from the Butte copper miners. New, uncontrolled fires burned on District One's Clearwater, Lolo, Cabinet, Flathead, Blackfeet, and Kaniksu forests. The Forest Service persuaded President Taft to deploy U.S. Army troops to aid in the fire fight.

On Saturday, August 20, a mighty Palouser, a forty-mile-per-hour whirlwind claimed to kill cows, blasted into the St. Joe River valley from the Palouse country to the south. The winds propelled flames out of the firebreaks and into timbered areas deemed saved. Flames reached one hundred feet into the sky and set the forest's crown ablaze. Swirling winds pushed the flames ahead with the speed of a locomotive. Firebombs of burning branches and red-hot, sap-soaked pinecones flew through the air to ignite more and more of the forest. The unstoppable firestorm leaped ahead eight miles in twenty minutes, uprooted trees, hurled them like matchsticks, and consumed every trace of living green in its path.

That evening the hills surrounding the city of Wallace erupted into a fiery inferno. The air filled with smoke and ash that stung eyes and lungs. Terrified parents pulled sleeping children from their beds and joined the crush at the station hoping to escape town on relief trains. Blazes raced in from the hills and reduced portions of Wallace to rubble. Weary men asleep in downtown hotels, unaware of their peril from the invading flames, never woke again. Townspeople burned alive, buried in the wreckage of their homes. Wildfires also threatened the mining town of Mullan and erupted along Canyon Creek, jeopardizing Burke. At Avery, packers refused to risk the flaming maelstrom to haul supplies out to the camps. They dumped their loads and fled back to Wallace with their animals. The racing flames surmounted the Bitterroot divide and crossed into Montana.

Telephone and telegraph wires melted. Poles crashed and burned. Information became difficult to obtain from remote places. The lack of communication hampered forest supervisors from mounting counterattacks to control the fire. Railroad bridges were incinerated, wooden ties turned to ashes, and metal rails twisted in the fire's red-hot forge. Rescue trains on their way to evacuate isolated mountain towns retreated from the flames and sought refuge in tunnels under the mountains.

Days before, Greeley had assigned the Army's Black 25th Infantry Regiment, stationed at Fort George Wright in Spokane, Washington, to guard Avery, Mullan, and Burke. At Avery, under the command of Lieutenant E.E. Lewis, Company G troopers dug pools and filled them with water, placed water-filled barrels near wooden buildings, and organized bucket brigades. Refugees who had fled fires that threatened their mines and homesteads crammed the town. Early Sunday, August 21, an impenetrable wall of fire twenty miles wide charged up the slopes as fast as a person could run and enclosed Avery.

Puget Sound Superintendents Marshall and W.R. Lanning had barely escaped burning to death the night before as they ran rescue trains near Falcon. Sunday afternoon the men directed two special trains to evacuate Avery. Troopers loaded water barrels onto the passenger cars and sealed the windows shut. Then they stood guard at the doors with orders to take passengers into the St. Joe River in an orderly fashion if the fire cut them off. The men's train headed east and arrived safely in St. Regis, Montana. The other train headed west more than fifty miles to Tekoa, Washington. The townspeople welcomed the women and children into their homes and provided them with food and clothing.

By dusk, Sunday, raging fires closed around Avery in an ever-tightening circle of destruction. Troopers and a few remaining men boarded another train and started west to escape. But flames, landslides, and fallen trees blocked every route. The heat-blistered train retreated to town. Frustrated and frightened, Avery business owners and those responsible for the railroad's property, convinced that only backfires could save the town, held Ranger Debitt at gunpoint to force him to institute their plan. The men ignited buildings around the outskirts. In less than five minutes, unbridled winds incited a charging backfire that plunged headlong into the encroaching blaze. The two conflagrations collided with a deafening explosion. Flames rocketed to the sky, then collapsed into nothingness. But Avery was still not safe.

At dawn, Monday, swirling winds rose again, picked up energy throughout the day, and rekindled surrounding fires. The fires joined to form another rampage that again threatened the town. Townsmen and soldiers formed a bucket brigade to battle this second wave. Then, as if their prayers were answered, the winds died, the persistent flames burned themselves out, and Avery was finally secure. Heroic efforts also saved the Idaho towns of Mullan, Burke, Kellogg, Murray, and Osburn, and Saltese, Montana. As if in a taunting reminder of the winter's deadly avalanches, unseasonal August snowstorms helped stop the Big Burn's progress across the Bitterroot Mountains like spit-wetted fingers pinch off a flaming candlewick.

Accounts of the fate of the Butte miners vary with the teller. One claimed that on Saturday afternoon Ranger Debitt managed the firefight from his cozy office in the North Fork ranger station. When the alert came that fires were racing up the St. Joe toward Avery, Debitt dispatched couriers to warn the firefighters encamped near Setzer Creek to flee for their lives. Local Avery firefighters received and heeded the alarm. They reached town around 6:30 PM Saturday, singed but safe. When later questioned about the firefighters from Butte, the couriers claimed that once warned, the entire crew had insisted they were in no danger and chose to remain in camp. A separate report raised the question: if they had been warned, why did the miners seem not to have posted sentries to watch for the fire's approach?

Butte miners detraining at Avery, August 1910
(Used with the permission of the Museum of North Idaho)

On Monday morning, Shoshone County Deputy Sheriff Sullivan departed Avery with nine men to search for the missing Butte firefighters. The men discovered Setzer Creek littered with ash and bloated fish killed by the heat. Little trace remained of the firefighters' camp. Searchers deployed into the wasted forest discovered twenty-four charred bodies. The firefighters were scattered where they fell, within a one-mile radius of their camp. Sullivan surmised that an instantaneous burst of flames had consumed the firefighters and they had suffered little pain. The tremendous heat had exploded them like shells and cracked their skulls. Watches found on two men's remains had both stopped at 7:30, the hour on Saturday night when the fire swept up the canyon. A burned-black miner, his watch stopped at 7:34, was discovered a half-mile from camp with his head turned backward, staring into his impending doom. Sullivan claimed that his search party made every effort to identify the men, then buried their bodies on the spot with military honors.

At first Coeur d'Alene Forest Supervisor William G. Weigle could name only four of the dead at Setzer Creek. The flames had obliterated the firefighters' distinguishing clothing and burned or melted their personal effects. Extensive decomposition rendered identification difficult. G.A. Blodgett lay on his back. Protected in his back pocket, searchers had found a red leather folder with his signed IWW card for Butte Workingman's Union No. 5. The charcoaled remains of a man lying next to a dog near a shredded tent littered with melted tin cans and cook pots were presumed to be Patrick Grogin, the camp cook. A gold ring, a watch, and a newly sharpened knife identified an Austrian, and a distinctive whetstone identified another firefighter.

Ranger Debitt, soldiers, and scout, Avery, Idaho, 1910
(Used with the permission of the Museum of North Idaho)

Pat Grogin, cook, and temporary firefighters at camp near Avery, Idaho, 1910
(Used with the permission of the Museum of North Idaho)

During those two days of searing hell, other victims who failed to outrun the unstoppable flames were cremated into heaps of ash. Desperate firefighters, miners, and homesteaders who sought refuge in tunnels, mineshafts, and root cellars breathed in superheated toxic gasses that evaporated their lungs. Or heat from the fire turned their hoped for haven into an oven and cooked the men, women, and children alive. Others died days and weeks later from burns, smoke inhalation, or crushing injuries they'd received from falling limbs and trees.

The Big Burn of August 20–21 was the largest, deadliest, and most devastating fire of the Great Fires of 1910. The blaze obliterated a swath of forest 160 miles long and 25 miles wide, an area roughly 4,000 miles square. One-third of Wallace, plus St. Joe City, Falcon, Grand Forks, and Adair, Idaho, and De Borgia, Haugan, Bryson, Henderson, Tuscor, and Taft, Montana, all lay in smoking ruins. Fire also destroyed the town of Wendling, Oregon. Smoke from the Big Burn darkened the skies across the northern tier of states as far east as Michigan. Fires raged into September on Idaho's Coeur d'Alene and Montana's Flathead Forests, and near Newport, Washington.

The United States Forest Service's "Annual Reports of the Department of Agriculture for the Year Ending June 30, 1911" presents the federal government's official accounting of land and timber burned in 1910. The report enumerates 5,201 fires that burned 4.86 million acres "within the boundaries of the United States National Forests."

In his "Annual Fire Report for the Coeur d'Alene National Forest," dated January 5, 1911, Acting Supervisor Roscoe Haines explained that not all the fires on the Coeur d'Alene that summer had been counted. New and inexperienced patrolmen had not been instructed how to report a fire, several fires were often reported as one, or extinguished fires were never reported. Haines admitted, because of the confusion that started on August 14, he made no record of new fires after that date to the end of the fire season. Similar conditions and circumstances existed on the other forests in both Districts One and Six during that tumultuous fire season. The 5,201 fires listed as occurring within national forest boundaries in 1910 is likely an undercount. Also not included in that accounting are the multitude of fires that burned outside of national forest boundaries from April into September across Montana, Idaho, Washington, Oregon, Nevada, and northern California.

The Department of Agriculture report lists the names of seventy-eight men who lost their lives in the fires, all temporary employees of District One. Temporary firefighters were poorly accounted for by an overburdened

Forest Service. Many of their names were recorded only on timekeepers' records. Indiscriminate flames burned up some timekeepers, along with their papers. Observer accounts of immolated fire crews were denied or never verified. Also not included in the Forest Service tally are fatalities of railroad, mine, and lumber employees, U.S. soldiers, state militia, homesteaders, independent miners, residents of burned towns, and campers reported missing in the back country and never confirmed dead or alive. The death toll for the Great Fires of 1910 far exceeds seventy-eight. The exact number will never be known.

Wisps of smoke still rose from the fallen timber as Puget Sound Railway workers repaired and replaced rail lines and burned bridges to resume its profitable traffic through Avery. Mine owners rebuilt mills to process ore and houses to shelter burned out miners. Avery businessmen constructed new storage buildings and stables. But the forests couldn't be repaired as easily. Mile after mile of mountain peaks stood as blackened wreckage. Carbonized skeletons of fallen western white pines up to two hundred feet tall littered the canyons and hillsides. The Big Burn had plundered every tree in its path, including inch-tall seedlings that would have grown to perpetuate the forest. It could take generations before lumbermen returned to work in that devastated environment. How would the vast burned-over expanse in north Idaho and western Montana begin to heal? How could forests filled with beauty, vitality, and value grow again on this sterile landscape? Where would the Forest Service find enough seedlings to replant the forests?

In 1906 Gifford Pinchot had appointed Lolo Forest ranger Elers Koch as supervisor for Montana's Lolo, Bitterroot, and Missoula Forest Reserves. Koch had married in 1907. He and his wife Gerda honeymooned in a charming, secluded, abandoned homestead on the Savenac Creek near Haugan, Montana. Elers had dreamed of building a forest nursery here, an ideal location to nurture thousands of seedlings to replant forests damaged by wildfires. In 1909 Elers received permission from Forester Greeley to establish the Savenac Nursery. Elers dammed Savenac Creek to form a reservoir, then dug open ditches to let the pooled water flow through to irrigate the seedlings growing in the valley's fertile soil.

The widespread 1910 drought also threatened Savenac Nursery. Insufficient water flowed from the creek to resupply the reservoir. By August no water remained behind the dam to irrigate the seedlings. Their needles fell onto the parched dusty soil. On Sunday, August 21, 1910, the Big Burn swept across the border from Idaho and eradicated every seedling growing in the Savenac Nursery.

Elers rebuilt his dream. He constructed a closed irrigation system to reliably deliver water, even amid drought conditions. He replanted the nursery, not with thousands of trees, but with millions. Young trees spent two years in a seedbed, then two more years in a transplant bed. By 1915 ten million young trees thrived in the nursery, trees to begin the recovery of the forests leveled by the fires of 1910. By the 1930s Savenac Nursery had become the largest American supplier of tree seedlings. In 1956 the facilities' duties transferred to the Forest Service's nursery at Coeur d'Alene.

Don and I shivered in the cool evening air as the setting sun sank behind the crests of the St. Joe's mountain ridges. Setzer Creek ravine stood completely darkened. Misty had stopped growling, but she was still jumpy. I hoped the ghosts of the Butte miners had bedded down for the night. I said a prayer for their souls to find rest. And I asked them to warn us if they spotted a fire headed toward the lookout.

Avery, Idaho, after the Big Burn
(Historic postcard from the Mike Fritz collection)

7

BLACK AND WHITE AND PURPLE

Dunn Peak Lookout stands eight miles northwest of Avery at latitude 47.29464(°N) and longitude 115.89955(°W) in Section 36, Township 46N, and Range 4E of Shoshone County, Idaho. A 1935 US Forest Service map shows Thunder Peak Lookout on Thunder Peak at the same section, range, and township. A 1939 map changed the name to Dunn Peak Lookout on Dunn Peak. The change likely honored Leon M. Dunn, a ranger at Avery District's Roundtop Workstation during the mid-1920s.

The original tower on Dunn (Thunder) Peak had been constructed in 1932. The standard fourteen-by-fourteen-foot precut L-4 cab on top of a twenty-foot-tall pole tower had a straight ladder access from the ground and a gabled roof with shingles. Heavy shutters sealed over the windows for winter protection and opened like flaps to provide shade during the summer. Dunn Peak's current lookout, erected in 1958, is a twenty-foot-tall R-6 TT flat cab. TT stands for a creosote treated, sawn timber tower. R-6 refers to U.S. Forest Service Region 6, Washington and Oregon, where the cab's design originated. R-6 cabs were constructed beginning in 1953 with a standard fifteen-by-fifteen-foot frame cab, a flat roof that extends a few feet to provide shade, and removable shutters.

In 1919 the Forest Service changed its districts from numbered to geographical designations. District One became the Northern District. In 1930 the districts were designated as regions. The Northern District became Region 1 (Northern Region). In 1972 Region 1 comprised northeast Washington, northern Idaho, Montana, North Dakota, and northwest South Dakota.

The grocery store in Moscow was my last stop on my way back to the lookout. The clerk behind the bakery counter had become accustomed to my early Friday routine. She bagged four apple fritters as I walked in. "I'll take a lemon meringue pie, too," I said. Don and I would celebrate our second anniversary this weekend. I'd planned a special dinner: a stuffed capon, Idaho russets mashed with milk and butter, fresh green beans with dill and garlic, Parker House dinner rolls, and a $3.00 bottle of Cabernet Sauvignon from a fledgling Washington winery. The night before the gas station attendant had checked the wagon's tire pressure, water, and oil, and cleaned the windshield while the gas tank filled.

I topped off the gas tank in St. Maries, emptied my bladder, and refilled my coffee mug. Two hours behind me, two hours to go. The Fourth of July campers had cleared out. The road was clear of the choking dust clouds that the Friday afternoon wave of RVs and pickups from Coeur d'Alene and Spokane would churn up. I parked at Hoyt Flat, ran in, and asked Wanda to radio Don that I was on my way. By this time on Friday, even though Don knew I was still miles away, he'd begun to watch the fireroad for my dust cloud. "Have a wonderful anniversary," Wanda called out as I left. I worried that if the entire forest knew it was our anniversary, they wouldn't let us have a minute to ourselves all weekend.

Days before our first anniversary I'd entertained grand notions about the delights my thoughtful husband had planned for a romantic celebration. The day before I couldn't detect that he was aware of the next day's importance. Don laid awake that night wondering what he'd done wrong to deserve my chilly demeanor. He apparently figured it out, because he jumped out of bed before the alarm rang, dressed, and raced out the door without so much as a good morning. When he snuggled back into bed, he presented me with a huge gushy anniversary card from the expensive top row of the Hallmark display. He promised to make up for his oversight on our second anniversary with a lavish dinner in a posh restaurant. Whenever other married couples reminisce about anniversary celebrations, I retell this story, just to keep Don on his toes. He's never forgotten another anniversary.

I rounded the last turn to the lookout. A Forest Service pickup was parked at the base of the tower. The fire control officer waved from the catwalk. I climbed the stairs. Wade said he'd come to tighten the stove's propane fittings. His crew would bring firewood tomorrow and water on Sunday. He asked if we needed anything else. I brushed past him and planted a long dusty kiss on my husband. Misty squeezed in to share our hug. Don told Wade he already had everything he needed and kissed me back. Wade blushed and headed for the stairs. Don closed the trap door and slid the bolt through the hasp to lock it. He bragged that he'd spotted my dust cloud when I was still six miles from the lookout. He pulled me into the cab. "Happy anniversary, Mrs. Hammond. We have the whole weekend alone to celebrate."

Saturday evening Don set the table for our anniversary dinner. No paper plates or plastic forks tonight. He laid out flatware and white china decorated with the green Forest Service logo that had come with the lookout. He set out two wine glasses I'd brought from home. Our centerpiece was wildflowers in a spaghetti sauce jar. A pine-perfumed breeze wafted in through the open windows and flickered the candle. Soft music played on the transistor. We made a toast. I reminded Don that he'd kept the promise he'd made to me one year before. He'd brought me to a special place for our second anniversary dinner. I didn't even mind that I had to cook. How blessed I was to be here, at exactly the right place at precisely the right time, thanks to my determined boy.

The next Friday Don hollered from the catwalk that I'd missed a doozy of a storm the night before. He'd logged eighteen ground strikes in one hour. The air around the guy wires had glowed neon blue from the static buildup. The closest strikes had zapped his night vision. It took his eyes a few minutes to adjust before he could write. He'd searched all night but didn't spot any flames or smokes that morning. He complained that he'd had to hunch over the Firefinder, twist to align the strikes in the alidade, and stretch to grab the logbook. He needed a good backrub. He was one sore puppy. He said Misty had laid on the bed and whimpered through the whole storm. She was taking a nap to recuperate.

I carried up two bags of groceries, impressed that I made it to the catwalk without getting winded. Misty got off her quilt and poked her nose through the bags, more curious to sniff what was inside than to say hello. Don showed me a piece of wood he'd found on a walk. He'd begun to whittle out an owl that he visualized inside. He hoped I'd brought hamburger and buns for sloppy joes. He confessed that he and Misty had eaten huckleberries for dinner all week because he hadn't felt like cooking. Misty picked the berries right off the bushes, like a hungry bear. Bright purple stains stood out against her black-and-white muzzle. I said we should call her Huckleberry Hound.

Don complained that he had to keep Misty on her leash when they picked berries because the bears were back at the garbage pit. He wanted to climb onto the abandoned generator trailer parked next to the pit and throw rocks at the bears to chase them away. He'd already loaded his ammunition on top of the trailer. He'd waited until I got back so I could radio for help if something went wrong. I asked Don when he'd lost his mind. But I knew I couldn't dissuade him from this insane mission.

Dunn Peak's garbage pit was out of view from the lookout. Misty and I paced the catwalk with the trap door firmly locked. Don hollered that he'd climbed on top of the trailer. I strained to hear any sound of human distress coming from the garbage pit, but all stayed quiet. After an hour Don came back to the lookout. He shouted with disappointment that no bears had arrived. I shouted that I'd never be on bear watch again. I wanted Wade to bring us two handheld radios so we could communicate just in case Don ever pulled another crazy stunt.

Idaho Fish and Game had studied black bears on the St. Joe forest. Captured *Ursus americanus* females, four years or older, weighed up to 165 pounds. Males that age weighed up to 260 pounds. Some males stood more than five feet tall. Black bears see full-spectrum colors. Their daytime vision is as good as humans'. Their nighttime vision is better. Their fur can be black, brown, cinnamon, blond, blue-gray, or white. Black bears lean from winter hibernation can run as fast as 35 miles per hour, climb trees, and swim rivers. Bears possess the most scent receptors of any terrestrial mammal, about 100 times more than humans. It's estimated their sense of smell is seven times greater than a bloodhound's. Black bears can smell a food source over a mile away. Bears for miles around could smell when ripe huckleberries, a major component of their diet, hung heavy on Dunn Peak's bushes. And they could smell when Don threw garbage into the pit. After Don's risky escapade I carried our garbage back to Moscow.

Early in our relationship Don and I had discovered that we were comfortable in each other's silence. We'd drive around the Pennsylvania countryside for hours and not utter a word. When a rock-and-roll song we both liked came on the radio, we'd sing along and be-bop to the rhythm on the Ford's bench seat. We'd resume our silence until another good song came on. This shared quirk in our personalities served us well on the lookout. During the day we tuned the transistor to the classical station, I read a murder mystery, and Don conducted his binocular searches. Unless the Motorola radio crackled to life, or Misty discovered something to bark at, hours slipped by in a comfortable silence.

Dalmatians were bred as coach dogs, designed to run long distances with a harnessed team of horses. The dogs cleared the road ahead of animals who might spook the horses, ran back to make sure the carriage or fire truck hadn't tipped over, and repeated the cycle. When fire stations upgraded to motorized trucks, they put their horses out to pasture but kept their Dalmatians. Misty traveled ten times further than we did on our walks. She chased off every chipmunk and ground squirrel that dared to cross our path. But I worried what might happen if she came across a mule, deer, elk, coyote, or black bear. She had no fear of large animals. I worried she'd fight to the death to protect us. With one exception, we didn't encounter a single threatening animal all summer.

One Saturday morning low clouds heavy with moisture blanketed Dunn Peak's summit. We were socked in. We couldn't see anything but whiteness beyond the catwalk. It felt odd to be inside of a cloud. There was no danger of fire or of anyone driving to the lookout in those conditions. Don sat on the safe bench and whittled. I slouched in the captain's chair and read.

A tortured bone-chilling scream jolted us to our feet. Don's fishing knife and the half-whittled owl clattered to the floor. "That's a baby screaming! We've got to find it!" he yelled. The cry seemed to come from the closest ravine. Misty charged off in that direction and disappeared from sight. I hadn't heard a car. There was no road where she was headed. I'd never heard a real cougar scream before, but in an instant I knew. We ran to the catwalk and yelled for Misty to come back. She had the good sense not to wrangle with a big cat. She bounded up the stairs. I grabbed her collar and held her tight until Don locked the hatch. We never heard another scream.

July stayed cool and the lightning storms disappeared. Good news for the forest, bad news for lookouts and fire crews hoping to earn overtime money. Sometime before we'd arrived on Dunn Peak, sawyers and bulldozers had gouged a straight, wide swath through the forest below the lookout. Two precisely aligned rows of gigantic high-tension transmission towers climbed the mountainside from Avery toward the lookout. No wires connected the towers, but Don speculated that the area, void of vegetation except for a low ground cover, looked too well-tended to have been abandoned.

One Friday Avery crawled with men in hardhats. I saw Bonneville Power trucks and a helicopter parked in a field near the railroad tracks. Don said he'd heard radio chatter about power lines being strung. He wondered if it would happen on the towers below the lookout. The next day an intricate aerial act began below Dunn Peak. The helicopter supplied endless strands of transmission lines to men perched on the towers at death-defying heights. The fearless high-wire acrobats precisely maneuvered and secured the lines into place. I watched in awe of the workers' talent and courage.

The Bonneville Power Administration was stringing Dworshak-Taft transmission line No. 1, DWOK-TAFT-1. The line would carry electricity generated at the Dworshak Dam near Orofino, 160 miles by road from Avery. The dam, to be completed in 1973, was named for Idaho Congressman and Senator Henry Clarence Dworshak. Dworshak Dam holds back the North Fork of the Clearwater River. It's the third tallest dam in the United States and the highest straight-axis concrete dam in the Western Hemisphere. The men and the helicopter soon moved out of our sight. Don and I experienced disappointment, like our favorite TV show had been cancelled.

Cooking our second anniversary dinner

Whittling an owl

Misty likes hugs

Reading a murder mystery

8

A FIREBALL, ANTS,
AND A SERIAL KILLER

Early in August soaking showers and cool weather reduced the fire danger to a Low rating. The St. Joe Forest would be safe from another disastrous fire season. Everyone searched for ways to fill the uneventful days. The district's sympathetic dispatcher now tolerated radio chatter. Lookouts filled the empty airwaves with their summer experiences. Don told everyone how he'd chased off a local who had parked his pickup in the middle of Dunn Peak's huckleberry bushes, yanked the bushes out by their roots, and threw them into the back of his truck to pick the berries at home. Another lookout related that he'd had to barricade his car with wire fencing to keep porcupines from chewing his tires to bits. And the couple on Middle Sister Peak Lookout announced they were expecting their first baby.

No roads reached Snow Peak Lookout at 6,738 feet of elevation. The Forest Service had packed in the lookout on horseback and mules at the beginning of the fire season and would pack him out at the end. The lookout had a long hike on a rocky trail to get water from a spring. Still gasping after lugging in his water, the lookout radioed to ask if anyone knew how much a "pound" of water weighs. We knew he meant to ask how much a "gallon" weighs. We all had our water delivered. We respected the effort he'd had to expend. No one laughed at his slipup. And no one knew the answer to his question.

Don usually greeted me from the catwalk. On Friday, August 11, he ran down the stairs and jumped into the wagon. I worried that something bad had happened. Don blurted out that he'd seen a UFO. I laughed in spite of my concern. He said the day before he'd been standing on the eastside catwalk and saw a massive white-hot fireball with a huge tail streak across the sky. It looked like a chunk had fallen off the sun. He asked if I'd heard anything on the radio about a low-flying spaceship. I said I hadn't heard about Martians landing, no news of anything unusual at all. But I didn't doubt that Don had seen something. He said the fireball had passed between Dunn Peak and Middle Sister. They were the only lookouts to call it in. The dispatcher had acted like they were pulling a prank. He said the fireball had come out of the south and disappeared to the north. The last he saw it, it was still moving. No crash, no sound at all. I assured him that something that unusual would make it into the newspapers. I'd check when I got back home.

I'd brought burgers from The Beanery. I told Don he should drink a couple of beers with his burger to relax. The beer had its calming effect. Don settled on the safe bench and unsheathed his knife and grabbed the unfinished owl. I curled into the captain's chair and turned back the cover on a new murder mystery. Don glanced out the windows to the north where the fireball had disappeared. He broke our comfortable silence to confess, "I feared the world might end, Nance. You read and I'll whittle. We're together and safe."

Don had witnessed a meteor, the Great Daylight Fireball of 1972. A near-infrared radiometer on a U.S. Air Force satellite had detected the cosmic streaker. Few newspapers reported the unique event. Tourists in Grand Teton, Yellowstone, and Glacier National Parks, with cameras at the ready, had filmed and photographed the fireball. The meteor had appeared over Salt Lake City, Utah, and disappeared from view north of Calgary, Alberta. It traveled the 900 mile path at an estimated 33,000 miles per hour. Its maximum brightness at the middle of its course, near Dunn Peak, exceeded that of the moon. Estimates of the meteor's diameter ranged from 13 to 32 feet, and its mass was estimated to range from 1,000 to 1 million metric tons. The meteor had been within 36 miles of the earth's surface near Dunn Peak. It had entered our atmosphere at a shallow angle and bounced back into space near Calgary. If the meteor had impacted the earth, the force from its lowest estimated mass would have been equivalent to the atomic bomb dropped on Hiroshima. If the meteor had impacted near Dunn Peak, Don's world might have ended as he'd feared.

On Saturday morning the invasion started slowly. A few miniscule, six-legged winged ants gathered on the windowpanes. As the day warmed, more and more ants flew from the ground onto their sky-high pleasure palace to breed. By afternoon there were thousands of them. I shut the windows. I didn't care if I roasted to death. I got itchy all over just thinking about those critters landing on me. Except for the closed windows the first swarms didn't do much to impact our routine. The temperature cooled near sunset and the ants disappeared.

The next Friday Don waved at me from inside the cab. "Run up fast as you can," he yelled. Halfway up I crashed into the second swarm of ant invaders. These were winged giants, three-quarters of an inch long. By the time I got inside, monster ants crawled all over my clothes, twisted through my hair, and tried to climb up my nose. Don brushed off the intruders and we stomped them into oblivion. Misty sniffed the gooey remains and decided that ants weren't to her liking.

In all the excitement I'd forgotten to use the outhouse. I wasn't going to sit on my emergency bucket in the middle of that swarm. I grabbed Don's sweatshirt, zipped it, tightened the drawstring on the hood until only my eyes showed through, put on sunglasses, and hooked Misty to her leash. The winged ants beat against my fleece armor as we dashed down the stairs. A few feet from the lookout no more ants swarmed in the air. I brushed Misty and myself clean of our hitchhikers, and we headed to the outhouse.

Saturday was warmer and the swarms were larger. Ants covered the windows on all sides of the tower and stayed on the windows longer. "The males die after they mate, Don. Aren't you lucky compared to ants?"

"You're lucky, too," Don threw back at me.

A dozen wasps arrived late in the afternoon to feast. They snapped off the ants' heads, discarded them, and gobbled the remains. I thought when the day cooled and the windows cleared there'd be a crunchy carpet of ant bodies to sweep off the catwalk. But tidy Mother Nature sent a brisk breeze. Every male that had sacrificed his life to ensure the continuation of his species sailed away in the wind.

That Sunday I was happy to leave the lookout and head back to our ant-free home in Moscow. That was the only time that summer I took Misty home with me. She couldn't stay on the catwalk with ants crawling all over her. Misty was a bad traveler. The wagon's backseat windows hinged open only a few inches. She rode the entire trip standing on the back seat with her head poked out my window. I arrived home with my left shoulder caked with a muddy mix of road dust and dog drool.

I researched our invaders in the forestry library at work. They resembled carpenter ants, or *Camponotus vicinus,* which nest in North Idaho's coniferous forests. As many as ten thousand ants swarm at once from all the colonies in an area. This encourages mating between different genetic lines to strengthen the species. And the large numbers help to protect them from predators, like the wasps, who'd eat their fill before all the breeding ants could be consumed.

The following Friday Don waited for us at the foot of the stairs. I thought the ants were still a nuisance until I saw his face. He looked pale and jumpy. "What happened?" I asked with worry. Don assured me it was nothing bad, just an odd encounter. He helped me unload the car. We settled in with a glass of wine and he told me the story.

Don had sat on the safe bench one evening to whittle the owl with his fishing knife. A motion outside caused him to glance up. A man's face stared through the window over the trap door. Don jumped off the bench. The owl clattered to the floor. Don hadn't heard any footfalls on the stairs or felt their vibrations. The man snaked along the catwalk toward the door and scanned the inside of the lookout. Don faced off with him through the windows before he reached the door.

"What do you want? What are you looking for?" Don demanded.

"Nothing," the man said. He continued to peer inside.

"Do you need something?" Don moved to block the door.

The man shrugged, turned around, and left. Don ran across the catwalk, shut the hatch, jumped on top, and slid the bolt through the hasp. Don's legs shook as he stood to watch the man leave. The intruder calmly walked down the road and never looked back. He veered left into the trees and disappeared like a ghost. Don listened but there was no sound. He peered into the forest until it was too dark to see. He double-checked the locked hatch, went back inside, lit a lantern, and sat on the bench to collect his senses. He hadn't heard a car coming or when the man left. He realized that until he'd locked the hatch, he still had his fishing knife gripped in his hand.

Don sat in silence as I took in his story. Then he gave me a tight hug. "Who walks up to a lookout near dark? I'm so thankful you weren't here, Nance. But I wish I'd had Misty with me."

We mulled over Don's scary experience for days. Then we forgot about it for years. I can't remember what I was doing when Don yelled, "Nance! It's that guy I saw on the lookout!"

I ran into the living room. Don had jumped off the sofa. He stabbed his finger toward a grainy black-and white photograph of a man's face that filled the TV screen. "That's him! That's the guy who came to Dunn Peak!"

The show was a retrospective on male serial killers. The police mug shot on TV belonged to Ted Bundy. The image had frightened Don as it did when he'd seen the face staring through the lookout window. Ted Bundy had brutally kidnapped, raped, and murdered young women. He targeted brunette, petite, Caucasian women aged twelve to twenty-six years old. He confessed to committing thirty murders between 1974 and 1978. Before his execution in 1989, Bundy had also confessed that on September 2, 1974, he'd raped and strangled a still unidentified hitchhiker near Boise, Idaho. And that same year he'd murdered a twelve-year-old girl in Pocatello. In both cases he said he'd disposed of the corpse in a nearby river. Bundy had hinted at committing murders starting in 1969, but no evidence tied him to crimes that early. In 1972 Bundy's psychology degree had earned him a job working with psychiatric outpatients at Seattle's Harborview Hospital. Bundy's cousin John had testified that the two of them had often hiked the forests behind Lake Sammamish, east of Seattle, that summer.

There's no way to prove that Ted Bundy was the intruder on Dunn Peak that August evening in 1972. Although Bundy had admitted to two murders in southern Idaho, there's no evidence of him being in the northern part of the state. From his known location in Seattle, it would have been less than an eight hour drive out I-90 to Wallace, south on Placer Creek Road and NFD 456 to Avery, and another hour to Dunn Peak Lookout. If he'd left Seattle early, he could have arrived at Dunn Peak close to the time Don saw the face in the window. Don remains resolute in his identification of Ted Bundy.

I'm thankful Don held his fishing knife in his hand that evening. I'm more thankful that I or a lone woman lookout wasn't in the tower when that stalking stranger appeared out of nowhere. I know that evil exists in our world. Evil might cross our path at any time. Nowhere is safe from evil.

9

THE LAST LOOKOUT
ON DUNN PEAK

Don's senior year at the University of Idaho would start in two weeks. We'd pared our lookout belongings to the bare necessities. I'd taken home our goose down parkas, sweatshirts, flannel PJs, winter slippers, bear whistles, berry buckets, my big roasting pan, a stack of murder mysteries, food we didn't need, and extra towels, toilet paper, and batteries. The one carload of stuff we'd brought to the lookout had grown to two.

The Avery District often rehired lookouts. They preferred married couples. But I worried that our time on the St. Joe could end with this single summer. Don pumped up his confidence for his close-out evaluation with the same fervor that had won him his dream job as a lookout. And he had the same luck.

Wade sat and listened politely as Don delivered his rehearsed speech. "On my first day as a fire lookout, you challenged me to be damn sure that the trees around Dunn Peak didn't burn again. The summer's over and the forest is intact. I hope I can return to Dunn Peak Lookout next year to continue to protect the St. Joe Forest."

Wade slowly shook his head. He said headquarters had cut his next year's fire control budget by 20 percent. Lookout towers would soon be a thing of the past. Air patrol had proven more effective at spotting smokes and was less costly. Wade told Don he was sorry. He had to close three lookout towers and Dunn Peak was one of them. There'd be no lookout on Dunn Peak after this summer. Don stood in stunned silence. He'd been certain that his diligence and sunny personality had earned him one more summer on the St. Joe Forest.

Wade continued. Middle Sister Peak Lookout would stay open as the communication contact when air patrol flew. The couple working there was expecting a baby. Babies were forbidden on fire lookouts. Don had proved himself capable and trustworthy. Wade wanted him back next summer as the lookout on Middle Sister. Was he interested?

"Wait until I tell Nancy." Don's enthusiasm flared. "This calls for a celebration!"

On our last night on Dunn Peak Lookout, the fire crew arrived ready to party. I'd fixed the food. They brought the beer and a pint of blackberry brandy for me. From the time I was a teenager, my Uncle Billy had poured me a shot of blackberry brandy every time my parents and I visited him and my Grammy Sule. Three dozen sloppy joes, four big bags of chips, two pans of brownies, and all the beer disappeared. The only leftovers were half a jar of kosher baby dills and half a bottle of brandy. It was past midnight when Don and I finished cleaning. "Grab a lantern, Nance," he said. "This is our final nighttime trek to the outhouse. I'm right behind you."

I stepped onto the catwalk. I worried I'd had too much to drink. Green lights swirled in the sky. It looked like the Chicago River on St. Patrick's Day. I promised Don I'd never doubt his UFO story again. Lightning had sparked our first night on Dunn Peak. The Northern Lights decorated the sky on our last. It was a perfect ending to our summer.

Don wondered if next summer on Middle Sister could be better than this. I told him I'd had my fill of living apart. I hated saying goodbye every week. I told him we'd follow a strict austerity budget all year so that I didn't have to work next summer. We'd be on Middle Sister together. I wouldn't discuss the matter. Don hugged me tight. He said he'd hated saying goodbye, too. But he really liked how we said hello. The next morning Don cleaned the ashes out of the wood stove from our last romantic fire. The lookout would stay open for a few more weeks. Wade might need to post one of his fire crews there if a thunderstorm came through or a fire started. When the fire season was over, his crew would turn off the propane, shutter the windows, and padlock the trap door from the stairs.

When I was a kid, my cousins made fun of me because I was afraid to go into the deep end of the pool to play water polo. When I was twelve, I'd learned to swim at Lake Mineola in the Poconos. I couldn't wait to show my cousins that I wasn't afraid of the deep end anymore. It surprised me how easy it was to leave Dunn Peak Lookout. The challenges I'd faced had given me confidence to take on risky situations. I'd learned that if something did go wrong, I had the courage to face what came my way. And the time I'd spent alone with Don had increased my certainty that I wanted to be married to him.

Don's mixed emotions showed on his face as we drove away from the lookout. He'd achieved the dream he'd pined for since he was a boy. He'd met the Forest Service's expectations. But it tore him up to leave his dream, even if only until next summer. He stopped our wagon at the last turn before the switchback descent into Avery. He took a long final gaze at the lookout. "Imagine," he said, "I lived all summer inside that little bump on top of a mile-high mountain. No other lookout will spend another summer there." Don left the St. Joe Forest around Dunn Peak as he'd found it—green and growing.

Don signed his termination papers at Hoyt Flat. We headed home. He said he hoped next summer would be drier so he could earn more overtime. We hadn't yet learned to be careful what we wished for. Back in Moscow I dug my keys from my purse and unlocked the front door. In June, two Pennsylvania steel workers' kids had walked out to seek adventures in a green, pristine forest. In August, two fire lookouts schooled and matured by Mother Nature's wonders and dangers walked in. Don carried himself with pride. I liked the difference.

In his book *Fire Lookouts of the Northwest*, Ray Kresek explains, "I've now discovered that numerous other folks too have inhabited the high world. Among the clan there seems to be a unity of spirit—once a lookout, always a lookout." That summer of 1972, Don and I paid our dues to join the clan who have inhabited the high world. We will always be lookouts.

After 1972 only temporary observers staffed Dunn Peak Lookout. Harsh winters scoured and faded the lookout's crisp white enamel to a dull gray. The cab's windows were boarded up. The tower was repurposed into a storage area and support for electronic communication equipment. Metal scaffolds with antennas and satellite dishes filled in the summit around the tower. As of 2023 Dunn Peak Lookout still stands. Donald Thomas Hammond was the last lookout on Dunn Peak.

Dunn Peak Lookout, August 1972

Dunn Peak Lookout, 1994
(Photo by Neil Hammond)

PART II

MIDDLE SISTER PEAK LOOKOUT, 1973

Middle Sister Peak Lookout

10

STEP NUMBER NEXT

Don had failed ninth grade, graduated high school in the bottom 5 percent of his class, and flunked out of his first try at college. But he never quit trying. He graduated from the University of Idaho in May 1973 with a bachelor's degree in history. He'd met the primary requirement to enter seminary. He'd have to earn a Master of Divinity degree to be ordained into Christian ministry. We worked on accomplishing this one step at a time.

Don's graduation from the University of Idaho, May 1973

I was proud of Don for being accepted into seminary. But I was upset that he'd chosen a Christian Church (Disciples of Christ) seminary in Indianapolis. I hated leaving Idaho for cornfield-flat Indiana. At our church in Moscow, I'd become accustomed to the Disciple's practices of weekly communion and baptism by immersion, but I couldn't accept their desire to achieve unity among the various Christian denominations. I'd wanted Don to attend a school affiliated with the United Church of Christ denomination I'd been raised in. But Don worried that the UCC's seminaries, like Andover Newton in Massachusetts and Lancaster in Pennsylvania, would be more scholastically challenging than he could manage. He feared failing again.

Don had notified Avery that the lease on our bungalow would expire at the end of May. We hoped to be on the lookout the first week in June. We had nowhere else to live. The previous summer Don and I had loaded our wagon and arrived on Dunn Peak in one whirlwind weekend. Our preparations this summer proved more complicated. We separated our belongings into three piles. Friends quickly claimed everything in the pile we no longer wanted. I'd compiled a four-page list of necessities to go to the lookout. We carefully checked off each item as we placed it in the second pile. The third pile would go into storage to be moved to Indianapolis. I looked at the three mounds and saw our past, present, and future laid out on the living room rug.

Our friend Jerry had asked if he could hitch a ride to Indianapolis with us. He'd be attending the same seminary as Don. He and his wife Tammy would also be lookouts on the St. Joe this summer. With a third driver, Don and I purchased a worn but serviceable brown 1959 Chevy pickup. The truck had almost-new tires, a trailer hitch, and rotted out floorboards. Its price fit our tight budget. We condensed the move pile down to what would fit into the back of the truck, a small, enclosed U-Haul trailer, and our trusty wagon. We bought citizens' band (CB) radios for both vehicles so we could communicate on the road.

The last morning in May, I locked the bungalow's front door with my key and pushed hard to make sure it was secure. We dropped off our keys at the landlord's office. Then we turned north onto the now familiar Route 95 to Avery.

Don radioed, "Head 'em up!"

I radioed back, "Move 'em out!" We were so pleased to hear our voices over the CBs that neither of us looked back as we left Moscow.

We checked in at Hoyt Flat. Wade gave us the bad news that the road to Middle Sister was snowed shut. He said because he was a nice guy, he'd let us stay in the bunkhouse again. He said it could be weeks until the snowbanks melted. We might be living with the fire crew for a while. He hoped we two lovebirds had brought a pile of books to pass the time. Don didn't mention that I was pregnant.

It was Amy's fault. Don and I had thought about getting pregnant. He was twenty-six, I was twenty-four. Past time, according to our parents, for having our first baby. But we'd hesitated. If Don didn't get a student pastorate, his GI Bill wouldn't cover seminary tuition. I'd have to work. Easier to do without a baby. But if we waited until Don graduated, I'd be twenty-seven. I didn't want to be that old when I had my first baby. One Friday night as we played Risk and drank wine, Amy encouraged us to start trying. "It could take a while," she baited. "Besides, it's a fun way to occupy your time on the lookout." Amy was a nurse. She should have known better. I got pregnant that month.

Don and I swallowed hard when the news of a baby came much sooner than we'd expected. What if something went wrong on the lookout? There was no doctor for miles. Would things change between us? There was no room to hide on a lookout. Would Don be a good dad, me a good mom? There was no going back.

My mother's voice repeated in my head, "It is what it is."

My grandmother chimed in right behind, "Do the best you can with what you've got."

The notion of a baby began to grow on us, even feel good. We could do this. I was strong and healthy. We had PhDs in living on an austerity budget. Last summer the couple on Middle Sister had gotten pregnant. She did fine. And no way in hell would Don call Avery to cancel going on the lookout!

I didn't look pregnant. I could still button and zip my blue jeans. I didn't feel pregnant. I had no morning sickness and no mood swings. I naïvely expected not to. With a biology degree I knew pregnancy's mechanical and technical aspects. But I had no real-life experience with pregnant women. I'm an only child. I'd never observed my mother pregnant. My aunts had older children or ones who'd arrived about the same time I did. The first time I held an infant in my arms, I was twenty-one years old. But I was acutely aware that I was now responsible for a being other than myself. I stopped drinking alcohol, I didn't swallow even an aspirin, and I didn't lift anything heavy. I thought through every action I took to make sure it wouldn't bring harm to either of us. Yet I'd rationalized away the risks of living on an isolated lookout. If Don headed off on an adventure, no way would I miss out!

That night in Avery Don and I slept on the same two skinny bunkbeds as the summer before. The next morning we lounged in our room until the fire crew cleared out for work. The bunkhouse kitchen had a plug-in aluminum coffee percolator, a toaster oven, a refrigerator, and no stove. We ate cold cereal and sipped hot coffee until we got bored. Don and Misty guarded the bathroom with no door while I showered, then watched the bedroom door with no lock while I dressed, in case one of the crew barged in for something he'd forgotten.

Passing time in a down-on-its luck railroad town proved a challenge. Don and I loafed on the bench next to the circular concrete pond in the center of town. We pitied the immense rainbow, brown, and cutthroat trout mechanically swimming in circles through the pumped-in river water. We strolled along the banks of the St. Joe. We put on our polarized sunglasses to spot trout lolling in the river's deep pools. I fished out a few sun-dappled rocks that glistened like raw gems of citrine and amber in the river's shallows. We drove upriver and played on the swinging bridge. We meandered through the campgrounds and admired or criticized how campers had arranged their vacation homes. The next morning I looked at my jewels from the river. They lay lifeless on the bedroom dresser, dried in the mountain air to a dull gravel gray.

Swinging bridge over the St. Joe River, east of Avery

For lunch and dinner Don and I circulated between The Beanery, Parker's Log Cabin Café, and the bar with a new permanent sign that still warned, "No Calks or Knives." Most afternoons Misty and I settled in for a nap. Don pulled the chair up to the desk and studied a Forest Service map to memorize the names of landmarks around the lookout. East Sister, West Sister, and Little Sister Peaks were the closest. Nugget Ridge connected Nugget Point to Hardpan Point. Sisters Creek, Prospector Creek, and Nugget Creek flowed nearby. Whistling Peak, Bluff Saddle, Dismal Lake, Mammoth Springs Campground, Pineapple Saddle, and Bear Skull sat to the southeast. To the northwest were Sisters Basin, Shoepack Point, Lower Shoepack Point, and Siwash and North Siwash Peaks.

Weeknights after dinner, the bunkhouse sprang to life. A portable record player spun out rock and roll from scratched 45s. Twangy country singers competed from a tabletop radio. Piles of worn nickels and dimes shifted around the kitchen table in the nightly poker game. One of the crew popped the cap off a longneck bottle of beer. "I remember you don't drink beer, Nancy. Sorry, but we're fresh out of blackberry brandy," he teased. I laughed along and held onto my secret that alcohol was off my beverage options.

Every morning for five days, Don had checked in at Hoyt Flat to find out if the road to the lookout was clear. Every day he received the same response—still snowed shut. Don joked with the dispatcher about how he and Misty stood guard while I showered. He spilled the beans that I was pregnant. The very next day the Forest Service moved us out of the bunkhouse and into a minimally furnished, un-air-conditioned, single-wide mobile home parked next to the ranger station in an open field with no trees. Our "upscale" new housing came equipped with privacy, a comfy queen-sized bed, and an operational kitchen. But I missed the crew's comradery.

Don and I had been stuck in the trailer for over two weeks. Unfiltered afternoon sun pounded onto Hoyt Flat and heated the metal trailer to broiling. But on Middle Sister's cold heights, that same sun didn't generate enough warmth to melt the persistent snow banks blocking the road to the lookout. Don had his fill of idleness, and our money was getting tight. He wouldn't be on the payroll until he was on the lookout. He asked if I wanted to go with him to check out the road to Middle Sister. No way would I let him go without me. The price of gas in Avery was insane, so we took the wagon instead of the gas-guzzling truck. Don rearranged the back to make room for Misty. I fixed ham and cheese sandwiches.

Don didn't want anyone at the ranger station to know his plan. We guessed at the best route to take. We turned south off the river road onto Fireroad 301 along Fishhook Creek. The lush mountain brook could have been on the cover of an Idaho Chamber of Commerce brochure. The dirt road widened and approached a new two-lane concrete bridge edged with shiny steel guardrails, the only guardrails we'd seen in the forest. The bridge led into the arched mouth of a short tunnel just tall enough to accommodate a loaded logging truck. Sharp points of rock protruded along the tunnel's entire see-through length. No interior supports held up the mountain overhead. It looked to me like the construction crew had shoveled out the rock debris from blasting and walked away.

The tunnel opened onto the northwest forest of Don's reveries. The devastating 1910 fires and later burns had spared this section of the St. Joe. Don shifted between second and third gears as the road curved steadily upward. We scanned lush tall-grass meadows to spot mule deer or elk or moose. We admired an elaborately engineered beaver dam. We passed a road sign that read, "Logging Trucks Use Channel 5." I tuned the CB to channel 5. We presumed that no chatter on the frequency meant a clear road ahead. But just in case, Don honked three warning toots at the next blind curve. Thundering jake brakes and a blinding dust cloud preceded a speeding logging truck trying to stop. The truck swerved one way and Don swerved the other. We prayed that the load of logs wouldn't tip over on top of us as the truck squeezed past. The driver keyed his radio and blasted out a warning in foul language about an idiot on the road. After all that excitement I needed a rest stop. The map showed a Forest Service workstation ahead.

The access road into Roundtop Work Station curved around a mowed lawn scattered with small red cabins and brown equipment sheds. I peeked behind doors until I found a bathroom. One of the fire crew who we knew told us he'd been on Middle Sister that morning. The road was still blocked. "But suit yourself," he said. I felt better that someone knew we were heading onto the mountain just in case something went wrong.

We negotiated nineteen more miles of twisted uphill dirt road. A large wooden sign at the Avery–Timber Creek Road intersection contained no mention of a lookout, and we couldn't see a mountain. Don and I got out of the car to stretch and get our bearings. An azure flash in the old clear-cut next to the road caught my eye—a mountain bluebird lit in a tree. It was my first bluebird sighting. I took it to be a good omen.

Fishhook Creek

Fishhook Creek bridge on Fireroad 301

USFS Roundtop workstation

Avery–Timber Creek Road intersection (my bluebird corner)

Fireroad 324 banked sharply upward, then divided into two equal forks. Our map didn't help. Don judged that the left fork curved down. We wanted to go up. He chose several more forks to the right. The road degenerated into two rock-strewn tracks. Wildflowers, instead of paint, marked the center of the road. Middle Sister Peak Lookout finally appeared, perched on the distant summit. I was sure the bluebird had been a good omen. Don wondered out loud why we didn't see any snow.

As he steered around another curve, Don asked if I was doing okay with all the jostling. I started to say I'd be happy to get to the lookout, but the words stuck in my throat. A snowbank barricaded more than half of the road in front of us, right where the road crossed a precipitous slope strewn with boulders. The frozen blockade rose about eight feet against the mountain on our right and angled to within two feet of where the edge of the road merged into thin air.

Don cursed, a lot. He'd have to back the car down the mountain about a mile to find a place wide enough to turn around. I prepared myself to not be surprised at what came out of his mouth next. He asked if there was anything in the wagon he could use as a shovel. Despite my effort, I was still surprised. I couldn't dissuade Don when he was determined, so I tried to help. All our kitchen gear was packed in the back. I suggested he use my big Teflon frying pan.

Don scraped his improvised shovel into the hard-packed icy blockade. He pitched one panful of snow after another into the sky over the boulder-filled precipice. The handle broke off the frying pan under the strain. Don continued to dig for about an hour until he'd cleared enough snow for the car to fit across the road. I got out and gulped at the (almost certain) death plunge Don risked. It scared me. I asked him not to go. I wanted our child to grow up with a father. But after he'd dug out all that snow, there was no holding him back. I kissed Don goodbye. I hooked on Misty's leash and took her out of the wagon. I didn't want to lose my dog, too, if the car fell over the cliff.

Don inched the wagon forward. I prayed for his stubborn soul and asked the bluebird for good luck. He steered the wagon so tight against the snowbank that the door handle carved a line into the snow. The tire edges hovered over thin air on the cliff side and dislodged rocks that careened and clattered down the precipice. I worried that the road edge might collapse under the weight of our loaded car. And then the wagon cleared the snowbank. Don pumped his fist out the window in celebration. I breathed again. I walked across with Misty in tow, climbed back into the car, and kissed my lucky fool. He drove on as if nothing extraordinary had happened.

We reached the summit and groaned in unison. A wider, taller snowbank blocked the fork to the left. It would take a plow to clear this giant. Don was crushed. The lookout stood so close behind that we could walk to it. But more unseen snowbanks could clog the rest of the road. The right fork curved so sharply that we couldn't see if snow blocked it, too. We agreed it wasn't worth getting marooned to find out. The road at the fork was wide enough to turn our wagon around. We headed back to Avery in a dark mood. We hated the thought of living in the trailer until all that snow disappeared. We'd have to tighten our belts until Don started work. We reached the boulder fall. The warm afternoon sun had melted away enough of the snowbank's battered edge for Don to drive across with all four tires firmly planted on the road. Misty and I walked across again just in case the road gave way.

Don suggested cheap hot dogs for dinner. On top of all the day's excitement my pregnant tummy roiled at the thought of frankfurters and beans. Instead, we splurged on cheeseburgers from The Beanery. Don and I recalculated our finances while we ate. The next morning Don checked in at the ranger station. He charged back to the trailer and shouted, "Start packing, Nance! There's no snow on the right fork. We're going to the lookout on Sunday. Head 'em up. Move 'em out."

Renowned baseball player Yogi Berra once advised, "When you come to a fork in the road—take it." Our roads in life had diverged often. Sometimes Don and I chose a fork after careful consideration. We'd planned for years to move to the Northwest. Sometimes a fork seemed to choose us. Don went to college in Moscow instead of Pocatello. Sometimes we stepped onto a path in excitement. We were going to be parents. Other times we stepped out in dread. We'd be leaving Idaho. Future circumstances would force us onto paths we never would have chosen. Sometimes Don would lead the way, other times I would. But every time we headed off to a new adventure, we did it together, for better or worse.

Middle Sister Peak Mountain

Approaching Middle Sister Peak Lookout

Middle Sister Peak Lookout behind snowbanks

North Fork Road with snowbanks

11

THE HIGH WORLD

A green Forest Service pickup headed our procession to Middle Sister Peak Lookout. Roy and Cody, from the fire crew, didn't take Fishhook Creek, but drove east through Avery and past Packsaddle, Turner Flat, and Tin Can Flat campgrounds. After twenty miles we turned south at the Bluff Creek Bridge. Fireroad 509 squeezed and curved between two perpendicular rock faces that the creek had carved away over the ages. The road left Bluff Creek, widened, and climbed steadily past abandoned logging roads, old clear-cuts glutted with tall grass, and an unoccupied lumber camp with a half-dozen derelict camp trailers and a rusting bulldozer.

No bluebirds greeted me at the intersection. I worried our luck had changed. Halfway to the lookout, Roy and Cody got out of their pickup. They pointed to a galvanized can an arm's length from the edge of the road. Icy, clear spring water burbled out of the ground, filled the can, flowed out a pipe near the top, and disappeared back into the ground through a cushion of greenery. The fire crew wouldn't deliver our water like they had on Dunn Peak. Don would have to fill our cans at that pipe. I eyed the water bubbling out of the dirt and worried, "I'm building a baby. It better be safe."

At the summit Roy turned onto the right fork along Middle Sister's sunny south slope. The Forest Service had cut this road because the snow-blocked north fork often delayed staffing the tower. Middle Sister Peak Lookout soon came into view, perched atop the peak's apex at the end of the road. Much of the rocky summit facing East Sister had been flattened for space to build the tower and to park vehicles.

Our water supply

Middle Sister Peak's original lookout, a ground-based log cabin with a central cupola for observation, had been constructed around 1923. Only six of the precision-carved, dovetailed log houses, called a D-1, were built. Fire managers had begun to recognize the advantages of elevated lookouts that were staffed full time. L-4 cabs, bundled in fourteen-by-fourteen-foot pre-cut kits, could be shipped by train, hauled up a mountain, and constructed onsite atop four tall poles. An L-4 cab on a thirty-five-foot-tall wooden tower replaced Middle Sister's log cabin in 1951. That lookout accidentally burned in 1953. The next year a thirty-foot, creosote-treated, sawn timber tower (TT) with a revised L-4 cab, known as an Aladdin, was constructed on the summit. Don and I arrived at the base of that tower precisely at 1:00 PM on Sunday, June 24, 1973.

Roy dug a key ring from his pants pocket. Don and I followed him up four steps to the lookout's first landing. Eleven open steps angled to the second landing. I grabbed the railing with my right hand to pull myself forward. My left hand instinctively cradled my belly. Thirteen steeper steps climbed to the third landing. My lungs burned from the unaccustomed exertion at close to seven thousand feet in elevation. Roy sprinted the final flight, unlocked the trap door, swung it open, stepped onto the catwalk, and hollered, "Come on up!"

I tilted my head as far back as it would go to take in my final fourteen challenges. I twisted sideways to fit my whole foot on the rung-like step. I grasped the rail with my right hand. With my left, I grabbed the step above my head and pulled. Don's hands nudged my hips from behind. I made it through the hatch and onto the catwalk. I doubled over and missed the view until I caught my breath.

Dunn Peak Lookout had been cleaned and organized before we arrived. Middle Sister's cab was still shuttered after a long, hard winter. Roy propped up the door's protective shutter and opened it. The light coming in weakly illuminated the inside of the cab. I looked in and lost my breath again. I'd heard of packrats. Now I saw how they lived. Roy attempted to cheer us. "Don't worry, they won't come back while you're here."

The packrats had mounded pine needles, branches, and grass into nests about twelve inches tall. A black carpet of dead flies covered the floor between the nests. A breeze through the door swirled the flies into tiny dust devils. The cab smelled like rotten cabbage mixed with fresh manure. My stomach churned. I turned to the outside and sucked in deep breaths of clean air. I turned back and studied the infested interior more closely. I yelled, "Roy, there's no stove! What are we supposed to cook on? At least Dunn Peak had a wood stove."

A cloud of curse words followed Roy down the stairs. "I'll radio Wade. We'll fix this."

I informed Don of three certainties. First, Misty and I would sleep in the car until every packrat pile and dead fly was cleaned out of the cab. I hoped he would, too. Second, I'd be moving back to Hoyt Flat if a new propane stove wasn't installed soon. And third, I meant it!

With the deftness of a future preacher, Don smoothed over everyone's ruffled feathers. We were all worn out. We decided to wait until tomorrow to carry our things to the catwalk. Roy and Cody said they'd be back early to connect the refrigerator to the propane tank. I hadn't noticed a refrigerator. Roy opened the cubicle below the cab. No packrats had nested in here. Inside sat a version of the 1940s Frigidaire in my grandparents' kitchen. It even had a small freezer. Roy said because Middle Sister's rocky summit didn't have room for a garbage pit, the campground custodian for Mammoth Springs would come once a week to haul off our trash. And he'd bring our mail. Roy bragged that Middle Sister Peak Lookout was a first-class operation. "Except for the packrats," I grumbled under my breath.

Bushy-tailed woodrats, *Neotoma cinerea*, are the largest and most cold-tolerant woodrat. They'd earned the packrat nickname because they store shiny objects. Males weigh as much as 1.3 pounds. They can grow to 18 inches long, half of that being tail. Packrats don't hibernate. They're active throughout the year. They use their thick, sticky urine to cement their feces, plants, bones, and other materials into quasi-structures called middens. Middens have persisted in arid desert caves for tens of thousands of years. They're botanical archives, a record of changing flora and climate that can be radiocarbon dated. The North American Packrat Midden Database contains information on palaeobotanical remains collected for more than 40 years. Packrats have sharp claws that make them excellent climbers. Middens have been found 50 feet high in coniferous trees, or 30 feet high on Middle Sister's lookout tower. Despite our mutual interest in plants, these packrats had to go.

Cody walked us along the south fork to Middle Sister's outhouse. It sat about twice the distance from the lookout as the outhouse on Dunn Peak. Two tippy rock steps shoved into the road's edge led to a bushy, overgrown footpath. The outhouse sat in a hollow, protected from the wind and intrusions from the road. It had tight boards and sturdy screens to keep out creatures that flew or skittered. The toilet box had been sanded free of splinters and painted. It had a plastic seat that didn't shift when sat upon. The outhouse didn't smell. There was a can for the toilet paper. Things were improving.

As we walked back from the outhouse, I noticed Don eying the snowbank beside the parking area. He said he planned to bury our cooler deep in the snow so our food would stay cold until the refrigerator was clean and running. He said no animals could dig it out, except maybe bears. He'd decided to take the risk. Don checked in with the dispatcher at Avery. His transmission confirmed that the Motorola radio operated properly. And it confirmed that he was on duty. He'd start getting paid.

Roy and Cody had plans for the rest of the day that didn't include us. Don and I were alone again on an isolated lookout in the middle of the St. Joe National Forest. We ate cold ham and Swiss sandwiches, chips, and pickles for dinner and Oreos for dessert. Misty supervised while Don buried the cooler. Our long day at seven thousand feet had exhausted us. We headed to bed before dark. The back of our truck and little wagon were still stuffed. Misty and I curled into the wagon's bucket seats, her under her quilt, and me in my mummy bag. Don stretched out on the pickup's bench seat in his bag. Sleep came so fast and hard on that chilly night that neither of us noticed the overhead display of the Milky Way's thousands of stars.

Middle Sister's outhouse

Blinding sunshine flooded through our windshields and rousted us at dawn. With no means to heat water, we sipped our morning caffeine from icy cans of cola chilled overnight in the back of the pickup. Misty wolfed down her kibble. Don and I munched leftover Oreos. He radioed his 8:00 AM check-in. The other lookouts already on the job were Conrad, Surveyors, and Snow Peak on the Red Ives District; Huckleberry on Calder District; Crystal on Clarkia; and our friend Jerry on Bald Mountain on the Palouse District.

Roy and Cody arrived early as promised. They got the fridge running, then unloaded four full water cans from the back of their truck, identical to the cans we'd had on Dunn Peak. Don eyed the cans with dread. He remembered hauling those one-hundred-pound cans up Dunn Peak's stairs by himself. Middle Sister was ten feet taller and had one more flight of stairs. Roy carried a long sturdy rope onto the catwalk. He strung the rope through a pulley attached to a beam that angled out from a corner of the roof and threw the ends of the rope over the railing. He yelled at Don to tie one end of the rope to a can's handle and the other end to our truck's bumper. Don inched the truck forward until the can reached the railing. Roy hefted the can over the railing, then threw back the loose end of the rope. They repeated this process until all four cans sat on the catwalk. Don was glad he'd learned to tie secure knots in Sea Scouts. I worried I might have to help lift the cans when Don and I were alone.

Two wood shutters on each wall of the lookout and a smaller shutter over the door protected the windows through the winter. The shutters were hinged at the top. A bolt with a wingnut secured each bottom corner tight against the wall. Don unscrewed the wingnuts on one shutter. Roy and Cody lifted it to engage with bolts that protruded from the ceiling joists under the roof. Don tightened on the wingnuts to secure the shutter in an open, flap-like position. Light filtered into the lookout through the grimy windows. I worried if I'd brought enough detergent and disinfectant to clean the cab. At least Don and I possessed an ample supply of the one cleaner my mother swore by—elbow grease.

Wade had told Roy and Cody to help carry up our supplies, suitcases, and bedding, maybe because I was pregnant. Those forest-hardened firefighters never broke a sweat or ran out of breath. Don directed them to put the food in the cubicle and everything else on the catwalk. Nothing would go into the cab until it was cleaned. But Wade had told them that Don and I would clean the lookout. With no update on our stove, we waved Roy and Cody goodbye with our thanks.

Misty headed off to scout her new territory. She pawed the rocks under the lookout, but no ground squirrels popped out to tease her. Maybe the squirrels hadn't liked living with packrats either. Don tightened a hoodie over his mouth and nose. He opened the door and the center windows. He draped the mattress over the railing and beat out the dust with a dustpan. He left the mattress to air in the disinfecting sunshine. He pulled the bed out from the corner and pulled the drawers out from under the bed. He swept up the packrat middens, the dead flies, and the dust. He dumped a generous measure of Spic and Span powder into the bucket I'd brought to use for cleaning. He scrubbed the bedframe, wiped the table and bench, cleaned the podium under the Firefinder, cleaned the cabinet and shelves that lined the walls, and scrubbed the floor. Our water supply quickly dwindled. Below in the cubicle, I wiped out the refrigerator, threw away the bulging cans of over-wintered food, and stacked our fresh cans on the shelves. I set aside our food packaged in cardboard or plastic to keep in the cab, safe from mice and packrats, I hoped. I scrubbed the garbage can with the tightest lid to store Misty's fifty-pound bag of kibble.

I thought about the packrats while I cleaned. Why hadn't Wade let us wait in the trailer until his crew had prepared the lookout? It felt like cleaning this rat-infested cab was a punishment. It wasn't a task listed on a lookout's job description. Maybe Wade didn't like that I was pregnant. Maybe a boss had given him trouble because he'd put a pregnant woman in the bunkhouse with the fire crew. Wade seemed anxious to have us out of Hoyt Flat. Maybe he thought that lowly lookouts and their dog didn't deserve to stay in a trailer. Maybe he'd promised the trailer to someone else. Maybe Don and I had run out of our bluebird luck. Maybe it was my pumped-up hormones. Maybe I was right. But I kept my opinions to myself. It could be dangerous to make waves. This had to be our home for the summer. Don and I had nowhere else to live.

I came out of the cubical to find that the June weather had turned to October weather. Don had put the mattress back on the bed, carried in everything from the catwalk, and closed the windows. I dumped my armful of food onto the bed. Dark clouds rolled in. The winds blew harder. A cold, gray mist condensed on the river and rose along the stream valleys. I thought it might snow. We pulled out our jackets from the suitcase. We ate another cold supper. Too weary to make the beds, we opted for a second night in our vehicles. The clouds and mist merged to sock-in Middle Sister's summit. This night we remembered to face our vehicles west in case the clouds scattered before sunrise. This night Don slept curled in the wagon's bucket seat. Misty and I stretched out in the truck.

We drank cold cola and ate the last crumbled Oreos for breakfast. Don radioed his check-in. Clouds still blanketed the mountain, so he had free time to help organize the lookout. And hooray, Roy and Cody arrived with a brand-new propane stove. Don and I washed our grubby selves with hot water. We ate a hot dinner of Dinty Moore canned beef stew. We assumed the same sleeping arrangement as on Dunn Peak. Don slept on the bed, Misty curled on her quilt on the floor, and I slept next to the bed on my cot, with elbow room.

The wind-up clock's luminous hands pointed to 2:30 AM. I cursed the mug of hot tea I'd drunk before bed. I slid my feet into my fuzzy slippers, zipped up my goose down jacket, and grabbed a flashlight and a wad of toilet paper. I scoured the catwalk with my flashlight for any passing packrats. I settled down to business on my emergency bucket's rim and turned off my flashlight. The clouds had cleared. Sparkling pinpoints of starlight coalesced into a silvery sheen that washed over the dark forest. I stared into the universe in amazed wonder until I realized that my bare ass was freezing onto the bucket. I went inside and slept soundly.

That summer air patrol flew as ordered, dependent on weather and fire conditions. Safety requirements mandated that the pilots radio location check-ins at fifteen-minute intervals. Middle Sister Peak Lookout had survived 1972's fire protection budget cuts because of the radio repeater installed near the tower's base. The repeater dependably received air patrol's wide-ranging transmissions and enhanced wireless communication throughout the forest. Don had to be within arm's reach of the radio whenever air patrol flew. They flew for the first time on our fourth day on the lookout.

We had very little water left. At 11:00 AM air patrol landed at St. Maries to refuel. Don announced he was heading to the spring. He promised to be back before air patrol flew again. He poured the water remaining in the last can into our biggest pot. He said anybody on the road would pass him, so I'd be fine.

At 2:40 PM air patrol radioed, "Middle Sister, air patrol, over." Don wasn't back. I worried that he'd get in trouble for leaving the lookout without permission. Air patrol repeated, "Middle Sister, air patrol, over."

Somebody had to respond. I lifted the microphone and depressed the switch. "Air patrol, this is Middle Sister, over."

"Our 4-16 is the mouth of Sisters Creek, over."

"The mouth of Sisters Creek, air patrol. Middle Sister clear."

"Air patrol clear."

I recorded air patrol's check-in time and position in the logbook. I searched the road. There was no sign of my AWOL lookout. Fifteen minutes later air patrol checked in from Point 81. I logged two more check-ins from the head of Beacon Creek and Surveyor's Peak. Don finally arrived. He answered three more calls until air patrol landed. Don still had a lot of work ahead to lift the cans to the catwalk. I kept my opinions to myself about how long he'd been gone. And nobody but me cared who answered air patrol's calls as long as someone was in the tower.

Don backed the pickup to the bottom of the stairs and unloaded the cans. I threw him the ends of the rope. He tied one end to a can and the other end to the truck's bumper. He edged the pickup forward. I steadied the rope. If the can started to swing, I hollered, "Slow down." If a wind gust threatened to tip the can, I screamed, "Stop!" When the can reached the top of the rail I yelled, "Whoa." I pulled the can in next to the rail to steady it. I couldn't lift one hundred pounds, besides the risk to our growing child. Don raced up the stairs, lifted the can over the railing, untied the rope, and ran back to the truck. We repeated the process. After all the cans sat on the catwalk, we grabbed cold sodas from the fridge. That water was too precious to expend one drop of its hard-gotten contents to quench our thirst.

Don soon had his water runs perfected: forty-five minutes to the spring, forty-five minutes to fill the cans and load them on the truck, and forty-five minutes to drive to a spot wide enough to turn the truck around and drive back to the lookout. It occurred to me that it would be a challenge to fit those cans in the back of our little wagon. Having the truck made us more self-sufficient. Don could get water without needing help from the fire crew. That would become important.

The weather in 1973 echoed the weather in 1910, a snow-glutted winter followed by a hot, dry, windy spring. On Thursday, June 28, the fire control officer radioed Don that air patrol would be flying on Saturday. We welcomed the overtime pay, but a kernel of worry sprouted in our brains. It was early in the fire season, and this was a tight budget year for the district. Fire management must be concerned about a growing fire danger to authorize overtime for Don and for air patrol. The only smoke Don had spotted on Dunn Peak was the bomb Wade had set to test Don's attentiveness. This summer could prove more dangerous. This summer the smokes could be real.

Digging a cooler into the snowbank, with Misty supervising

Morning on Middle Sister

12

THE BURNING INDEX

Middle Sister Peak Lookout had no daily delivery of mail or newspapers, no television, no telephone, no grocery store, hairdresser, doctor, or restaurant around the corner, no tap water, no electricity, no hot showers, and no toilet that flushed. Middle Sister had peace and quiet. It had solitude for relaxing, reflecting, and dreaming. Stunning vistas spread to the horizon in every direction. The lookout could have become a womb for Don and me, a safe haven with nothing to do but prepare for becoming parents. But Middle Sister wasn't a TV lookout. We lived surrounded by nature in the raw, not on a Hollywood sound stage. There was no script, we lived each day as it came. There was no guaranteed happy ending. We faced real dangers. It would become the most memorable summer of our lives.

The sun rose at 4:51 AM on July 1 and its light blasted into the lookout. One contraband roll-up shade did little to block the glare. Don braved the chilly morning to make coffee, tour the catwalk with binoculars pressed to his face, and radio in to Avery at 8:00 AM. I curled inside my sleeping bag to stay warm. A knot of regret formed in my chest. I realized that after this summer I might never again be surprised by the flash of a mountain bluebird. I might never again count the age rings on the stump of a western red cedar as big as a kitchen table. I might never again see the pattern the Vibram soles on my boots had pressed into the dusty road behind me. Don and I had worked so hard to come to Idaho. We'd fallen in love with the west. Moving to Indiana felt like going backwards, like erasing our progress.

Most mornings Don and I fixed a catch-as-catch-can breakfast. A wireframe campfire toaster worked great on the stove if I turned off the gas before the bread burned. I edged down the narrow path to the outhouse. My emergency bucket sloshed at my side. I ducked under low-hanging branches of fir and hemlock. I brushed against prickly grass and knocked dew onto my clothes. On special days when the weather and my timing coincided, I propped open the outhouse door with a heavy rock to indulge myself in the alpine view. Photons that had traveled ninety-three million miles from the sun transformed the liquid dewdrops to vapor. The mist floated skyward to vibrate leaves and needles and generate soft swishes and sighs. The cool upper air reconstituted the vapor into droplets. The droplets coalesced into puffy white clouds that contrasted against the Idaho-blue sky. I enjoyed the view from my throne until Don hollered from the lookout to make sure I hadn't fallen in. One morning the sunlight angled in just right. I saw that previous lookouts had lingered here, too. They'd carved their names into the outhouse wall to record their presence. Don used his fishing knife to add our names to that unique logbook: D and N Hammond, 1973.

Lunch was a sandwich or canned soup. We brewed sun tea in a glass jar set on the catwalk and iced it with cubes from our tiny freezer. I cleaned the lookout and settled on the bed with a murder mystery or a crossword puzzle. Sometimes my eyes grew heavy and I turned them to look inside myself. My body was no longer mine alone. Changes within me progressed with every tick of the clock. Hormones swung my emotions. I wasn't just Don's wife; I'd become the mother of his child. I worried how a third person would affect our balance. I worried how our lives would be different in Indiana, in ministry. My growing uncertainties made me short-tempered. Some afternoons I escaped with Misty to keep the peace. I'd rest on a smooth warm rock with a good view. Misty sat and leaned against my leg and listened to my ramblings. I lived in a wonderland others dream about. My family had taught me how to find happiness in simple pleasures. I decided to immerse myself in nature, to fill my memory banks with moments few people experience. I worked on resetting my balance. I returned calls to the birds. I studied ants hauling a bit of food ten times their size. I noticed the distinct smell of the first raindrop hitting a dusty roadbed. I stared deep into our starlit universe. I kissed my husband hello every time I came back from the outhouse or from a walk.

Don spent his afternoons pacing the catwalk in search of any anomaly in the landscape. Around 2:00 PM a composed female voice aired the daily fire weather forecast from St. Maries. The broadcast was new this summer. We paid little notice to the humdrum predictions of temperatures, wind speeds, and thunderstorms. Don clocked out of work at 5:00 PM. We ate supper soon after because of the setting sun; the stove faced west. If I cooked after 5:30, I had to wear sunglasses and a broad-brimmed hat to block the intense light. And the lookout's glass walls acted like a greenhouse. If we waited to cook and heat wash water when the sun poured in, the temperature inside the lookout grew hot enough to cook us, too.

Our evenings hardly varied. Don carried the garbage to the cubicle, locked the trap door, and lit the propane lanterns mounted on the walls. We set up my cot. Secure for the night, we played cribbage and listened to classical music. Don had discovered that if he dialed the transistor's tuner past the radio frequencies, it received transmissions from a local television station. Sunday evenings we pulled the bench out onto the catwalk and sat and listened to *Bonanza* reruns until dark. I headed to my bucket before bed. Don relieved himself between the catwalk railings, positioned at just the right height. The annoying downside of his convenience was that the local elk herd often woke us around 3:00 AM, clattering across the loose shale under the lookout to partake of his salty seasoning.

Some nights, zipped inside my mummy bag on my wobbly cot, I lay in dread that my grandfather had predicted my future. "What does she need to go to college for? She'll just get married and have babies." When I'd called my parents to tell them I was pregnant, I sensed disappointment in my father's voice. I wanted to reassure him that he hadn't wasted his money on my education. I wanted to promise him I'd become more than a by-product of Don's calling, more than a minister's wife. I wanted to have it all, to be a wife, and a mother, and have my own career. But I couldn't put my finger on what it was I wanted to be. My career had no form or substance. I'd scream if one more person advised me to follow my passion. I had no passion, no ambition, no desire, nothing. I did have the need to prove my grandfather wrong, to prove myself right. I decided that would be enough for now. But I worried I might disappoint myself, too.

The Fourth of July fell on a Wednesday. Campers had arrived the Friday before to reserve their favorite spot. Like the summer of 1910, a respite of cool, damp weather late in June had kept the fire danger Low. No fires spoiled the holiday. Don and I walked out the north fork to the last snowbank that still blocked the road. He snapped a photo of me holding a sign I'd made to mark the day.

The last snowbank

The view from the outhouse

The weather turned hot, dry, and windy. St. Maries moved the daily weather briefing to first thing in the morning. And they added a new data point—the burning index (BI). The BI is a measure of fire intensity. The number has no units and no upper limit. Dividing the BI by ten predicts the length of the flames at the head of a fire. A BI of seventy predicts a flame length of seven feet. The higher the BI, the more difficult a fire will be to control. The first BI stood at sixty-seven. The next day it rose to seventy-two.

July 11 would be our third anniversary. I asked Don what we should do the next day to celebrate. He said he was sorry. Avery had called while I was in the outhouse. Air patrol was scheduled to fly an extended route around Middle Sister. He had to work until dark that night and the next. He promised me we'd go into town and celebrate with a nice dinner when we could. An incoming cold front made the temperature drop fifteen degrees. Neither of us remembers how we spent our chilly third anniversary.

On July 12, Don radioed Roundtop that he'd spotted a smoke at eighty degrees, fifteen minutes on Black Mountain in Montana's Lolo Forest. He asked if the Lolo had reported it. Roundtop radioed back that the Lolo was already working the fire. It was a big one. They were dropping borate to get it under control. There was nothing for Don to do but keep Roundtop posted if he observed anything unusual.

In the 1930s the Forest Service had dropped a wooden beer keg filled with water from a Ford Tri-Motor airplane onto a forest fire. Water bombs proved more dangerous to the firefighters they fell on than they were effective at putting out the fire. In 1955 a Boeing Stearman 75 Kaydet dropped 170 gallons of free-flowing water onto the Mendenhall fire in California. But water drops proved ineffective unless delivered from a dangerously low altitude during perfect weather conditions. In 1958 a General Motors Avenger TBM dropped a sodium calcium borate slurry onto a fire at Lake Elsinore in California. Borate slurries were most effective when dropped onto a new fire to create a firebreak before firefighters arrived. In the early 1970s ammonium sulfate and phosphate compounds were being studied as replacement retardants.

Avery radioed to complain that Middle Sister's signal was weak. Air patrol was scheduled to fly morning and afternoon routes that weekend. Don changed out the battery to ensure a strong signal, critical for both the safety of air patrol and for communication for the whole forest. At 11:02 AM air patrol radioed in their fifth location check over Elbow Ridge. Eleven minutes later St. Maries radioed that they hadn't heard from air patrol. They reminded Don to notify them if he didn't get a check-in every fifteen minutes. Don politely informed St. Maries that they'd missed the check-in. At 11:15 Don logged in air patrol over Indian Dip. We worried about why St. Maries had become so jumpy. The BI rose to ninety-nine with no rain forecast. Fire crews adjusted the Smokey Bear signs from Low to Moderate—which meant that fires were not likely to become serious and that control was relatively easy.

Warming temperatures brought on another problem, one we'd hope to avoid on the taller Middle Sister. The winged ants were back. We closed all the windows. Being pregnant, I minded the heat more. I felt like I'd melt. A disconnected exhaust pipe from the departed wood stove hung from the ceiling in the corner above my chair. A plastic sheet wound with duct tape closed off the pipe's inside open end. Ants found their way into the pipe from the roof and crashed onto the plastic. A noise like popcorn popping filled the lookout for hours every afternoon and drove me crazy. There was no escape. Male ants fertilized female ants on the windows, on railings, and on towels we'd put out to dry. Dead males piled into heaps on the lookout's catwalk and on the roof. Like on Dunn Peak, evening breezes swept the piles high into the air. But Middle Sister's prevailing winds crossed the setting sun. For a few magical seconds, thousands of prisms on transparent ant wings fractured the sunlight apart into a swirling cloud of minute, glittering rainbows.

On July 19, St. Maries reported a 50 percent chance of thunderstorms, the BI at 127, and the fire danger at Very High—which meant that fires would start easily from all causes, spread rapidly immediately after ignition, and quickly increase in intensity. Don began to worry. It had been three weeks without rain and none was predicted. At 4:15 PM Don radioed in the St. Joe Forest's first lightning of the summer. Except for a few ground strikes, most of the lightning that night was cloud-to-cloud.

The next morning Don spotted no smokes. The all business weather voice radioed out a "Red Flag Alert" for the forest: a 60 percent chance of thunder-showers, strong winds, and the BI at 134. No one had informed Don what a Red Flag Alert actually meant. Don had been stationed on a Navy ship on the hurricane-prone Virginia coast. He at least understood that a Red Flag Warning meant fire conditions on the St. Joe had deteriorated from bad to worse. My mood had deteriorated, too. We'd been on the lookout for almost a month without a break. The fire crew was busy with control duties, so no one had brought our mail or collected our garbage. The cans in the cubical were full. We'd attract bears if we stored our garbage in the back of the truck. It had to go into our wagon with the windows closed. The bears would tear our wagon apart if they got in. We were out of bread and sandwich meat. I was low on clean clothes. A hot shower would improve my cranky disposition. I pestered Don to ask for time off so we could go into town, or at least go to Mammoth Springs to dump our garbage. He radioed St. Maries for permission to leave the tower for half a day. They told us to wait until the weather improved. Who knew when that would be? We started to wear our underwear for three days at a time, our jeans for a week.

St. Maries had begun to radio Don every morning before the weather report to get information on Middle Sister's weather and lightning activity. Air patrol continued morning and afternoon flights. The fire crew quickly extinguished a small fire of unknown origin reported by the public. Don's overtime accumulated. Maybe we could afford to sleep in motels instead of in the pickup on our drive to Indiana.

Don radioed his morning check-in on July 23. He reminded everyone in hearing range that Middle Sister NEEDED a day off. With the probability of thunderstorms at 10 percent and low winds, Avery granted Don permission to leave the tower at noon. That wasn't enough time to drive to St. Maries. We drove our trusty wagon to Avery, showered and washed clothes at the bunkhouse, stocked up with whatever fresh food, canned goods, and kibble we could find, and enjoyed our twelve-day-belated anniversary dinner. The fire crew had invited us back to the bunkhouse. Don sat in for a few hands of poker. I listened to the Rolling Stones' new album and caught up on the latest gossip. Suddenly, the room began to reel. I felt terrible. I told Don we needed to go.

We made our excuses and started back to the lookout. I felt worse with every mile. I grew anxious about being farther and farther away from medical help. I had horrible cramps. I worried about losing our baby. I told Don to take me to St. Maries. At the first spot wide enough to turn around, Don headed back toward the only doctor for more than seventy-five miles. He drove too fast in the pitch-black night. He navigated the narrow dirt road and sharp curves along the river, with one eye on the road and one eye on my pale face twisted in agony.

"Pull over, pull over. I have to throw up." I bent in half and wretched. My anniversary dinner hit the road so hard that it kicked up clouds of dust and splattered onto my best slacks. I prayed our baby held on tight. If it came undone there was nothing in the car to swaddle it in. We drove on. I felt a little better. Scattered lights appeared from cabins and farms and helped me to relax. I suggested we head back to the lookout. Don pressed harder on the gas and said I was going to see a doctor. The clinic in St. Maries was shut tight. Don rattled the locked door in frustration until he noticed a telephone on the wall. The doctor who answered was unhappy to be rousted in the middle of the night. Don explained my symptoms and our circumstances—pregnant, cramping, vomiting, and living on a lookout in the middle of nowhere. The doctor agreed to examine me. "You ate something bad, you'll both be fine. No charge, happy anniversary," he said, and showed us out. I slept while Don drove back along the river through what remained of the night. We parked on Middle Sister's summit in the nick of time for his 8:00 AM check-in.

The rest of July fell into a tense acceleration of the fire danger. Winds continued to be strong, no rain fell, and the BI rose. Air patrol flew two routes every day. On July 29 a BI of 175 combined to push the St. Joe's fire danger to Extreme—which meant that fires would start easily, spread furiously, burn intensely, and that all fires were potentially serious. The fire control officer sent an emergency observer into Dunn Peak. On the last day of July, the BI climbed to 189.

My anxiety elevated in proportion to the BI. Forests ready to spark an uncontrolled wildfire lined both sides of our only escape route from the lookout. I laid awake worrying that a raging firestorm would turn us into charcoal like the Butte miners. I worried that our baby might never draw a breath. Since I was awake, I decided to be useful. I thought about an emergency evacuation plan. The next day I packed a go-bag and wrote two lists. The first was for necessary items we could throw over the railing to retrieve when we got to the ground. The second was for things we'd carry with us when we left. Don loaded a full can of water into the back of the pickup in case we had to douse a fire blocking our escape. We hated the idea of abandoning our trusty wagon, but the truck had better visibility, a higher clearance, and a powerful granny gear that could push aside fallen trees blocking our way. Then we decided that what we needed to do next was to calm down, quit worrying, and enjoy our time on Middle Sister. This was our last summer to be fire lookouts. We had no intention of squandering this opportunity on what might be needless worry.

13

VISITORS

An official Forest Service sign had been posted next to the stairs on Dunn Peak Lookout. It stated:

NOTICE TO VISITORS—THIS TOWER IS MAINTAINED FOR THE DISCOVERY OF FOREST FIRES. You may climb it if you wish but the Forest Service United States Department of Agriculture cannot assume any liability for accidents. For your own safety not more than four persons should be on the tower at any one time.

I'd read the sign once to see what it said, then ignored it. Dunn Peak Lookout didn't appear on Idaho road maps from gas stations. No road signs pointed to the lookout. Other than that one mysterious stranger who'd appeared out of nowhere one evening, we'd had no visitors on Dunn Peak. When Don and I arrived on Middle Sister, I noticed an identical sign posted next to the stairs.

Middle Sister Peak Lookout was our home for the summer. We had a baby on the way. We'd be moving to Indiana. Don would be starting seminary. We'd counted on having time alone to adjust. Our first visitors surprised us. They'd stopped at Hoyt Flat and asked about places to see. They were given directions to our lookout. They'd like a tour. I'd just finished my bath in the plastic basin. I ran onto the catwalk and moved my used emergency bucket out of sight. No one had informed us that the Forest Service expected lookouts to be goodwill ambassadors and welcome the public. It wasn't in our nature to be rude to visitors. We just wished we'd been told what to expect.

We had a steady parade of visitors every weekend. Don prided himself on noticing an approaching vehicle's noise or dust at least three miles away. He scrutinized the arrivals with his binoculars as they drove along the fire road. He greeted them from the catwalk with the hatch closed. Most were campers at Dismal Lake and Mammoth Springs. Most were polite. Families and scout troops climbed the stairs and asked questions about life on a fire lookout. Newlyweds cuddled on the catwalk. But some visitors were having a bad day. A station wagon full of people stopped in the parking area. The driver got out, screamed obscenities at everyone in the back, got back in, and drove off. If visitors appeared belligerent or drunk, Don politely explained from the catwalk that this lookout was our home. If they asked reasonable questions, he gave them an overview of the lookout's history and pointed out landmarks. If the visitors got rowdy, Don wished them a good day, made a show of going inside, and loudly closed the door. Deprived of their audience, they took in the view for a few minutes, then left.

Because Don and I would be leaving Idaho, friends came to wish us goodbye. Don's personality attracts people. He makes friends without effort. I'm not easy to be friends with. I'm an only child who doesn't share well. I'm introverted, prideful, gruff, opinionated, stubborn, and a perfectionist. I'm a walking contradiction. I require alone time to function, but I become depressed if no one seeks my company. I challenge bullies without thinking, but I abhor confrontation. I do the best I can because it's my nature, but I fall into depression if no one recognizes my efforts. I rely on my own counsel, but I lay awake for hours tormented by regret. I assess the efficiency and effectiveness of every step in a process before I proceed, but I lose control of my emotions, jump the gun, rush to judgement, and blurt out inappropriate comments at inopportune times. Our friends' visits would disrupt my routine for an entire weekend. I couldn't wait to see them. I cherish the people willing to put up with me.

Early in the summer, while the fire danger was still low, the Avery dispatcher radioed that our friends Ron and Amy from Moscow would arrive that evening. They'd camp at Dismal Lake. After a tour of the lookout, their daughters took Misty out to play. The four of us shared the latest news from our lives. Nurse Amy made certain all was well with my pregnancy. The evening sped by. Knowing the road to Dismal Lake could be treacherous after dark, I urged them to head back to camp. Amy invited us for a charcoal-grilled steak with fresh salad the next evening; we gratefully accepted.

After our steak dinner, Ron and Amy showed us a rickety raft they'd found and floated out onto the snow-melt lake to fish. Amy complained the water was so clear they could see the trout nibble their bait, then swim away. Don and Ron paddled the raft out onto the lake. Amy and I set off to scout the ripening huckleberries. The girls stayed at their tent to play with Misty and their two German Shepherds. I stopped at a clearing and scanned across the lake to check if the guys were still afloat. Amy whispered from down the hill for me to slowly turn around. I did and stood too close for comfort to the nose of a magnificent bull elk. The brown hulk of muscle and fur sniffed and pawed. I nearly peed my pants. While Amy and I whispered ideas about how to save ourselves, the elk disappeared back into the forest without a sound.

Our friend Jerry, who'd be driving back to Indiana with us, and his wife Tammy were lookouts on Bald Mountain, about forty miles away as the crow flies. Jerry was competitive, and claimed he'd driven for hours on dirt roads just to say hello. Don believed he just wanted to compare the accommodations between his lookout and ours.

Mike and Shirley, our next-door neighbors in Moscow, arrived with their two teenagers and two toy poodles. Three rifles hung on a rack in their pickup's back window. Mike had served as an Army sniper in Vietnam. Before we'd left town for our lookout duty, Mike had taken Don to a quarry and shown him how to load and fire and clean one of his rifles. He said he'd feel better if Don had it for protection on the lookout. When the pleasantries of greetings were over, Mike asked to see his rifle. Don moved the bench next to the Firefinder, stepped up, pulled open a small trap door in the ceiling, and angled out the rifle. He assured Mike that he checked it regularly to make sure it stayed dry. Don told Mike he was right; Don did feel better having the rifle available in case there was a problem.

Before we knew it, the visit was over. I hated when our friends left. My emotions swung between sadness, because I might never see these dear people again, and joy at having my alone time back.

The church Don and I had attended in Moscow was a merged congregation. Mainline Protestant denominations had experienced a decline in membership during the 1970s, partly because young adults had lost interest. The small congregation of the Christian Church (Disciples of Christ) had sold their building and moved in with the American Baptist congregation. Their beliefs were similar enough that they held joint Sunday services. Soon after Don and I had started attending, the church conducted a program to acquaint its members

Don and Ron on the raft at Dismal Lake

Our friend Jerry on Middle Sister

*Tom Wilkinson (right) with unidentified
Forest Service worker*

with each other. Ten of us gathered weekly at our house. Don and I were the youngest in the group. The other members were the lead physician at the University of Idaho's clinic and his wife, a PhD chemistry professor, a wheat farmer's wife, a couple working toward their PhDs in mathematics, and a crop duster pilot and his wife. One evening Don and I shared experiences from our summer on Dunn Peak and our plans for Middle Sister. Someone asked what we missed most while living on top of a mountain. Don said he missed reading the Sunday newspaper. Keith, the pilot, straightened up from his usual disinterested posture. He queried Don for details on Middle Sister's location and altitude. He teased, "Don't be surprised if you see me some Sunday morning with a newspaper." We presumed he and his wife might drive to the lookout one day to visit us.

Early one Sunday, a small yellow plane buzzed the north fork road, uncomfortably close to the lookout. We ran onto the catwalk, still in our pajamas. The plane banked sharply and turned to make another pass. It came so close we feared it could crash into the tower. Don yelled that the pilot was an idiot. The plane buzzed by again, even with the catwalk. We recognized Keith at the controls. We waved frantically. Keith tipped his wings. He banked into another turn, buzzed the road, and threw a bundled Sunday newspaper out the window. "What a delivery," Don crowed. He raced down the stairs to retrieve his treasure. He waved the paper in thanks as Keith flew by on his final pass. Don and I read every article, worked all the puzzles, and wished we could shop for the juicy steaks and fresh vegetables pictured in the colorful grocery store ads. We never got to thank Keith for the newspaper. He died the next summer when his crop duster crashed into a field.

Our most extraordinary visitor was one of two Forest Service workers whom Don and I hadn't met previously. We offered the men cold sodas and they introduced themselves. The older man said he'd worked for the Forest Service for years. The younger man admitted that this was his first summer on the forest. Don asked what he'd done before. Our visitor's answer was anything but expected. "I worked in the mines, the Sunshine Mine," he replied in a self-effacing manner with no hint to the fact that he was a walking miracle. Don and I shared a glance in silent stunned recognition as the name Tom Wilkinson registered. Wilkinson and Ron Flory had survived after being trapped underground for eight days following a fire in the Sunshine Mine, a little more than one year earlier. The mine was located eight miles southeast of Kellogg, Idaho, and approximately forty air miles north-northeast of Middle Sister Peak. Tom said he didn't care to talk about his experience. We respected his request. The four of us passed a pleasant hour chatting about anything except the horror that had suffocated ninety-one of Tom's fellow miners.

The Sunshine Mining Company had begun operation in 1884. From 1904 to 2001, the Sunshine produced more than 364 million ounces of silver, making it one of the world's most profitable silver mines. On May 2, 1972, 173 miners on the day shift were lowered down the No. 10 shaft to their work levels in the 6,000-foot-deep mine. Around 11:35 AM two electricians on the 3700 level smelled smoke. The unseen fire burned in the worst possible location, on the intake air side of the mine. Smoke and toxic concentrations of carbon monoxide quickly contaminated most of the airways. But the miners weren't overly concerned when they first smelled smoke. Prevailing lore held that hard-rock mines never burned.

Foremen Jim Bush and Harvey Dionne decided to evacuate the mine. Dionne removed insulation from over the No. 12 borehole to allow fresh air to reach the lower levels. Bush carried three men near exhaustion toward the Jewell shaft until he also became exhausted. Bush abandoned the men to find help. The crew on the 4400 level telephoned the chippy hoist operator to get them out, but they got no response. The operator had abandoned his post because the smoke had become so thick, he couldn't see the controls. The drum hoist operator was ordered to reconfigure his machine from hauling muck to hauling out miners. At 12:13 PM the drum hoist began to lift men off the 3700 level.

Locomotives pulling cars full of miners derailed when they crashed into dead bodies lying across the tracks. Hoisting ceased at 1:02 PM when the drum hoist operator died at his post. No miners working on the 4200, 5200, 5400, 5600, or 5800 levels survived. In little more than one hour and fifteen minutes, ninety-one miners died underground in the Sunshine Mine. The last of the eighty miners evacuated alive reached the surface at 2:30 PM. Rescue operations shifted to recovery. Bodies were discovered seated against the mine's walls next to open lunchboxes. The miners had taken off their self-rescue respirators that changed the deadly carbon monoxide into harmless carbon dioxide because they didn't know it was normal for them to get hot. They'd sat down and poured coffee from their thermoses while they waited for the hoist that never came.

On May 9, a rescue capsule, loaned from the Atomic Energy Commission's Nevada Test Site, descended into the enlarged No. 12 borehole to the 4800 level. A rescue crew found Tom Wilkinson, 29, and Ron Flory, 28, alive and in good condition. Wilkinson and Flory had waited at the 4800 level shaft station to evacuate. When the hoist didn't arrive, their group had driven a tunnel transporter back to where they thought the air was fresher. Wilkinson passed out. Flory recruited another worker to help them find a better location. They came to an intersection where the smoke dissipated into a tunnel above. Flory stayed there with Wilkinson. The third man left to bring the others. They never arrived.

Flory and Wilkinson took turns sleeping to monitor the wall of smoke outside their refuge. They drank from a nearby waterline, ate leftovers from their fallen comrades' lunch pails, and breathed fresh air because Harvey Dionne had uncovered the vent hole when the fire started. The men only turned on their battery-powered headlamps when absolutely necessary to break the total darkness. They passed the time talking about their families, hunting, and fishing. They speculated what their wives might do with the insurance money if they didn't make it out. They repeatedly phoned for help, but no one answered. After eight days in darkness, Wilkinson and Flory saw a beam of light come down the tunnel. They beat on the water pipes until help arrived. No one else alive remained inside the Sunshine Mine to be rescued.

Our two visitors got ready to head back to work. Don asked Tom what he planned to do in the future. Tom explained he was glad for his job with the Forest Service so he could earn some money, but he got nervous working this high in clean air and bright sunshine. I remember he said that Flory swore he'd never go back to the mine. But Tom said he'd go back as soon as the mine reopened, because mining was what he did.

14

THE BIRDS AND
THE BEES ... AND A BEAR

Ornithology was one of my favorite college courses. It opened this city kid's eyes to avian wonders that exist beyond pigeons, robins, and sparrows. I'd sit for hours at the crest of Hawk Mountain Sanctuary near Kutztown, Pennsylvania, mesmerized by the circling raptors. I'd packed my bird book and binoculars for Middle Sister. I'd planned to add birds to my sighting list that I might never again have the chance to observe.

On hikes through the underbrush, Misty and I sometimes tripped over a pair of dusky grouse. When our fresh meat ran low, I was tempted to wring the neck of one of those plump, free-range, organic birds, known locally as mountain chickens. But it wasn't a fair match. The birds froze like statues, depending on their coloring to camouflage them into the forest floor. But the male's eyebrows glowed a neon red-orange and betrayed their position.

A sleek peregrine falcon often perched on the tall antenna pole next to the lookout. This side-burned aerial speedster seemed to find it entertaining to watch us. One warm afternoon Don hollered from the catwalk. Two golden eagles leisurely circled in a thermal rising over Middle Sister Peak. We traded Don's binoculars and craned our necks back so we didn't miss a second as the eagles circled ever higher. I wondered how far above seven thousand feet those birds could climb before they ran out of warm air for support. They rose so high they faded from sight into the unclouded sky.

A flurry of tiny, yellow-streaked pine siskins often ruffled through the tall conifers next to the lookout. I wondered how many siskins it would take to equal the weight of one golden eagle. A noisy Clark's nutcracker often chased off the siskins. That boisterous bad guy tolerated no interlopers in his territory. One day a splash of yellow and orange in the same trees caught my eye. I grabbed my binoculars and bird book to confirm a male western tanager in full breeding plumage. Dark-eyed juncos and Cooper's and sharp-shinned hawks flew past the lookout. The evening's abundance of flying insects attracted clusters of swooping tree swallows and a solitary nighthawk who slid by gape-mouthed to collect his dinner.

I didn't realize at first how deeply quiet it could be on Middle Sister. One day, as I walked to the outhouse, I was surprised to hear a low-flying airplane approach. I turned to search the skies. The fattest, hairiest bumblebee I'd ever seen brushed the brim of my hat. The incoming roar abated as it flew past. How did this bee make so much noise that I thought it was an airplane? I decided it wasn't the bee's enormous size, but the lack of interfering noise around me. I heard no cars, no motorcycles, no planes, no buses, no barking dogs or screeching cats, no screaming kids, no yelling parents, no radio or TV, no lawn mowers, and no sirens. I heard only the breeze whispering through the pines, the harmonizing hum of pollen collectors in a sun-drenched field of wildflowers, and the staccato cry of a hawk on the hunt. I could hear the outhouse door close from more than two city blocks away. I heard tires crunch rocks on the final turn half a mile down the south fork road. Dirty dish water dumped from the catwalk crashed like a mighty stream onto the rocks below. At night, the gentle hiss from the propane lanterns occupied every millimeter of space inside the lookout.

One night a strong wind dumped my emergency bucket. We hated using precious water to wash the catwalk. Don put a heavy, flat rock into my bucket to keep it from blowing over. Certain bees discovered they had a convenient spot to land and sip my urine. Even on cold nights I shined my flashlight into my bucket to check for pee bees before I settled on the rim.

Mountain goats lived across the valley on East Sister's rocky slopes. We never spotted one, though not for a lack of trying. Other than those clattering nighttime elk visits, we had just one other four-legged encounter all summer. Misty patrolled the catwalk to spy critters who dared to trespass on her territory. One day her alarm of "stranger-danger" barks rushed us to the windows. "Holy shit, it's a bear," Don yelled. A scrawny mess of matted brown fur had lumbered out of the trees onto the north fork. He sat on the road and sniffed the air, trying to figure out what all the fuss was about. Don raced out the door to grab Misty's collar as she scrambled toward the stairs. The hair on her spine stood erect in full attack mode. Misty ducked under Don's reach and tore down the stairs straight for the bear. Nothing stops a Dalmatian on a mission to chase an intruder.

"Get the rifle!" I screamed. "That damn bear's not going to eat my dog!"

Neither of us had experience with dogs or cats when we were children. Misty was our first pet. When she was a few months old we'd hooked her leash to our front doorknob so she could enjoy our Fourth of July fireworks. We set off the first firecracker and turned to see her reaction. Misty's collar and leash hung empty from the doorknob. Our ignorance had created a gun-shy dog.

"Misty's halfway down the road. Shoot that bear!" I yelled.

"I might wound the bear and make him mad, or shoot Misty," Don yelled back.

He fired the rifle into the air. Our fireworks fiasco saved the day. Misty's fear of loud noises superseded her need to chase the bear. She turned tail and retreated back to the lookout. I guessed the bear didn't like gunfire either because he hightailed it back down the ridge from where he'd come. Don radioed Roundtop. He said the bear had come and gone of its own accord. The Forest Service prohibited firearms on lookouts. A few days later the Roundtop crew showed up to report they'd caged the bear. He was on his way to a more remote part of the forest. They pushed Don to retell his story. They nodded knowingly when Don fessed up to having a rifle. They said it was a good thing he did.

That bear had looked thin and ragged. He may have risked coming close to the lookout because he couldn't find huckleberries to eat. I couldn't either. I'd stopped draping a berry bucket around my neck on my hikes because so few berries grew in the bone-dry weather. When Misty did dive off the trail ahead of me to push her nose into a huckleberry bush, I raced to collect my share before she scarfed down every tasty morsel. First come, first served. The law of the forest. Sorry, bears.

15

AUGUST ON FIRE

The previous summer on Dunn Peak, the fire control officer had assured Don and me that the Great Fires of 1910 could never be repeated. He said he'd trained his fire crew to carry out the Forest Service's 10 AM Policy, which decreed that every forest fire should be suppressed by 10 AM following the day it was reported.

The four men in charge of the Forest Service through 1939 had witnessed the death and destruction inflicted by the Great Fires of 1910. Forester Henry S. Graves, who'd succeeded Pinchot, was succeeded by District One Forester William Buckhout Greeley from 1920 to 1928. Robert Y. Stuart served as Forester from 1928 to 1933. Ferdinand Augustus Silcox had been District One's Assistant Forester and head of the district's quartermaster corps. He served from 1933 until his death in 1939.

Forester Silcox had introduced his 10 AM Policy in 1935. He espoused that, to prevent a repeat of the 1910 disaster, science, technology, manpower, and enough money could and should eliminate fire from national forests. Some of his contemporaries deemed his strict fire suppression policy as folly. Former Lolo Forest Supervisor Elers Koch argued in favor of letting backcountry fires burn themselves out. Yale Forest School Professor Herman Chapman debated that fire had an important, if yet little understood, ecological role in the landscape. And Secretary of the Interior Richard Ballinger advocated that national forest land should be allowed to burn to reduce fuel loads, following the established practice of Native American tribes who had lived in harmony with the forests for eons.

President Franklin Roosevelt dispatched an army of Civilian Conservation Corps carpenters to erect more than 8,000 fire lookout towers across America to spot forest fires while they were small. Many towers overlooked lands devastated by the Big Burn in the Pacific Northwest. Idaho led the tally with 992, most densely packed into the Coeur d'Alene, St. Joe, and Clearwater National Forests. Oregon had 849 towers, Washington had 656, and Montana had 639. In the 1940s the first parachuting smokejumpers landed on a fire in Idaho's Nez Perce National Forest, hotshot crews formed in California's Cleveland and Angeles National Forests, and roads were constructed into the remote backcountry to quickly get crews to fires spotted by the lookouts. And the Forest Service launched an ad campaign to involve the public. Smokey Bear urged the nation that "only you can prevent forest fires."

By the 1960s, Silcox's 10 AM policy had created unintended consequences. Undergrowth and dead trees clogged the forests. Fuel loads had built up to critical levels. Without fire to contain them, harmful insects and plant pathogens had flourished and added more dead material to the fuel loads. No new Giant Sequoias grew in California because their seeds needed fire to germinate. Bison and elk herds had diminished in overgrown woodlands. And because the Forest Service worked to control every fire in one day, expensive houses were built near ski resorts or in the back country, far from community fire protection.

From my view on Middle Sister, I developed a new perspective of the St. Joe Forest. I saw clear-cuts, hundreds of acres in size. Loggers had cut down every tree, hauled away the commercially valuable timber, and left the debris to decay on the ground. I thought the clear-cuts looked like scabbed-over wounds. Clumps of pines with red needles, dying from blister rust, stood out against the green forest canopy like warning flares of decay. On our hikes Don and I had to push aside thick underbrush. Fallen limbs and trees clogged the trails. The summer's high temperatures, lack of rain, and drying winds had turned the St. Joe Forest into a tinderbox ready to spark, like the forest in 1910. I worried if even our well-trained fire crew could douse a blaze that ignited near Middle Sister Peak. Don and I checked our evacuation gear and rehearsed our escape plan.

On August 1 the St. Maries fire weather broadcast predicted a high of 92 degrees, a 40 percent probability of thunderstorms, and a BI of 210. Headquarters authorized all lookouts to work ten-hour days. In June the logbook's two-page format had easily accommodated one day of Don's activities.

Now he added extra pages to record his entries. His day circulated around air patrol check-ins, message relays from crews in remote sections of the forest, and nearly constant binocular surveillance of the miles and miles of increasingly dry, vulnerable forest. Every morning the fire control officer radioed Middle Sister to gather real-time cloud conditions. Wade used the information to adjust his fire control strategy.

Clear cuts, logging roads, and cloud shadows viewed from Middle Sister Peak

Middle Sister Peak Lookout was equipped with extra radio batteries, but no backup radio. At 8:10 AM on Saturday, August 4, Don called Avery to report that his radio was failing, a precarious situation given the forest's hazardous conditions. Five minutes later, St. Maries broadcast alarming but not unexpected news:

THROUGH PROPER AUTHORITIES THE FOREST WILL BE CLOSED AS OF 11:00 PM, AUGUST 5.

Closing a national forest, especially one as popular and complex as the St. Joe, was a monumental undertaking. The St. Joe's more than 860 thousand acres were measured on a flat map. They didn't include the thousands of up-and-down acres on the steep, fan-folded ridges that run across the forest. All non-fire related activities would cease: logging, mining, road repair, and

Snow Peak viewed from Middle Sister Peak

The locked-down St. Joe National Forest

forest research, including the University of Idaho's entomologists who'd asked us to keep our eyes peeled for gypsy moths. Only Milwaukee Road trains and maintenance crews would be allowed to work in the forest after it closed. Fire crews would locate and evacuate all commercial and recreational users and clear all campsites of hazards. Manned roadblocks would be erected at all intersections connecting to St. Maries and Wallace, and to St. Regis, Montana. Patrols would canvass the forest to eliminate all possible sources of ignition, and to remove anyone who had evaded the roadblocks.

Headquarters instructed lookouts to maintain clear air waves except for necessary fire-related transmissions. Lookouts now required permission from the district ranger to leave the tower when on duty. And if a lookout absolutely had to exit the forest, they'd need a written pass from the district office to get out through the roadblocks and back in again. Each forest worker had received their assigned tasks to keep people safe and protect the forest should a fire break out. We didn't wait long.

That afternoon Craig Frank, a Red Ives District fire prevention guard, spotted a wildfire. A crewman named Bledsoe called the fire in to Middle Sister at 2:15 PM, 1 hour and 45 minutes after air patrol had landed from a clear morning surveillance route. Don raced to the Firefinder, pointed the alidade in the direction Bledsoe had given, spotted the smoke, pinpointed its location, called Avery on his just delivered replacement radio, reported the pertinent information, and recorded the data in his logbook: "FIRE (smoke) N.F. Clearwater, Spotted Louis, T43N, R6E, Sec. 35, SE of NW. Azimuth 186°30'." The fire burned between Spotted Louis Creek and the North Fork of the Clearwater River at Township 43 North, Range 6 East, and Section 35, southeast of northwest at azimuth 186 degrees and 30 minutes. The Spotted Louis wildfire burned about 10 air miles south of Middle Sister. Staring into the face of a burgeoning blaze, I rechecked our go-bag and rehearsed our evacuation plan.

Nonstop transmissions crackled across the airwaves until a spotter crew arrived and confirmed the fire's location. The firefighters switched to their operational frequencies to assess how best to allocate the forest's limited resources to control the rapidly growing blaze. Within three hours of Frank's report, the Spotted Louis fire had consumed one hundred heavily forested acres. From our well-positioned observation point, Don and I watched low, slow-flying, retired, gray Air Force propeller planes carpet bomb Day-Glo pink retardant onto the flaming forest. A helicopter resembling a misshapen metal mosquito dangled a dripping canvas cylinder on a long tether below its belly and deluged river water onto hotspots along the fire's perimeter. Darkness temporarily suspended the battle. Despite the firefighters' best efforts, the wildfire raged uncontrollably. Headquarters announced that because all their resources were dedicated to controlling the wildfire, they'd postponed closing the St. Joe Forest.

Air patrol flew at 6:00 AM Sunday morning and scoured the forest for additional smokes. The BI stood at 217, a rough indication that flames at the head of the Spotted Louis wildfire shot out more than twenty feet. The fire weather report predicted increased winds but held out a slim hope for some relief with a 10 percent chance of wetting rain and showers through Wednesday.

"They're dropping smokejumpers!" Don hollered. I grabbed binoculars and watched black dots fall in quick succession from a low-flying propeller airplane, likely a DC-3 or Beechcraft Model 18. The parachutes billowed and the jumpers descended (with our prayers supporting them) into the dense smoke behind a ridge that blocked our view.

The smokejumpers, their cargo boxes, and fire boxes had flown from Region 1's Aerial Fire Depot in Missoula, Montana, about 75 air miles southeast of Middle Sister. They descended on round FS-14 parachutes, specially designed for use in western forests with tall, close conifers. From the cargo box they unloaded chainsaws with fuel and oil, tree-climbing gear, and Pulaskis, firefighting tools with an axe and an adz on one head. They immediately set to work clearing fuel away from the front edge of the fire to slow its progress. The fire box contained first aid kits, sleeping bags, food, and water to make them self-sufficient for 48 hours. More supplies could be dropped to extend their time on the fire. When the smokejumpers were released from duty, they'd load their jump gear, tools, and trash, weighing up to 110 pounds, into pack-out bags. The bags could be retrieved by a longline from a helicopter, packed out by mules, or carried out by the smokejumpers.

From our perspective we couldn't see if hotshots had been sent in. The St. Joe's Interagency Hotshot Crew was based in a tent camp at the Clarkia Work Center, approximately thirty air miles west of the Spotted Louis fire. Hotshot crews earned their name because they specialized in suppressing the hottest part of a fire by constructing firebreaks with only the tools they carry. The hotshots at Clarkia exceeded the experience, training, and physical fitness required for a Type 1 Crew firefighter. They'd passed the Work Capacity Test at the Arduous Level by completing a three-mile hike with a forty-five-pound pack in forty-five minutes. The crew must be available twenty-four hours a day, seven days a week, during fire season. The St. Joe's hotshots packed in all the water and supplies they needed for work shifts that could last for twelve hours or longer, depending on fire conditions.

By 1:00 PM on Sunday, the Spotted Louis wildfire had crossed the Lower North Fork of the Clearwater River. Winds at thirty miles per hour created an impenetrable smoke plume and drove the fire's front edge toward Stubtoe Peak. By 2:30 PM, just over twenty-four hours after it had been called in, the blaze had doubled in size. Don wrote in the logbook, "Already thinking of getting out of here if this pace continues."

The only building visible from Middle Sister was the lookout on Snow Peak. The R-6 flat roof cab, built in 1963, sat on a ten-foot-tall concrete base. Smoke from the Spotted Louis had completely obscured Snow Peak's sharply pointed rocky summit, within two air miles of the fire's origin. Its lookout debated over the radio whether to stay or leave, then hiked out in zero visibility. Don and I watched planes drop more retardant. I wondered if the pink powder crashed on top of the smokejumpers and hotshots. At 4:00 PM Don logged rain showers evaporating as fast as they fell, and the volume of smoke lessening.

An urgent voice reached out over Middle Sister's radio. Every communication on the forest fell silent. He desperately pleaded, "The wind shifted and the fire's coming right at us. Somebody, please, get us out now!"

A calm, commanding voice countered the smokejumper's fear. "I'm on my way. Keep a sharp eye out for my helicopter."

The smokejumper zeroed in the pilot to their perilous location.

The calm voice said, "I don't see an opening to land where you're at. Visibility's closing in. Can you move your position to the clearing to the east?"

"No, that direction's blocked. Please help us." Everyone in hearing range could only pray for them.

"Okay, I see an open spot, right behind you. Get ready to board, I'm coming in." That courageous pilot rescued the entire crew and landed them safely at Roundtop Work Station.

Don and I went to bed before dark. The smoke was still thick but seemed to be dissipating. I fell asleep worried that St. Maries would wake us in the middle of the night to evacuate. And I worried what tomorrow could bring.

Misty's steady, low growl woke me at the break of dawn. She was a serious dog, and protective of her people. When she barked we paid attention because an undeniable issue had alerted her concern. Misty lunged toward the door, barking hysterically. The lookout shook to a deafening drum beat that pounded in my ears.

"Don, wake up. You need to move the truck. A helicopter wants to land." Don groggily asked what in the hell I was talking about. The events of the fire had so exhausted him that he'd slept through Misty's barking and the helicopter's hammering noise as it hovered overhead.

I answered slowly and distinctly, to convince him, and myself. "Move the truck, now! It's blocking a really big helicopter that wants to land. It looks like a Huey from Vietnam."

The helicopter landed to the pulsing beat of its rotor blades and the yelping counterpoint of one pissed-off Dalmatian. The khaki-green airship loomed like a brontosaurus the closer we approached. We ducked and ran below the rotor like we'd seen people do on TV. The copilot cranked down his window like he was a passenger in a family sedan. He chuckled at Misty's bravery. He shouted that they were lost. They'd flown from Alaska to fight the Spotted Louis fire, but they couldn't find it. He asked for directions. Don pointed toward Roundtop and described the buildings they should look for.

"Thanks," the copilot shouted back.

"Good luck," Don and I wished them in return.

The three of us watched from the safety of the tower as the pilot revved the massive front rotor. The lookout shook to its wooden bones again. The Huey lifted tail-up off Middle Sister and flew toward Roundtop. Don shook his head. He'd just given directions to a lost helicopter pilot. They couldn't find the fire because the cold air the night before had held down the smoke. It would rise again as the day warmed. We'd never considered it could cause a problem to park on that convenient, flat helispot. From that day forward no one was allowed to park there.

I worried that for fire management to call in a helicopter from Alaska, they must have expected this blaze to get worse. And that they expected that other fires could start. Monday's BI continued its climb to 224. Air patrol switched its check-ins to Crystal Peak on the Clarkia District, 30 air miles west of Middle Sister, to keep Avery's airwaves clear for firefighting traffic.

A second fire erupted. Planes already loaded with retardant made two quick drops and extinguished the burning railroad trestle over Storm Creek. Don logged the fire and noted, "Turned in by Dave Brown. Another min. or two and I would have had it. I was searching with my binoculars moving that way (was at Shefoot)." Earlier that morning St. Maries had asked Don to confirm who had first called in the Spotted Louis fire, and at what precise time. Competition ran high on the forest for who got credit for spotting a fire. The spotter's name got entered into the official record and, traditionally, that person received naming rights for the fire. Wildfire names usually reflected a nearby landmark. Sometimes, to the spotter's chagrin, a higher-ranking fire officer usurped naming rights.

The Spotted Louis' fire boss announced that twenty retardant drops had slowed the wildfire's progress. Given the high temperature of sixty-four degrees with low wind conditions, he believed his crews could contain the fire by the end of the day. Given his favorable projection, Headquarters broadcast forest-wide at 7:00 PM:

THE ST. JOE FOREST WILL CLOSE AT MIDNIGHT TUESDAY, AUGUST 7

On Tuesday morning St. Maries announced that the Spotted Louis was still uncontained and had been designated as a project fire. This Forest Service category for serious fires enabled the affected forest to access emergency budgets for extra firefighting personnel and equipment. A bonus for the St. Joe was that they'd retain equipment purchased with the allocations. And if firefighters needed to replace personal items like boots or gloves, those costs were covered, too. St. Maries attributed the Spotted Louis' cause to a camper. The fire had already burned 450 acres. Five helicopters and 400 firefighters had battled the blaze. Tuesday's BI stood at 229. At midnight the St. Joe National Forest locked its doors.

Don and I had gotten to know the Forest Service workers on the St. Joe. We respected their knowledge of forestry, their integrity, and their determination to avoid a repeat of the disastrous 1910 fires. We'd witnessed the skill and courage of the firefighting crews who risked their lives to save trees. We trusted they would save us, too.

16

PUT BACK THE TREES

By the middle of the Civil War, the conflict's lethal effect on the environment had appalled America's emerging conservationists. East coast forests, once so thickly treed that horses couldn't move through them, had fallen to axes and saws. The Northern and Southern armies were mobile communities bigger than many cities. They required wood for warmth, for cooking, and for building ships, railroad bridges, and corduroy roads constructed of logs laid side by side. War profiteers produced crucial timber by-products like turpentine, resin, pitch, tar, and paper—lots of paper. President Lincoln supported the conservation movement. On June 30, 1864, he signed the Yosemite Grant that ceded the Yosemite Valley and the Mariposa Big Tree Grove to the state of California. The act required that "the premises shall be held for public use, resort and recreation; [and] shall be inalienable for all time." It was the first land set aside by the federal government for public use, resort, and recreation.

The war's effects endured after the guns fell silent on April 9, 1865. New York State lost 75 percent of its forested areas to feed America's booming economy. New Yorker James Wallace Pinchot had earned enormous profits from the manufacture of wallpaper. He belonged to influential clubs and rubbed elbows with New York's wilderness preservationists, including landscape architect Frederic Law Olmstead, artist Sanford Robinson Gifford, and politician Theodore Roosevelt. Pinchot's first child was born into wealth and comfort four months after the end of the war. Pinchot requested Sanford Gifford to be godfather to his son, whom he named Gifford.

One year later, in 1866, Sanford Gifford debuted his oil painting "Hunter Mountain, Twilight." In contrast to its romantic title, the work's bleak brown tones depict a mountain vista of sawed-off tree stumps rotting away in a dying woodland laid to waste by generations of loggers, leather tanners, and farmers. James Pinchot purchased "Hunter Mountain, Twilight," hung the painting in his home, and became an ardent conservationist, perhaps in acknowledgement of his personal contribution to the large-scale ecological destruction of the lower Hudson River Valley. Gifford's painting influenced Pinchot and other New York society elites to sponsor landscape artists. They built monumental venues to display the artists' romanticized renderings of the unmolested, pristine Hudson River, Adirondack, and Catskill Mountain landscapes. They hoped the art would persuade the viewing public that, unless conserved, the country's precious woodlands might be lost forever.

Conservationists helped influence President Ulysses S. Grant to reserve and withdraw from settlement, occupancy, or sale, a certain tract of land lying near the headwaters of the Yellowstone River. In 1872 Yellowstone National Park, the first national park in the United States, gained protection from damage and private exploitation. Four years later Congress approved the Commissioner of Agriculture to produce a statistical study on the nation's forest supply, consumption, preservation, and renewal. Physician Dr. Franklin B. Hough was appointed as the nation's first forestry agent. In 1881, under President Chester A. Arthur, the Congress provisionally established the Division of Forestry in the Department of Agriculture and named Hough as its Chief. Clergyman Nathaniel H. Eggleston succeeded Hough in 1883.

Grover Cleveland secured the presidency the next year. Congress granted permanent status to Agriculture's Division of Forestry in 1886, but with a narrowly scoped mission to gather information on forests and conduct scientific experimentation. Prussian immigrant Dr. Bernhard Eduard Graf von Fernow, the lone technically trained forester living in America, headed the division. Fernow crafted a Forest Reserve Act to expand Forestry's mission and give the president authority to create forest reserves to protect western woodlands in the public domain. But Fernow's act languished unapproved by Congress.

In 1889 incumbent Cleveland lost to Benjamin Harrison. Six western states joined the union during Harrison's single term: North Dakota, South Dakota, Montana, and Washington in November 1889, and Idaho and Wyoming in July 1890. Millions of acres of timbered land became available for presidential protection, action strongly desired by conservation-minded Americans desperate to preserve the nation's forests from unconstrained exploitation.

Fraudulent timber companies had misused the Timber Culture Act of 1873 to trespass on or purchase public lands to harvest public timber. Congress revised Fernow's Forest Reserve Act to control their cut-and-run practices that had rapidly diminished the western and midwestern forests. Fernow and the American Forestry Association noted that the proposal contained no provision to protect forested lands from sale or homesteading. They convinced Interior Secretary Noble to add a single sentence to authorize the president, at his discretion, to set apart public land–bearing forests in any state or territory as public reservations, whether of commercial value or not. Section 24's limited scope withdrew these lands from any use, but didn't provide authority or funds for managing the forest reserves. Congress voted the Creative Act into law on March 3, 1891. President William Henry Harrison created fifteen forest reserves encompassing thirteen million acres in Colorado, Arizona, California, Oregon, Washington, and Alaska. Harrison placed the reserves under Noble's purview in the Department of Interior's General Land Office rather than under Fernow's Division of Forestry in Agriculture.

The federal government's annual spending exceeded $1 billion for the first time in history. Harrison lost the 1892 election back to Cleveland, in part because of America's lackluster economy and a strong attack on the "Billion Dollar Congress." During America's Gilded Age, corporate magnates had driven unsustainable footloose financial schemes that set the stage for an economic downward spiral. Banks failed in the Panic of 1893, the federal government teetered on bankruptcy, and the economy dived into a deep depression. Unemployment rates stubbornly remained above 10 percent for the next four years. Newly enfranchised western Populists wanted their state lands to remain open for private development. They joined with eastern industrialists looking to expand their lumber, railroad, and mining operations into the west. This unlikely alliance unsuccessfully opposed President Cleveland's addition of twenty million more acres to America's forest reserves.

Gifford Pinchot graduated from Yale University in 1889. Because no American school taught forestry as a program, his father sent Gifford to the L'Ecole Nationale Forestiere in Nancy, France. He directed Gifford to learn how to put the trees back. Gifford dropped out of the French school after one year. James Pinchot called on his friend and prominent landscape architect Frederick Law Olmstead to employ Gifford as the property forester at Biltmore, George Washington Vanderbilt II's estate near Ashville, North Carolina. For four years Gifford gained practical experience as Biltmore's head forester. He and Dr. Fernow developed a friendship through their common interests in scientific forestry.

Despite the depressed economy, Fernow had persuaded Cleveland to appoint a commission to study forestry conservation. Fernow recommended his protégé, Pinchot, as one of the commission's five members. Pinchot backpacked through western forests to gather data for his well-received reports. But Agriculture Secretary Julius Sterling Morton, who had initiated Arbor Day in 1872 to grow more trees in Nebraska, ardently believed it wasn't government's function to conduct experiments. He drastically reduced Fernow's budget and exiled him to an office in the attic. The Division of Forestry languished through the remainder of Cleveland's term.

Incumbent Cleveland lost the 1896 nomination to William Jennings Bryan, endorsed by western Populists. Bryan lost the election to William McKinley, Jr. President McKinley designated seven million more acres as forest reserves. He supported the Sundry Civil Appropriations Act of 1897 (Organic Act) that authorized the Secretary of Interior to open the nation's forest reserves for public use and to enact rules and regulations bearing the force of law for their management. After twelve years in office, Fernow looked for a replacement. In 1898 McKinley appointed thirty-three-year-old Gifford Pinchot as Chief of Agriculture's Division of Forestry.

Carl Schenck had replaced Pinchot as Biltmore's head forester. On September 1, 1898, Schenck opened America's first forestry school, the Biltmore School of Forestry, endowed by Vanderbilt. A few weeks later the New York State College of Forestry opened at Cornell University with Dr. Fernow as its first dean. Yale University graduates Gifford Pinchot and Henry S. Graves, with financial endowment from Mary and James Wallace Pinchot, established the Yale Forest School in 1900. In 1908 Fernow moved to Canada to fill the newly created Chair of Forestry at the University of Toronto.

New York State had elected Spanish-American War hero Col. Theodore Roosevelt as its governor. Roosevelt's anti-patronage exploits to cleanse the state's political party of corruption had so aggravated the party machine that they foisted him onto McKinley's 1900 reelection ticket as his vice president. The slot was open because McKinley's first term vice president, Garret Hobart, had died of a heart attack at age fifty-five. Due in large part to Roosevelt's strength as a campaigner, McKinley again defeated the second-time running William Jennings Bryan.

On September 6, 1901, inside the Temple of Music at the Pan-American Exposition in Buffalo, New York, anarchist Leon Czolgosz, born in Alpena, Michigan, shot President McKinley twice in the stomach. Given a rosy prognosis for the president's recovery, Roosevelt departed on a family vacation to New York's Adirondack Mountains. But McKinley developed gangrene and died on September 14. That same day, wearing borrowed formal clothes, Roosevelt took the presidential oath of office at Ansley Wilcox's house in Buffalo. A mere 45 days after McKinley's death, an intermittent series of 300- and 1,800-volt jolts electrocuted the convicted Czolgosz. Following an autopsy, prison authorities placed Czolgosz's body in a plain black coffin, doused his corpse with sulfuric acid, and 12 hours later buried what was left of him in the ground at New York's Auburn Prison.

Soon after President Roosevelt took office, he proposed to Congress that the forest reserves would be better managed in the Department of Agriculture's Division of Forestry under professional forester Gifford Pinchot than in the Interior Department's General Land Office. The House defeated Roosevelt's proposed transfer bill in 1902. That year the General Land Office spent a meager $2,036 fighting forty-eight forest fires throughout the west. Only three rangers protected more than two million acres in Washington's Mount Rainier Forest Reserve when raging wildfires consumed an estimated seven hundred thousand acres around the town of Yacolt. The deadliest of those fires killed thirty-eight people. In the face of such devastation, Congress did nothing more than double the General Land Office's miniscule firefighting budget for the next year.

South Dakota's Senator Kittredge championed Roosevelt's stalled campaign to move the forest reserves into the Department of Agriculture. Sixty-three million acres were transferred on July 1, 1905. Forester Pinchot named his organization the United States Forest Service to emphasize his philosophy that federal forests were a renewable resource to be managed and cultivated to serve the people, not to be reserved from use.

Interior's General Land Office had hired rangers and forest guards using the political spoils system. But Pinchot organized his Forest Service into a tightly managed agency staffed with qualified professionals. Applicants had to pass standardized Civil Service exams that included questions on forest conditions, ranching and lumbering methods, surveying skills, mapping, and cabin construction. Applicants also had to demonstrate their ability to saddle and ride a horse, pack a mule, pace the perimeter of a measured course to compute the area in acres, use a compass, and accurately fire a rifle and a pistol. Rangers and forest guards worked six days a week, sunup to sundown, for $60 a month. The Forest Service provided an axe, a notebook, and Pinchot's "Use Book" of regulations. New hires furnished their own equipment, guns, horses, pack animals, and subsistence for themselves and their animals. The Forest Service frowned on married rangers and often laid off rangers through the winter.

A few constitutionalists noted that the federal government lacked authority to purchase private land for public use. Their challenge rose to the U.S. Supreme Court. The Court upheld the precedent of an 1895 law that had enabled the federal government to purchase or condemn private land to establish a battlefield park at Gettysburg, Pennsylvania. Then, Colorado's delegation, recognized as the most rabid anti-conservation contingent in Congress, questioned whether the federal government possessed the constitutional right to hold public lands within the borders of new states in perpetual ownership under municipal sovereignty without consent of the state. Oregon Senator Fulton introduced an amendment on the agricultural appropriations for 1907. The sole power to create additional forest reserves in Washington, Oregon, Idaho, Montana, Wyoming, and Colorado would be ceded to Congress. And the name of forest reserves would become national forests to emphasize that the forests were to be used and not preserved. The bill was scheduled for ratification on March 7, 1907.

Roosevelt and Pinchot had just enough lead time to skirt the upcoming limitations. Pinchot and an assistant blue penciled boundaries for new forest reserves onto maps. They prepared a proclamation for each new addition under the presidential powers provided in the Forest Reserve Act of 1891. Roosevelt signed the documents as soon as they were laid on his desk. In two days, on March 1 and 2, 1907, Pinchot and Roosevelt established seventeen new or combined forest reserves containing over six million acres inside the six soon-to-be-closed-off western states. The press dubbed the new national lands the "Midnight Reserves."

Roosevelt declined to run in 1908. His hand-picked successor, William Howard Taft, was not a committed conservationist and forced Pinchot to resign on January 7, 1910. Taft also fired Pinchot's Associate Forester, Overton W. Price. Pinchot's law officer, P.P. Wells, resigned in protest. Pinchot's close associate, Henry Graves, Dean of Forestry at Yale, was appointed as the new head of the Forest Service. The United States Forest Service entered

1910 under new unproven leadership, under investigation by the Secretary of Agriculture, and under threat to move the Forest Service back into the Department of the Interior.

In 1905, 60 forest reserves had covered 56 million acres. In 1910, 250 national forests covered 172 million acres. The Great Fires of 1910 are cited as the tragic events that reshaped United States Forest Service firefighting policies and added portent to the growing national sentiment for protecting and managing our wild lands and natural resources.

17

LOCKED IN A FOREST

Don and I woke on Wednesday, August 8, locked in the St. Joe Forest. At 10:00 AM St. Maries declared the Spotted Louis fire contained. One hour later air patrol called in a large, new wildfire. Coordinates placed this blaze at Deer Creek on Montana's Lolo National Forest, about twelve air miles northeast of Middle Sister. Although in empathy with the dangers unfolding on the Lolo, everyone on the St. Joe heaved a sigh of relief that this wildfire belonged to another forest.

The Rocky Mountain's Bitterroot Range forms much of the physical border between Idaho and Montana. The view east from Middle Sister encompasses Montana's Cabinet Mountains near Glacier National Park, established May 11, 1910, to the north, the Bob Marshall Wilderness, established in 1964, due east, and Idaho's Mallard Larkins Pioneer Area, designated in 1969, to the southeast. Don wrote in the logbook that in the hour and a half since the Deer Creek fire had been spotted the volume of smoke had become tremendous. He noted that the requirement to spend twenty minutes of each hour looking was no longer adequate. He was on constant vigil because a new blaze could explode into a project fire in just hours.

Don estimated that two hundred acres had burned in the four hours since air patrol had called in the Deer Creek fire. The wildfire was also designated a project fire. Its smoke boiled up heavier than what we'd seen off the Spotted Louis. The fire-generated convection currents carried moisture aloft from the burned trees. The moisture condensed in the cooler upper air to form a huge mushroom shaped cloud, called a pyrocumulus, over the crest of the Bitter-roots. It frightened Don and me to look at a cloud which perfectly resembled ones created by an atomic blast.

If another fire were to erupt on the St. Joe, Don couldn't leave the tower. He drove to the spring and filled our water cans. We washed less often to conserve water. There'd be no visitors to offend with our body odor. We conserved toilet paper. We conserved paper towels in case we ran out of toilet paper. We ate every bite of food before it spoiled, and to make less garbage. If our garbage overflowed the cubical, it had to go into our wagon again. The fire crew would only collect our garbage if they delivered mail that looked important. The BI rose to 234.

Thursday morning Roundtop radioed to ask if we needed any supplies. The request caught Don off guard. He mumbled that we could use a loaf of bread. Roundtop said, "See you soon," and cleared the transmission with a chuckle. I judged that I had more than an hour to change out of my bathrobe before the crew arrived. I sat on the chair under the closed-off stove pipe to knit a cap for our baby.

To keep myself occupied on our first drive back to Bethlehem from Moscow, I'd bought a teach-yourself-to-knit magazine, two skeins of white acrylic yarn, and a pair of size eight knitting needles. I cast off my first knit hat, stitched the seam, and attached a pom-pom just as we arrived. My mother assessed my handiwork and concluded she could tell it was homemade because it had mistakes. It took me a lot of growing up before I appreciated that my mother's back-handed compliments were intended to be instructive. She proudly snapped my photo in the Easter coat I'd hand-tailored, then commented that I'd sewed the hem crooked. She attended every one of my glee club concerts, then complained she couldn't hear my voice. If I mentioned that the TV show we were watching had gaping holes in the plot, or the trees cast sharp shadows in a rainy scene, she'd say, "You gotta use your imagination." With those few words my mother taught me how to solve problems, make art, make love, cook, make trash useful, find beauty, find peace, rebound from disappointment, recover from despair, and reconcile myself to the world.

For months after Don and I had moved to Moscow, we couldn't afford a telephone. We'd call our parents from the pay phone booth across the street in the grocery store parking lot. No one in our families was a letter writer. Our ten-minute phone calls gave our parents little insight into how Don and I were adapting to our life in Idaho. To them we were still the same Don and Nancy. The first day of each visit to Bethlehem was a joyous reunion. Conversations stalled on the second day. Don and I didn't care about the latest development in their long-standing family feuds. Our families showed little interest as we described Idaho's amazing geography. By the third day everyone bit their tongues to not offend. We concurred with Ben Franklin that "guests, like fish, begin to smell after three days." Don and I still belonged to our families, their love and caring remained strong, but we didn't fit in anymore. We existed on the fringes of their daily lives, no longer intimates. We would visit Bethlehem often, but we couldn't go home again.

Knitting a baby's cap

Twenty minutes after the radio call from Roundtop, the unexpected thump of helicopter blades alerted us to incoming visitors. I jumped off my chair, threw my knitting on the bed, pulled off my robe and pajamas, rubbed on deodorant, combed my oily hair, spritzed on cologne, and threw on clean jeans and a sweatshirt. I thought the Huey pilots were stopping to say goodbye on their way to the next fire. But instead of that bulky green behemoth, a sleek, powder-blue jet ranger landed on our helispot like a dainty bird.

The Roundtop caller squeezed out and circled two bags of sliced bread over his head. A gaggle of chattering young women followed, like circus clowns unstuffing themselves from a tiny car. I hadn't seen that many females in one place since we'd arrived in Avery. Everyone looked like they'd showered that morning. I held down my arms as we chatted. The pilot explained that he and the girls had wanted to see a lookout. Don gave them a tour. My unspoken wish came true when the pilot offered us a ride. Don sat in back. I buckled in next to the pilot. The rotors revved and the helicopter lifted nose down off the summit. In a split second nothing but hundreds of feet of empty air showed through the glass under my feet. My stomach dropped. I crossed my arms protectively over our growing baby. I gulped hard and gathered my wits. No way would I miss enjoying this aerial spectacle of Middle Sister Peak.

"Where's the wind coming from, Don?" the pilot hollered over the rotor noise. He calculated Don's response, circled the lookout far too close for my comfort, and hovered just off the catwalk. Everyone inside smiled and waved. I waved back. The pilot toured a few turns around the forest as Don pointed out landmarks, then landed. The gaggle loaded back in the helicopter and flew off. I pulled in a deep breath to collect myself after all the excitement, opened a loaf of bread, and made ham and cheese sandwiches.

The next day Snow Peak's lookout, back on duty, called in a lightning-strike fire. The seasoned fire crew quickly extinguished the small blaze. The Spotted Louis' mop-up crew was demobilized. Air patrol resumed calling their check-ins to Middle Sister. Don's overtime pay piled up. No measurable precipitation had fallen on the St. Joe for 47 days. The BI stood at 241.

I wondered if the locked-down forest troubled the lookout on Snow Peak. He'd gone in knowing he'd be alone for the entire summer. Maybe he'd purposely chosen to work on an inaccessible tower. The isolation was putting a strain on Don and me. We were stranded behind guarded barricades, not by choice. We felt separated from the world. We withdrew from each other. Don spent hours on the catwalk absorbed in his single-minded search for smokes. I read or knit or took long walks. But Misty and I couldn't go to Dismal Lake anymore. It was too dangerous to be that far from the tower. And Don couldn't get away to drive us back to the lookout. My stress level grew with the rising fire danger. I looked out over the dry forest in dread. I imagined a firestorm reducing it to an ash-covered expanse littered with limbless black tree trunks.

Taking off from Middle Sister's helispot

At 5:00 PM Saturday, August 11, the first storm on the Avery District since June 22 dropped a single lightning bolt. Snow Peak called in the fire on East Butte at azimuth 199 degrees and 45 minutes, Township 43N, Range 6E, Section 32, about 10 miles southwest of Middle Sister. The Roundtop crew doused the blaze before it had time to grow. The BI jumped 11 points to 252.

I had to get out of the forest. I craved a shower. We didn't have much food left. We had piles of dirty clothes and bags of garbage. Avery grudgingly gave me permission to go to St. Maries to restock supplies, about a 170-mile round trip. Don packed our wagon with coolers, dirty clothes, laundry supplies, snacks for the trip, garbage, and a handheld radio with fresh batteries. His bear-chasing escapade on Dunn Peak had taught us to be in communication whenever we were separated, in case something went wrong.

I didn't pass a single vehicle on my dusty, bumpy run. No logging trucks roared around blind curves. No oversized RVs hogged their half of the road out of the middle. I was on my own in a blockaded forest. The reality of my isolation loomed large in my mind. Miles and miles of mountainous forest at the ready to spark a wildfire stood between me and Don. He had risked his life edging our wagon between a cliff and a snowbank to get us on the lookout.

What if I was risking myself and our child to get food and do laundry? We could wear dirty clothes all summer, but we needed to eat. I urged our trusty wagon not to fail me now.

The wagon stuttered and dragged in the deep dust on Bluff Creek Road. The problem continued when I drove onto a hard-packed section. I got out to check. The driver's side rear tire was flat. No point worrying Don, I thought. I'll just change the tire myself and be on my way. I unloaded the back of the wagon and dug out the spare tire and the jack. But no tire iron. That tire iron wasn't where it should be, and it wasn't anywhere else I looked. I radioed Don. I'd already checked every place he suggested to look. But I looked again to pacify him. I was hopelessly stranded. I grew angrier with every minute that I couldn't fix that damn flat tire by myself. Either Don had to come off the lookout to bring me the tire iron from the truck—not likely—or Avery had to send a guard.

Avery told Don to stay in the tower. I sniffed the air for smoke while I waited. I regretted not bringing my binoculars. The guard dispatched to fix my flat was a new-hire contractor, not one of our friendly Roundtop crew. Naturally, before he arrived, I'd found the tire iron stashed under the driver's seat. It was right where Don had forgotten he'd put it, in case he needed a handy weapon for protection. Truth be told, by the time the guard arrived, I was sweaty and exasperated. I was thrilled to let the strong manly man jack up the wagon and change the tire instead of doing it myself. He clearly didn't share my sentiments. I thanked him profusely. He snorted in return and drove off.

I had the flat repaired and remounted in Avery. I stopped at the ranger station to collect my road pass and drop off our garbage. The dispatcher gave me a frosty reception. It seemed to me that she thought I'd fabricated my missing tire iron to get someone to change the flat. I'd been on the forest long enough to observe that some full-time workers viewed summer lookouts as "citified" intruders and overpaid amateurs.

The flat tire had gobbled up so much time that I didn't get a shower at the bunkhouse or get our laundry done in St. Maries. Other than that, the rest of my excursion went as planned, until I arrived back at the roadblock. A different contractor than the one who'd been there on my way out manned the two wooden sawhorses at the barricade. He'd never heard of Middle Sister Peak Lookout. He thought my pass looked suspicious. He radioed Hoyt Flat to check me out, but the dispatcher had gone home. No one in the office would vouch for me. "The ice in my coolers is melting," I fussed. "Can't somebody call the dispatcher at home to clear me through?" *Or I'll ram my trusty wagon over your puny sawhorses and you can chase me all the way back to the lookout*, I thought. The guard radioed his boss. He grumbled and pulled back one sawhorse to wave me through. I didn't wave back.

Two days later one of the Roundtop crew arrived at the lookout. "The dispatcher forgot to give you your mail on your way out," he said.

"Here's my pass," I traded him. "I forgot to return it on my way in." Avery was a close-knit district. Everybody knew my flat tire story. We shared a good laugh and got on with our day.

Don and I didn't have a single clean towel. We bathed with a used washcloth dipped in a small amount of hot, soapy water in a plastic basin set on the table. We didn't feel much cleaner. On Thursday, August 16, the BI stood at 285. Despite the increasing danger, Don received permission to leave the tower for half a day to go to Roundtop. We grew giddy at the prospect of hot water coursing over our grubby bodies and getting our clothes laundered for free. Don's replacement logged in at 12:30 PM.

The pickup sat ready to go with a can of water and emergency supplies. It seemed the prudent choice to drive to Roundtop. We soon regretted that decision. The truck joggled my bones over every rock. With no rain in fifty-two days, the truck's heavy-duty tires churned up clouds of dust. Don turned on the windshield wipers to see the road through the roiling dust storm. Despite the temperature being over ninety degrees we closed the windows. But dust boiled in through the holes in the floorboard and obscured Don's view from the inside, too. I pulled dirty towels and hooded sweatshirts from the laundry bags. I shoved the towels into the holes in the floorboard. We zipped the sweatshirts over our noses and tightened the hoods to the point where we could barely see out. I was glad we'd left Misty in the tower.

I'd never enjoyed a shower so much. We scrounged plastic garbage bags and duct tape and sealed in our clean laundry. We blocked the holes in the floorboard with newspapers and cardboard to keep out the dust. Our jerry-rigged repairs failed miserably. We arrived back at the lookout, exhausted from hours of being bumped around inside an oven-hot truck, plastered in dust again, and in need of another shower. But we had clean clothes!

An uneasy calm settled over the St. Joe Forest. On Sunday, August 19, air patrol had the day off. Don wrote in the logbook that it was the first day with no radio traffic. The predicted rain showers never materialized. Wailing winds swayed the lookout and further desiccated the tinder dry forest. The wingnuts on the shutters had loosened; the shutters banged up and down in the wind and set our nerves on edge. Except for the shutters, the forest was eerily quiet. We worried that a disaster had occurred and we were the only two people left in the world. We switched on the transistor to reassure ourselves that no cataclysm had taken place, that other people were still alive out there. It was time to get off the St. Joe. The pressure of the lockdown was affecting our sanity.

Headquarters announced a Red Flag Alert on Monday morning, August 20. There was a 50 percent chance of thunderstorms for the next two days. The BI stood at 305. Conrad Lookout called in a smoke. Azimuth checks from Don and the emergency spotter on Dunn Peak concurred that the smoke rose from the 2,000-acre Twin Creek fire on the Coeur d'Alene Forest. A huge fire about 15 miles away further heightened our fear. Conditions on the St. Joe were perfect for an unstoppable conflagration.

Don drove the truck to the spring to refill our water cans. I took binocular and radio duty. When he returned, he only pulled one can up to the catwalk. He left the others in the truck to use as fire extinguishers if we needed to make a run for it. We repacked our go-bag, loaded everything we didn't want to lose into the pickup, and ate a hearty dinner to finish off leftovers. We congratulated ourselves on being prepared to evacuate. Don and I realized with dread that the Big Burn had erupted on this date, August 20, in 1910.

Tuesday morning's fire weather report reduced the thunderstorm probability to 10 percent and cancelled the Red Flag Alert. We relaxed and sipped our coffee. Fifteen minutes later towering gray and purple thunderheads erupted from nowhere and converged on Middle Sister. We monitored the cloud-to-cloud lightning for an hour until the clouds dissipated. Even though we didn't observe any ground strikes, Don searched until dark for rising smokes. I'd had my fill of living on a lookout locked in a forest ready to explode.

St. Maries woke all the lookouts at 3:30 AM, Wednesday, August 22. Lightning was on the way. Don dressed and made coffee. Roundtop radioed at 4:00 AM to ask if he'd spotted any strikes. "10-4, near Dunn Peak," Don replied.

I recognized the strain in Don's voice. I dressed and grabbed a flashlight and Misty's leash. "Come on girl. We're going to the outhouse while the getting's good."

All hell broke loose at 6:30 AM. "Wammo! Lightning," Don logged. Thunder god Thor parked that hammering storm directly on top of Middle Sister Peak. Blinding flashes and deafening claps came so close together that they seemed to erupt from inside the windows. Wind gusts shook the tower. Misty and I curled together on the bed. We gave up any pretense of being battle-hardened veterans of Thor's pounding barrages. I whispered in her ear that the howling wind wouldn't blow the lookout over. "We'll be okay," I promised. "You gotta use your imagination."

Don whirled around the Firefinder to align one rising smoke after the other. He narrowed the smokes' locations with sightings from the other lookouts, wrote the locations into the logbook, and radioed Avery. By 9:00 AM he'd logged seven fires:

1. Section 16, T43N, R6E, Montana Peak, Az 203°
2. Section 35, T44N, R6E, Trimmed Tree Hill, Az 198°
3. Section 24, T44N, R6E, NE-NE, East Sister, Az 158°15'
4. Section 34, T44N, R6E, SE-NE, Bear Skull, Az 000°20'
5–7. Three smokes in Miller Peak area (turned in by Snow Peak)

I watched in fear and wonder as a bolt of lightning struck a tall fir on East Sister Peak. The bolt was still attached when the tree's entire trunk glowed from the inside out like a red-hot charcoal briquette. The bolt pulled away and smoke tendrils curled into the air in seconds. Flames emerged and ate a hole in the bark. Two more direct hits ignited two more trees. The three torches shot red-orange flames high into the air. Fiery needles, cones, and branches dropped onto the dry forest floor. Yesterday's BI of 310 meant the flames could grow to thirty-one feet in length.

Don radioed Roundtop as calmly as he could muster. "Please prioritize East Sister's fire to the top of your list. Thank you. Middle Sister clear." The fire burned half a mile from the lookout, next to our only road off the mountain. I hoped that fast-flying, aqua-blue jet ranger was still on the St. Joe, in case we needed a lift off the mountain. I rechecked our emergency go-bag. Prenatal vitamins, check. Truck keys, check. My purse and Don's wallet, check, check. Mike's rifle, check.

"Slow your pace, Nance," Don announced. A lumbering plane dumped pink clouds of fire retardant. A smaller plane dropped smokejumpers so close I could see their faces. We thought the retardant and smokejumpers were overkill for a small fire, but we were filled with relief to see them. I knew we'd be fine. At 1:00 PM Don logged a fire in Section 24, on Whistling Peak, about two miles south. This fire didn't pose a danger to our exit road. The crew quickly extinguished it, too. In one long day of firefighting, the St. Joe's Johnny-on-the-spot fire crews had controlled every fire ignited by that lightning storm. I thought air patrol chose his check-in locations to add some humor to our tense situation. He checked in from the mouth of Wisdom, the head of Red Raven, and the south fork of Santa. The BI reached 317.

I was exhausted. I stretched out on the bed for a nap, but I was too wired to sleep. Day-Glo pink bombers, aqua-blue helicopters, white parachutes, and red flames did a jig across the black screen of my closed eyelids. I straightened the blanket under me, tugged the pillowcase free of wrinkles, slowly pulled in a few deep breaths, looked inside myself, and tried to unwind. A flutter I wasn't sure I felt popped my eyes open. I focused inward to recapture the feeling, but it was gone. Was it gas? Was it my imagination? A fuzzy twilight memory carried me off. I was about seven years old. It was New Year's Eve and my parents had gone to a party. I was trying to fall asleep in a strange bed listening to strange noises at my Aunt Betty's house. I tried to recapture the sensations that had comforted me in other worrisome times. I'd feel myself shrink. I'd float up from the bed surrounded in a red-black warmth. I'd drift off to sleep. But on that New Year's Eve, those sensations stayed beyond my grasp. I never experienced them again, though I tried. Had I remembered being in my mother's womb? Another flutter opened my eyes. This time it wasn't my imagination; it was the baby.

In a few days Don's dream job as a fire lookout in the clean, green wilds of Idaho would be over forever. In a few more days we'd move away from our beloved Idaho not knowing if we'd ever return. We might never again hike along a mountain trail or set foot in a national forest, never inhale the perfume of pines, and never watch a golden eagle soar in an Idaho-blue sky. We withdrew into ourselves in grief. Neither of us wanted to admit how sad we were to go—how sad we were to leave home. Organizing and packing forced us to interact with each other. We had to make plans more involved than what to fix for lunch and dinner. We had to consider options more complex than robotically counting to twenty-nine in our nightly, repetitious cribbage games. Where would we stay when we went back to Moscow? Would we take everything from the lookout back to Indiana? How would we get rid of things we didn't want? How many suitcases and boxes were Jerry bringing?

Making plans took our minds off our sadness and our worries. As much as we hated to leave Idaho, Don and I grew excited to be free, to not live in a locked-down forest. We were ready to put the fear of fire behind us. We looked forward to resuming a normal lifestyle. In Indianapolis we could go where we wanted, when we wanted. We could drive on paved roads with painted lines and streetlights. We'd speak on private telephone calls instead of public radio transmissions. We'd have electricity, TV, and curtains on the windows. We'd wash dishes in a sink and have a bathroom down the hall with hot water, a shower, and a toilet that flushed. Best of all, we'd sleep together in the same bed. That amenity-filled lifestyle waited for us in Indiana. Maybe it wouldn't be so bad.

The BI spiked at 326 on Friday, August 24. A cold front had come through during the night. Misty had covered herself under a fold of her quilt. She didn't budge from her warm spot all morning. Thick low clouds socked in the lookout. It was an easy workday for Don. He couldn't see anything past the railing. He underlined "<u>Rain at last</u>" in the logbook. It got colder. Just as unexpected August snows had snuffed out the Big Burn in 1910, it snowed on Middle Sister. A soggy layer of white flakes covered our vehicles and clung to the lookout's windows. We dug our jackets out of the suitcases. The rain, snow, and cold broke the fire danger's grip on the St. Joe Forest. The BI plummeted to 189 on Saturday. But despite the precipitation and the lower fire danger, the St. Joe Forest remained locked down tight.

Misty wrapped in her quilt

Socked in by August snow on Middle Sister Peak

When Don had thirty days left of active duty in the Navy, he'd bought a short-timer's calendar. He'd marked off each day until his release with a big X. Now Don was a short-timer on the lookout, and it showed in his attitude. He no longer tried to be the best lookout he could be. On Sunday, August 26, he penciled in the logbook, "Usual stuff, didn't feel like writing." Roundtop radioed to ask how much rain had fallen. Don answered that he didn't know. On Monday he requested Avery to have his replacement at the tower by noon.

On Tuesday, August 28, 1973, Don wrote in the logbook, "Today is my last day here. Whoever reads this I would like to wish the best and hope that they enjoy Middle Sister to the fullest extent as I believe I have." During our last soggy, cold days on Middle Sister, Don and I had reminisced about our unforgettable experiences as U.S. Forest Service fire lookouts. But over the years we did forget. Neither of us remembers driving away from Middle Sister. I took no photographs to mark the event. And neither of us remembers if we looked back.

Don stopped at Hoyt Flat to relinquish duty. The station overflowed with forest workers taking advantage of the foul weather to do their paperwork. Sentiments of "sorry to see you go," "you did a great job," and "good luck in Indiana" bounced around the office. Don signed his papers and then cleared his throat. He told the group how his boyhood dream of being a fire lookout in the great Northwest forests had come true. He expressed his luck at being on Dunn Peak. On any other lookout, he might never have learned of the Big Burn of 1910. On Middle Sister he'd spotted fires and been locked in the forest. He was closing this chapter of his life and moving on to a new adventure in the seminary. It was time for other dreamers to follow their star to the top of Middle Sister Peak, to experience life on a fire lookout. Don bade the group goodbye and wished them good luck. The last lookout on Dunn Peak strode out of the Avery ranger station to a chorus of fond farewells.

Years later Don acquired a photocopy of Middle Sister's 1973 "Daily Log and Diary—Dispatchers, Lookouts and Other Semifixed Guards." His copy ends on the day his replacement logged in at noon. The replacement called in a fire on Bear Skull and recorded that the fire crew arrived and pronounced it small. The BI rose slightly to 198. Don and I know nothing more of what happened on Middle Sister Peak Lookout after August 28 that summer.

Beginning in 1990 Middle Sister Peak Lookout was staffed by volunteers. The lookout was placed on the National Historic Lookout Register, number US151, ID10, on October 2, 1995.

PART III
BETWEEN
MOUNTAINS

The Hammond Family, 2014 (left to right): Jason, Don, Nancy, and Neil

18

INDIANA, IDAHO, PENNSYLVANIA, AND WASHINGTON

When I was young I dreamed of traveling to Mars. Each turn of a page in my pop-up book, titled "The Jolly Jump-Ups Journey through Space," opened a three-dimensional scene of the Jump-Up family traveling in their spaceship to the Red Planet. I imagined that one day such a journey could be possible. I hoped that one day it would be me flying through space.

Don and I faced a future living in the in-between, the interim. We had lived in the east and the west—now we'd live in the Midwest. We faced big adjustments between lookout life and life in a metropolis, between being a couple and becoming parents, and between a home we loved and not knowing where our next home would be.

Two weeks after we arrived in Indiana, Don was hired as a student pastor in a small town two hours south of Indianapolis. We happily moved into the parsonage next door to the church. The only jobs in town were at a small shoe factory, but they wouldn't hire me because I was five months pregnant. We'd have to manage on Don's $90-a-week salary plus the few months of eligibility he had left on his GI Bill.

Don couldn't commute four hours a day to classes. He stayed in a seminary dorm. We couldn't afford long-distance phone calls, so we didn't talk during the week. I had no friends in town. Parishioners only phoned or visited when Don was home. If I fell down and died, I'd have laid rotting in the parsonage until Don came home on Friday. I felt abandoned. I felt more isolated than I had on the lookout. I felt like I'd landed on Mars.

The seminary's winter break was nearly over. My doctor measured that I was one centimeter dilated. No way would Don miss our baby's birth. I'd taken Lamaze classes, determined to experience a natural childbirth. But I compromised out of necessity. The next morning I checked into the hospital and had my labor induced. Hours later a nurse laid a beautiful baby boy on top of my empty belly.

I worried when we brought Jason home that Misty might not accept him. Silly me. I sat on the sofa in the parsonage with Jason on my lap. Misty poked her cold nose into every open space she found in his blanket and sniffed him from head to toe. She laid her head across his chest. Jason was now her baby to protect.

That summer Don and I went to a fair fifty miles from town. I wore red-and-white checkered hip-hugger slacks and a red halter top. I carried Jason in a red backpack. Someone from town spotted us and complained about my appearance to the chairman of Don's pastoral relations committee. He confronted Don. He said we needed to buy a baby stroller. Don told him we couldn't afford one. He told Don to tell me that my outfit wasn't acceptable for the wife of their minister. Don told him if he wanted me to dress differently, he should tell me himself. He never did. The parishioners stopped having us to their houses for Sunday lunch. One man disrespectfully snipped his fingernails with clippers while Don preached. The offering declined. Don's year-end evaluation didn't go well. The council complained that he told too many stories in his sermons. They wanted more Bible. Don didn't do enough home visits. His salary might be reduced.

I couldn't take it. I told Don to bring home an *Indianapolis Star*. I intended to find a job in the want ads that paid enough so we could move into seminary housing and live together full time. Don admitted that he'd wanted to move, too, but hadn't said anything because we needed his salary to eat and the parsonage to live in. I was hired for a job posted in the want ads. Just before Jason's first birthday, we moved into one of the student-housing duplexes across the driveway from Tammy and Jerry. I ran a one-person laboratory that analyzed electroplating solutions and wastewater. I liked my job. I made friends. Jason and Misty were happy. Don preached at a small church with an outhouse near the Illinois border.

Our parsonage in Indiana, 1974

My mother called one day—she only called long distance to give me bad news. My father was in the hospital. I had no idea he'd been ill. My mother had no skill at dishonesty. I knew she was lying when she said the doctors couldn't determine what was wrong with my dad, when she said he was too sick to talk to me. She never said that he'd get better. A few days later my mother called again. My dad was dead. I was heartbroken and furious at the same time. My heart broke because I'd counted on my dad to be around to love our children like he'd loved me. My anger flared because my mother had lied to me and my dad had shut me out. If I'd known he was dying, I'd have gone right to Bethlehem to say goodbye. My parents had never hurt me like this before. I wondered if I'd done something wrong.

Don, Jason, Misty, and I drove to Bethlehem for my dad's funeral. Don parked behind the funeral home where my mother had worked. I let myself in the back door. My dad lay in his coffin in the empty viewing room. I knelt at his casket and laid my hand on his. I'd never touched a dead person before. The feel of his cold, hard hand shocked me. Grief and anger mixed in my heart and poured out in my tears.

We arrived at my mother's. It was obvious that she was weighed down with grief, but she had no tears. She was relieved to have me home. I knew then I'd done nothing wrong. My grandmother came downstairs and I introduced her to Jason. My grandfather stayed in his bedroom. Don, Jason, Misty, and I slept the next few nights at Don's parents' house, in the same bedroom he had shared with his two brothers.

The day after my dad's funeral, I drove my mother to the cemetery. She rearranged the flowers laying on his fresh grave. We stood in silence, absorbed in our thoughts. Then my mother spoke to my dad's grave, loud enough to make certain I heard. "I hope you're happy. You got what you wanted." She turned and walked to the car. I followed, wondering what she'd meant. She never said, and I never asked.

Years later I found my dad's death certificate in my mother's papers. I'd always imagined that he'd died of lung cancer or liver cirrhosis. But he'd died of kidney failure. Now I understood my mother's words at his grave. My father had decided to not undergo dialysis. I was certain he'd made her promise to never tell me that he'd chosen to die. He knew I'd have fought with everything in my power to convince him to live. My mother did her best to let me know his choice without breaking that promise. My dad had cheated all of us out of precious time to have him in our lives. My heartbreak and anger, while honest, didn't persist. What persists in my heart is the tenderness, respect, and love I have for my dad.

Don completed his course requirements for graduation four years after we'd arrived in Indianapolis. He had to pass the seminary's faculty oral exam to be ordained. A panel of professors quizzed Don. He felt bad about his responses. They asked him to come back the next day. He answered more questions. They asked him to wait outside. Don feared that he'd failed again. The faculty called him back. No one looked him in the eyes. The head of the theology department shook his head and told Don that he'd decided to pass him, but he didn't know why. Don graduated with a Master of Divinity degree in 1977. God works in mysterious ways.

Don received boatloads of advice to preach at a small church in the Midwest to build his skills. But we were homesick. We decided to return to Moscow. I laid awake with worry. We had no jobs and nowhere to live. We'd survived that before, but this time we had a child. We bought a 1968 Dodge pickup, the same color green as the Forest Service trucks on the St. Joe. Don built a tall plywood box on the back and painted it to match the truck. We piled all of our worldly goods inside. We packed a Coleman canvas cabin tent and gear in the back of our wagon so we could camp on our way back to Idaho. I followed Don's truck out of Indianapolis with Misty and Jason in the back seat of our trusty wagon. I took a long look in my rearview mirror, delighted to see Indianapolis fading away behind me.

We were thrilled to be back in our beloved Idaho. Don's ordination would take place in the church we'd attended in Moscow. We stowed our belongings in a rented locker and pitched our tent at Laird Creek campground near Moscow. We had nowhere else to live. I worried how Jason would react to living outdoors in a tent. But as long as he was with Don and me, he was happy anywhere.

On Sunday, July 17, 1977, we showered at Jerry's parents' house and dressed in our finest for Don's ordination as a minister in the Christian Church (Disciples of Christ). After the service and reception, we went back to our tent, changed into blue jeans and tee shirts, and waited. Two months later, with the nights growing chill, a community church affiliated with the denomination offered Don a job.

Their parsonage was a three-bedroom, two-bath ranch one block from the church. I sewed café curtains on my grandmother's treadle Singer and hung them on the kitchen windows. I got a part-time job at the university. We made friends in the church. We were thrilled to settle into our new home. We didn't expect that we'd feel out of place back in Idaho. Or that it would happen so soon.

A parishioner who lived across the street phoned me to complain that because I'd hung the kitchen curtains, she couldn't look inside the parsonage. Don and I had decided, now that we had a steady income, it was time to have another baby. The woman across the street complained to the church council that she'd had to learn from strangers that I was pregnant. I wasn't then, but I got pregnant a month later. I lost that baby at twelve weeks. I quit my job because I worried that the bacteria I was working with might have been the cause. Two months later I was pregnant again.

Don and I had decided that with another baby coming, we needed a car with four doors. We bought a 1979 green Datsun 810 station wagon and placed a newspaper ad to sell our trusty Opel. A young man with dreadlocks, Jesus sandals, and a tie-dyed T-shirt rang our doorbell. He was interested in buying our car. He didn't look over the engine or kick the tires. He just asked to sit in it. He sat, and he sat, and he sat some more. It started to turn dark. We began to think he might need a hot meal and a place to sleep. He rang the doorbell again. He handed Don our asking price in cash, without any haggle. Don asked if he had any questions. "No, the car has good karma," he answered. We affirmed his judgment, happy that our trusty wagon would have a new owner who appreciated it.

The church council was comprised of wealthy farmers whose families had owned large parcels of land surrounding the community for generations. The council expected their minister to acquiesce to their will, as if he were a hired farmhand. They expected Don to bring back their children and relatives who'd left the church. Instead, Don's preaching attracted new residents who were neither family nor farmers. The council disliked that Don dared to preach that the congregation only welcomed new members who were just like them. Tensions mounted. The council agreed that no uppity, inexperienced, young punk, especially an outsider from the east, was going to come into their town and rattle their traditions. Don had to go, and he had to go now! We had to be out of their parsonage by Don's last Sunday in the pulpit, in fourteen days, even though it might be months before they hired a new pastor.

Jason would start kindergarten that Thursday morning. Don and I had talked about getting a good night's sleep for the next day's excitement. But a bright full moon hung centered in our living room's picture window. We decided to stay awake for what could be our once-in-a-lifetime opportunity to watch a total lunar eclipse from indoor comfort. At 1:21:36 AM the earth's dark shadow touched the edge of the moon. At 1:21:37 AM I went into labor.

By the next morning my contractions had progressed to three minutes apart. Don helped Jason dress for school. I took a picture of him seated in the maple rocking chair where I'd nursed him as a baby. On our way to the hospital, we dropped Jason off at our retired military friend's wheat farm. I hated missing sending Jason off to his first day of school.

Don and I drove along the dirt farm road that connected with the highway. The silver harvest moon, freed from earth's shadow, hung just above the rolling Palouse hills and glistened in contrast to the ice blue sky. Stalks of golden winter wheat stood tall in the still dawn air. Later that morning our friend Martin would drive one of the giant combines to cut and gather the stalks in his field. Martin and Don and I all had a busy day ahead, reaping what we'd sown months before.

Our wagon bumped across the railroad tracks on the outskirts of town. My contractions jumped to one minute apart. I went straight into the delivery room. At 8:02 AM a nurse laid a beautiful baby boy on my empty belly. I saw tears in Don's eyes. He bent over and kissed me hard.

The next morning, back at the parsonage, I sat on the sofa with Neil on my lap. Misty pushed her cold nose into every opening on his blanket and sniffed him from head to toe. She laid her head across his chest. Now she had two boys to protect.

Martin intervened with the reluctant church council. We could stay in their parsonage until Neil was six weeks old. Don had filed his profile for the denomination's job openings, but it could take six to nine months until he was hired by another church. When our six weeks expired, our friend Jerry's caring parents provided us refuge on their farm until the new year. Weekday mornings Don drove Jason to his new kindergarten on the university campus. Then Don went to work at a grocery store produce department. His morale hit bottom the day the woman who lived across the street from the parsonage ordered him to bring her a fresher head of lettuce from the back.

Days after Christmas our new trusty wagon carried the four of us and Misty to Bethlehem through a Chicago blizzard that shut down the freeway. We all slept in the same bedroom Don had shared with his two brothers. Jason settled into his third kindergarten class at the same elementary school Don had attended. Don, Neil, Misty, and I toured the countryside during the day to stay out of my mother-in-law's way. After dinner we and the boys visited relatives and friends. And we waited for a church to call. We had nowhere else to go.

My grandparents had sold their house so they could afford care in a nursing home. My mother had moved into an apartment complex for seniors. For the first time in her life, she answered to no one but herself. Her face glowed with her newfound freedom. "I'm baking a cake for your grandfather's eighty-ninth birthday. Will you come?" my mother asked in a way that left me no choice. My grandfather and I still didn't speak. I didn't want to dredge up old hurt feelings that had settled over the years. But I knew this was important to my mother, so I agreed to go.

Don and I and our boys followed my mother into my grandparents' room at the nursing home. My grandmother smiled vacantly, hunched on the edge of her hospital bed, her face to the door. My grandfather sat erect and sharp-eyed on a chair backed into the far corner. He held his cane in front of him like a king with a sword, deigning his subjects to kneel before his throne. I kissed my sweet Grammy's cheek and sat Neil on her lap. She asked me many questions, but it was the same question repeated every two minutes: "Whose baby is this?"

Each time I forced the same answer around the lump in my throat: "That's my baby, Grammy." She gazed lovingly at her great-grandson, a stranger to her like I'd become.

Papa caught my eye and waved his cupped fingers for me to come over. Don signaled with a shrug that the decision was mine alone. But my mother raised her chin ever so slightly, an unspoken order that she expected me to walk seven paces across the polished tile floor to break the entrenched silence that had persisted between my grandfather and me since I was in high school. It had been many years since I'd let my mother tell me what to do.

I stood before my grandfather. We each swallowed our pride. I congratulated him on his birthday. He complimented me on our children. My grandfather and I spoke more polite utterances I no longer remember. Papa never moved his cane aside to make room for me to approach any closer. We never touched. My mother said she wanted a picture of Jason and Neil with their great-grandparents. I moved aside. Then we all headed to the recreation room.

We ate yellow cake on paper plates and sipped grape drink from plastic cups. It felt to me like communion, like eating bread and drinking wine in remembrance of being a family. My mother smiled at me. She whispered she was happy that Papa and I had made our peace. I felt like I'd presented her with a long overdue gift.

I never saw my grandparents again. My grandmother died in December 1980. My grandfather died just three months later, I think because, after sixty-nine years of marriage, he didn't know how to live without her.

Don accepted a call to a church near Seattle, Washington. We left Pennsylvania early in April 1980 and headed west. We rented a house with views of Mount St. Helens spewing tons of roiling volcanic ash into the air. Jason settled in at his fourth kindergarten. This congregation sat on metal folding chairs in a repurposed building originally meant to be their parsonage. We understood each other. We shared the same beliefs about equality, inclusion, and social justice. We practiced an extravagant welcome for all. We believed that God was still speaking. We shared meals and drank wine. We fit in.

For the next eleven years, our lives revolved around work, school, activities, and church. We bought a cozy three-bedroom, mid-century style ranch on a cul-de-sac two miles from the church. We felt at home. Sadly, we lost Misty to cancer.

Our boys with their great-grandparents, January 1980

A church member recommended me for a job at Boeing's Kent Space Center working on the Inertial Upper Stage (IUS) program. The IUS was a rocket that carried satellites from a Titan-34D rocket, or from the Space Shuttle, into orbit. I eventually worked for the system safety group and analyzed hazards when workers interfaced with IUS flight hardware. Instead of flying through space myself like the Jump-Up family, I got to work inside the payload bay of the shuttle to prepare the IUS for launch. My father had pushed a broom in a steel mill. My mother had pushed a vacuum cleaner in a funeral parlor. She liked to brag to her lady friends in her senior apartment building that her daughter worked with NASA astronauts on the Space Shuttle. That proved to me that, in her mind, I'd fulfilled my promise to use the education she and my dad had sacrificed to provide me. I wished I could tell my father.

I flew to Bethlehem, where my mother had been undergoing chemotherapy for several months. Her friends said my mother had been waiting for me to come home. I steeled myself for what I'd find. Cancer had stolen the woman I knew. My mother was thin and wrinkled. She leaned on a metal walker with yellow tennis balls on its feet. She let me in and went right back to sit on the couch. I sat next to her and kissed her cheek. It felt cold. We talked about memories into the night. The next morning she woke up vomiting, and I drove her to the hospital. She had surgery, then was transferred to a nursing home. I'd used almost all of my vacation and sick leave. I had to go back to work in a few days. My mother hadn't told me what she'd wanted done with her belongings. She was on so much morphine that I couldn't ask her. I packed her belongings that I wanted to keep and shipped them home. I gave other things to family who could use them. I decided to sell the rest. Her neighbors pushed to be the first to come into her apartment for the sale. They haggled for bargains. It was an ugly scene. Her friends called it breaking up housekeeping. It made me sick to do it. That night I lay awake worrying that a miracle might heal my mother, that she'd come home to find that I'd gotten rid of everything that had been hers. But she never came back to her apartment.

I wasn't ready for my mother to die. I said goodbye and flew home, knowing I'd never see her alive again. I'd never before had to do anything so difficult. Don's plane passed mine on his way to Bethlehem. He cared for my mother until the end. My mother loved Don like a son. Sometimes I thought she liked Don more than me. My mother loved God like her best friend, but she became furious with God for not letting her die. One night she got her wish.

The woman I'd known as my mother had lived a simple, quiet life. Don and I had expected her funeral to be the same. I stood at my mother's casket for more than an hour to greet all the family, friends, and neighbors who came to pay her their respects. The viewing room filled to capacity. The air buzzed with shared memories of her kindness and concern. I told my sons to pay attention to what they were seeing. I told them it matters how you treat people. I hoped my mother could see everyone who had gathered to honor her. I hoped she was watching with my dad at her side.

After eleven years Don and the congregation arrived at a fork in their road. A faction had decided it was time to move out of their renovated parsonage and erect a larger building that was recognizable as a church. They told Don they were dissatisfied with his pace at moving the project forward. They asked him to leave. He hadn't seen it coming. He was crushed and angry. He felt like he'd failed again. He found a job managing a nearby camping resort.

Tensions at home rose to such a level where we sought family counseling. The sessions helped. I realized that sending objects into space wasn't what I wanted to do with the rest of my career. I wanted to apply the hazard identification methods I'd learned in system safety to help workers stay safe and healthy. Don affirmed that he'd return to ministry after his wounds and his pride had healed. Our boys' behavior improved: they had no doubt felt neglected because of the time and energy we'd spent on our jobs. I think that since we took the time to go to counseling, it reassured them that they were the most important things in our lives.

The timing seemed right for our family to move. Jason was graduating from high school. Neil would be going into middle school. Once more we headed into the unknown. I'd been hired as an industrial hygienist at Pacific Northwest National Laboratory, located next to the Hanford Nuclear Reservation in Richland, Washington. Don went to work for a nonprofit organization. We bought a house on the edge of the desert with nothing but sagebrush and grass behind us for miles. On dark summer nights we sat in the backyard and watched planets set on the horizon. We competed to be the first to spot a satellite passing overhead. We attended a church where the minister from our college church now preached. We bought a Dalmatian puppy and named her Sheba. We settled into our new home and our new life. It felt good to be making a fresh start.

PART IV
A ONE-NIGHT
STAND, 1993

View from Middle Sister Peak Lookout

19

THE KABUKI DANCER'S SWORD

Neil was almost fourteen. He sat on the staircase at home and stretched out his right leg. He had a purple lump on his shin, about the size of a half-dollar. He said it hurt and it was getting bigger. His pediatrician Dr. "Smith" made an appointment at the hospital for an MRI that Friday.

"Your son has Ewing's sarcoma. Bring him back on Monday for a biopsy," the radiologist deadpanned with no further explanation.

My stunned brain fixated on the word sarcoma. "Cancer! How can Neil have cancer? He leaves for summer camp on Monday," I agonized aloud.

Don's defensive mode kicked in. He pushed back at the doctor. "You're not touching my son's leg. We'll take him to Children's Hospital in Seattle where they have specialists to work on him!"

"Suit yourself," the radiologist threw back at us. And he walked out the door.

It was late afternoon on Friday. We prayed that Dr. Smith hadn't left his office yet. We had one advantage in this horrible situation. In Don's job he'd come to know physicians in the area who specialized in children's medicine. A dedicated Dr. Smith answered his own phone. I listened with guarded hope as Don described Neil's diagnosis and asked for recommendations. "He'll call us back soon," Don could only whisper as he hung up. Thanks to Dr. Smith, we got an appointment at Children's Hospital early Monday.

During Sunday's service our minister called the campers forward for a prayer. I hoped Neil didn't see me leave. I couldn't bear to hear a request for a safe, happy summer adventure. I couldn't bear to think that next year, Neil might be missing from that group. Grim statistics in 1993 gave boys Neil's age a five-year survival rate of less than ten percent. I found myself next door in the backyard of the parsonage. I gulped out sobs of fear that tore through my heart. The first notes of the recessional hymn sounded. I dried my tears on my sleeve, forced my feet to carry me back to church, and pasted a smile on my face. I told Neil I'd left to pray alone. We packed Neil's camp gear in the car because, no matter his diagnosis, we wanted him to have what might be his last chance to attend summer camp.

Neil, Don, and I stood like soldier's facing a firing squad, waiting for the hospital's sliding glass door to open automatically. We stepped into a massive complex filled with sick children and terrorized parents just like us. A woman who exuded calm authority greeted us. She checked her clipboard for our names, waved over a woman with a gentle smile, and handed her a paper filled with Neil's appointments. "I'm your guide for today," she informed us. "Please tell me if there's anything I can do to help." I hoped she had a cure for Ewing's sarcoma typed on her list.

Neil walked into his first test alone. Don and I collapsed onto cushioned club chairs in the waiting room. A sad-faced woman watched a boy, about three years old, as he silently played with toys piled in the corner. The frail boy suddenly pivoted toward us. With the choreographed moves of a Japanese Kabuki dancer, he swept a silver plastic sword out from under his belt. He waved the weapon in Don's direction. "I don't think he likes you," I observed.

The sad-faced woman explained to Don, "You're wearing a coat and tie. My grandson thinks you're a doctor. He's worried you'll poke him with needles. That sword has been his only protection for the past year he's been sick." With an aching heart Don explained to the brave little boy that our son was sick, too. The Kabuki dancer slid his sword back under his belt without a word and returned to the toys.

Our guide returned often to escort us through the long day of appointments. We had to be back at 11:00 AM the next morning to hear Neil's results. She told us that Dr. "Jones" was one of the best Ewing's specialists in the country. She encouraged us, with hope in her voice, that Neil was in good hands.

Don and I attempted to make that evening as normal as possible, for Neil's sake as well as ours. Neil requested his favorite Seattle meal: fish and chips at Ivar's on Pier 54. We squeezed into the crush of summer tourists to order at the sidewalk counter and squeezed back out without dropping a single

French fry. Don and I grabbed a table along the pier that juts out into Puget Sound. Neil headed to the chain-link fence alongside the waterfront. He flipped a French fry toward a gaggle of noisy gulls circling overhead. One sharp-eyed opportunist swooped down with precise timing, snatched the fry in midair, and flew off with his reward to Neil's delight. Don and I resupplied Neil's fry bait from our own dinners. When all was carried off, we returned to the hotel for a restless night of worry.

The next morning a nurse escorted us into an examination room. Lighted panels for viewing x-rays and MRI scans filled the walls. She instructed Neil to climb onto the examination table. Don and I sat on hard, cold metal chairs. We waited for what felt like an eternity. A scuffle rose in the hallway. The door flew open. A tall doctor in a white lab coat with a stethoscope draped around his neck barged into the room. A gaggle of residents crowded in behind him. Don and I held our breath.

Dr. Jones briefly introduced himself. Like a circus juggler he threw black-and-white x-rays and scans onto the panels. One image showed Neil's entire skeleton in miniature. "See this?" Dr. Jones queried the room in general as he jabbed a finger at a long dark shadow on Neil's right tibia. "This is a stress fracture." He turned to Neil and said, "Son, you don't have cancer, you have a broken leg."

Dr. Jones gifted us with the answer we'd hoped for beyond hope. I stuttered, "Are you sure? Are you sure?" I scanned every face in the gaggle for confirmation. Heads nodded, their faces adorned with big smiles. They convinced me that I'd heard the doctor's diagnosis correctly.

"Does Neil play sports?" Dr. Jones asked.

"Track," Don replied. "He usually runs long distance, but the coach also started him on sprints. Why?"

"Pick one kind of running, Neil. Your growing bones can't handle the stress of both," Dr. Jones directed. "Go home. You're fine. Your leg will heal on its own."

We three sat in stunned silence. The gaggle departed as Dr. Jones collected the images off the lightboards. "Neil, your x-rays and MRIs will become famous," he said. He explained that the radiologist had missed an obvious indicator in his diagnosis. Dr. Jones would use Neil's images to teach other radiologists and cancer specialists to not make the same error. Then he thanked Don and me for making his day. He explained that he didn't often get to give parents good news. He disappeared out the door before we could thank him back.

Tuesday afternoon we drove Neil to summer camp, near Spokane, Washington. We hugged him goodbye and told him to have a crazy good time. Don and I had booked a room at a bed and breakfast across the Idaho border in St. Maries. If Neil's diagnosis had been different, we wanted to stay close in case we needed to retrieve him from camp. We hoped that St. Maries' gritty charm we remembered from our lookout days would work healing magic on our frazzled souls.

I found the B&B homey and relaxing. But Don had nervous energy to wear off. He suggested we spend Wednesday on the St. Joe. I was tempted, but I was exhausted. I told Don to go by himself. I'd rather stay in town and recuperate. He loaded snacks and drinks into the car and drove off. I rocked on the breezy front porch immersed in the twisted plot of a murder mystery. I sipped icy glasses of the best sauvignon blanc St. Maries had to offer.

"Telephone, Nancy," our hostess hollered out the front door. My heart jumped into my throat. Only Neil's camp director and Don had the B&B's phone number. I worried that something had gone wrong.

It was Don. He'd stopped at the Hoyt Flat ranger station to chat. A storm was coming in. They needed someone on Middle Sister, just for that night. "And I'll get paid!" Don said. "Are you OK if I do it? I never expected to be on a lookout again, especially not on Middle Sister."

What were the odds that Don would stop at Hoyt Flat and they'd need an observer on Middle Sister? I couldn't say no. I told him to have a crazy good time.

Don relieved two men from the fire crew who were in the lookout. They left to get some sleep in case the storm dropped any fires. Wind and lightning arrived as predicted after midnight. Don still remembered how to be a lookout. He circled the Firefinder and recorded the position of every ground strike. He woke at dawn, grabbed the binoculars, and paced the catwalk in search of smokes. A thin blue spiral curled from the forest floor into the chill morning air. "Hey, I found a fire!" Don hollered out to the empty mountain. He ran inside, determined the smoke's coordinates, and radioed Avery.

"You haven't lost your touch, Don," Avery radioed back. "Stay on the air until the fire crew arrives." The crew quickly extinguished the small fire. No other smokes appeared. Don's replacement arrived in the afternoon and told him he'd done a good job. Don said that was worth more to him than his pay. He arrived back in St. Maries, tired but refreshed. On Friday we retrieved Neil from camp and headed home.

We tried to resume our everyday lives, but we were still in shock. Nothing seemed ordinary anymore. We realized how fortunate we'd been compared to others in that hospital who had also hoped for good news. People asked how I felt about it all. I said it was like we'd been run over by a bus and the driver got out and said, "Just kidding!"

It took more than a year for our anger to cool toward the radiologist who'd misdiagnosed Neil. We made an appointment to talk with him. He sat in a brightly lit meeting room at a long table next to a well-dressed woman we presumed to be the hospital's attorney. She never introduced herself. Neither of them had greeted us when we walked in. Don told the radiologist that we'd come to learn if he had educated himself on the difference between Ewing's sarcoma and a stress fracture. We wanted to be sure he'd never put other parents and their children through what we'd experienced. The doctor assured us he had. The woman next to him seemed relieved. Don and I walked out without saying goodbye. And we didn't look back.

PART V
MIDDLE SISTER PEAK
LOOKOUT, 2010

Returning to Middle Sister Peak Lookout, 2010

20

WHAT WERE WE THINKING?

Rows of magnets on our refrigerator door replicate the path through the ten states that Don and I have lived in since our marriage: Pennsylvania (two times), Idaho (three times), Indiana, Washington, Maryland, Hawaii, Nebraska, Massachusetts, Michigan, and Maine. Don stayed part-time in Delaware for work. I did the same in Florida and Nevada. Before we were married Don spent two years in Virginia with the Navy. We've tallied thirty-two moves—so far. I discovered a word that describes our lifestyle: peripatetic.

Years after we'd left Middle Sister in 1973, Don admitted a secret to me. During his first weeks on the lookout, he'd sorted through questions and doubts he harbored in his heart, mind, and soul. He'd debated what it was he wanted to do for his life's work. His seminary education would begin at the end of the summer. But he'd discovered pleasure and satisfaction working in the mountains and forests. He thought maybe he should stay in Idaho and work for the Forest Service instead of going to Indiana for seminary. Through those long days isolated in the locked down St. Joe Forest, Don realized that he needed to be among people, not trees. He chose the church rather than the forest because trees don't talk.

Soon after I went to work at Hanford, Don felt the call to return to ministry. He was hired by a small United Church of Christ (UCC) congregation to preach while they searched for a permanent minister. Early Sunday mornings Don drove 110 miles from Kennewick across the desert. One Sunday as he drove, he reviewed his sermon on the ways of love. He wondered how our sons would react if he only told them about the ways of love but never spoke the words that he loved them. At the end of that service Don told the congregation that God loves them, and there is no power anywhere that can change God's love for them. As he processed out the aisle, he noticed people in tears. He realized that this congregation was starved for reassurance. He wondered whether the church at large was also in need of such a reminder. He promised himself he would never conclude a worship service without telling the congregation they are loved, and that nothing could ever change that. Don noticed that after he had delivered those words every Sunday, the congregation became more empowered and more courageous in how they carried out their faith in actions.

Now, at the end of every service, wherever he preaches, Don assures the congregation, "You are loved." It has made a difference. I noticed that when Don began the benediction, parishioners stopped putting away their hymnals and putting on their coats. They wanted to make sure they heard him say those words of assurance.

Don discovered that in coping with his past failures, he'd developed abilities to help congregations heal, recognize their strengths and weaknesses, focus on their mission in ministry, and identify the leadership skills they needed to move forward. Don realized his calling had changed from being a settled pastor to being an intentional interim minister, one who serves congregations during the time between their previous minister and their next one.

Jason had moved to attend college. Neil would be starting high school. Don had developed issues with his full-time job. I had issues at my job, too. It seemed time to move on again. A contractor I knew at Hanford also contracted with the worker safety and health group at the headquarters of the U.S. Department of Energy (DOE). He'd recommended me for an opening they had for an industrial hygienist. Don, Neil, Sheba, and I moved from Washington state to Maryland. We bought a house on a quiet cul-de-sac. Fifty-seven trees, mature oaks, maples, a few firs, and one immense tulip poplar grew in our yard. I named them "Hammond's 57 Varieties."

Despite Don's awareness that he was better suited for interim ministry, he took on a settled pastorate in a small town in Maryland. A congregant baked pies in the church's kitchen to subsidize the church's budget. He said that gave him, not Don, the authority to make major decisions for the church. Don soon returned to interim work. He ushered congregations in Maryland and Delaware through successful searches for their settled pastors.

I'd been working on a special assignment in Nevada. They offered me a transfer. Don and I missed living in the west, in the desert. I started to house shop. But I'd been at the job long enough to hear about cars in the parking lot being scratched with keys. Some people I worked with resented me because they thought I'd come from DOE headquarters to change the way they did things. Others leaned on me like I was their emotional support counselor. I told Don I had to turn down the job. He said to come right home. I thought about the golden eagle as she'd soared off the cliff near Dunn Peak. Don's unquestioning support held me up when I risked jeopardizing my career. I was happy to come back to Maryland.

Congregations in Don's settled churches had expected things of me. To some it mattered that I didn't serve on committees, or teach, or prepare communion. Don's interim congregations didn't expect much of me at all. We'd be there for two years or less. Some were in grief because their beloved pastor had retired or died. Others were in shock and angry because their minister had run off with the organist. Don's interim congregations liked that I came to church. They appreciated that I listened with sympathy and without judgement to their pain. I smiled and gave them hugs. I found myself willfully changing into what I'd avoided. I'd found my purpose as a minister's wife. It made me happy.

During our ten years in Maryland, we lived through the events of September 11, 2001. We drove past the Pentagon, still smoking days later from American Airlines Flight 77 crashing into it. From our back deck we watched three military helicopters flying back and forth from DC to Camp David, one presumably with President Bush on board. We also lived through the DC snipers. We didn't know what the snipers' car looked like, or where they'd strike next. A woman had been shot in a store parking lot. For protection we zig-zagged between parked cars, then ran for cover into the store. When we pumped gas, we used our open car door as a shield. We were ready to leave Maryland, to leave all the tension and drama behind. We prayed to return to the west. We discovered that God has a sense of humor.

In 2004, a church in Hawaii called Don to be their interim minister. He moved into their New England–colonial style parsonage alone. I had to work for three more months before I was eligible to retire. Neil decided to move to Hawaii with us. I signed my retirement papers, locked our house in Maryland, and Neil, Sheba, and I flew to Hawaii. But the leisure life of a Hawaiian beachcomber didn't suit me. I'd been offered a job to replace an Army industrial hygienist going to Afghanistan. I'd asked for one day to make my decision. That night gusty trade winds blew in from the beach through our bedroom window, ruffled my hair, and kept me awake. The more I tossed the clearer it became that I'd turn down the Army and return to Maryland to sell our house. I worried that the bottom was about to drop out of the housing market.

I flew from Hawaii to Twin Falls. We missed its sunny desert climate and its big-sky views. We could afford a nice house. Twin Falls' population of about 40,000 suited us for our life in retirement. I'd scheduled only four days before I flew from Idaho to Maryland to put our house there on the market. After every showing I told the increasingly frustrated realtor that I didn't want the house; it didn't feel like *our* house. The third night I laid awake, worried I'd have to fly back to Twin Falls to continue the hunt for our new home. I swear that as I fell asleep, I heard in my head, "I'm out here. Come find me." The next day I bought our Idaho home on a handshake with the builder. I'd never bought a house by myself before. I worried if Don would like it.

We returned to Twin Falls from Hawaii. Don commuted for two years to an interim in western Idaho, 130 miles one way. I had to find something to occupy my time. I joined a writing group. I got positive feedback on my work. In March 2009 *IDAHO Magazine* published my story about our drive from Pennsylvania to Idaho in 1970. I thought, "Hell, if I can publish a story on my first try, I can write a book."

I'd bought Ruby El Hult's *Northwest Disaster* to read more about the Great Fires of 1910. She wrote that in the spring of that year, America's most deadly avalanche had occurred in Wellington, Washington. I researched 1910's other weather-related tragedies. The year had opened with a vicious January storm off the Oregon coast that had caused the state's deadliest shipwreck. The storm system that had caused the Wellington avalanche also caused Canada's deadliest avalanche at Roger's Pass. The hot, dry summer weather that had set the conditions for the Great Fires of 1910 also caused devastating and deadly fires in Canada. Weather-related disasters of the 1910s would be the storyline for my first book.

Don completed his interim in western Idaho. Neil and Jason lived in Seattle. Sheba had succumbed to dementia. Every morning Don checked his computer for another interesting position. Four months later we locked up our house and moved to Nebraska, our twenty-sixth move. After Don's first church had fired him, we swore a solemn oath that we'd always have our own home as a backup, in case we got kicked onto the street again.

Don and I rented a one-bedroom apartment in a gated complex with a pool. I did research and worked on my book about 1910's record-setting weather-related tragedies. The few books about those events, and the few internet sites available then, focused almost entirely on the Big Burn of August 20–21. I wanted more information on the Great Fires that had burned across the western states from April to September. I wanted to know why copper miners from Butte, Montana had gone to Idaho to fight fires. I wanted to go back to the source. When it was time for Don's vacation, I suggested we go to the St. Joe, with a side trip to Butte to dig through the Butte-Silverbow Public Archives.

On our first drive to Hoyt Flat, we'd bumped along a dirt road on the south side of the river. In 2009 we drove along a macadam thoroughfare on the north side. Nine years earlier the Forest Service had consolidated the administration of the St. Joe, Coeur d'Alene, and Kaniksu National Forests under the newly named Idaho Panhandle National Forests. The combined forests cover 3.2 million acres and are managed through four ranger districts: Bonners Ferry, Sandpoint, Coeur d'Alene, and the St. Joe. The former Avery District ranger station had been modernized and expanded. Polished fire trucks and water tankers sparkled inside halogen-lighted vehicle bays in a new building behind the station. High-tech antennas and solar panels sprouted from every roof. Duplexes that looked like ski lodges housed the permanent staff within walking distance. The reception area inside the station marketed national forest promotional T-shirts, hats, and stuffed Smokey Bear toys. Posters for sale advertised the next summer's one-hundredth anniversary of the 1910 Big Burn. Don and I felt out of date and out of place.

We put on smiles and introduced ourselves to the receptionist. She introduced us to the fire control officer. Minutes into our conversation about Don's time on Dunn Peak and Middle Sister Peak Lookouts the officer walked back to his desk. He returned carrying a circular laminated map from a Firefinder. He'd just upgraded the map on Middle Sister. He'd stuck the old map under his desk until he figured out what to do with it. Would we like to have it? Would we ever! Feeling more at home, we told him more lookout stories. A quizzical look grew on the officer's face. He said no one was scheduled to staff Middle Sister next summer. Would we like to come back? It would be a volunteer position, no pay. But, he enticed, it would be the one-hundredth anniversary of the 1910 fire, as if we didn't know. Don blurted out his four-word resume for the job, "I'm available and experienced."

Driving back to Nebraska, Don bounced in his seat like a kid who'd scarfed down all his candy on Halloween night. Neither of us had imagined we'd ever live and work on a fire lookout tower again, let alone in Idaho, and especially not on Middle Sister. Don told anyone who'd listen that we were going back to the same lookout where we'd spent the summer of 1973. We were in our twenties then, now we were in our sixties. We'd be forty-five miles from town on a mountain nearly seven thousand feet in altitude and living thirty feet off the ground. Listeners responded with mixed curiosity and derision. "You two enjoy your amenities. Yet you're choosing to live off the grid in the wilds of Idaho? Without pay? At your age! Why?"

Why not, Don and I agreed. We wanted to go back because we could. We had the time, the resources, and almost a year to get in shape. As Mrs. Funk had taught me in high school Latin, *tempus fugit*—time flies. I used to laugh at my mother when she told me that time goes by faster when you're old. Every night I worry that I won't wake up the next morning. I listen to my blood rhythmically pulsing through my ear pressed against my pillow. I pray the heartbeat I hear isn't my last. I wonder if I'll experience anything when it is. Or will it be a permanent lights-out nothingness like when the anesthesia kicks in on your way to the operating room? I don't want it to be over yet. There's so much more I want to do, to see, to learn. So much more I want to share with Don. We've talked about who'll go first. We promised that the one left behind won't throw time away on grief, won't miss another chance at love or companionship. Tick tock. Every day our *tempus* seemed to *fugit* a little faster.

Don would soon complete his interim in Nebraska. The church's settled pastor would arrive a few weeks before we were scheduled to be on Middle Sister. I flew home ahead of Don to take care of the house and pack for the lookout. I poured a glass of chardonnay on the airplane. I took a sip and shook my head. Going back on the lookout had seemed like a good idea last summer. Now I wondered what in the hell we'd been thinking. We were old. We were out of shape. Why had we decided to live in a fourteen-foot square box without plumbing or electricity, without computers or cell phones? We had an air-conditioned, roomy new home we'd hardly lived in. I took another sip and shook my head again. No going back now. No way would Don call the St. Joe and tell them we weren't coming. I decided to be useful. I got out a pen and paper and wrote down things we'd need to take. At least this summer we could afford amenities. My list grew to ponderous proportions.

I wanted a cot that didn't sag or wobble. Instead of squeezing and sweltering in winter weight goose down mummy bags, we'd sleep in mid-weight fiberfill bags with plenty of room to stretch out our feet. We needed a shower tent, solar bags to heat water, a battery-powered shower wand, a camp stove drip coffee maker, battery-powered lanterns, an odor-free flushable portable toilet, and a fold-up propane grill. Don had to grind coffee beans every morning and I had to have a hair dryer and my curling iron. I'd buy a small gasoline-powered generator. We'd need propane tanks and cans of gasoline. I'd buy a rack that attached to the trailer hitch of Don's white 1996 Jeep Grand Cherokee to haul them. I'd scrounge thrift stores for serviceable red wine glasses, cookware, flatware, and unbreakable dishes. Don wanted a pair of sixteen-by-fifty, high-powered binoculars. We had a tripod from our old video camcorder stashed in a closet. He'd need that to steady the binoculars. I'd dig through the garage for tools and Don's chainsaw. We'd need a few cases of a decent Washington Merlot. And we'd decided that rather than buying a shotgun, we'd borrow one.

After a few more sips, my thoughts shifted to worries about our future. We had no solid plans after the lookout. Don said he'd take another interim if one looked interesting. That could take months. We'd be at home together all day. We didn't know our neighbors. They'd built houses in our development and moved in while we were gone. Our one friend in town, now a widower, wintered in Arizona. We didn't have a church. We had no hobbies. We could lie dead in the house for days until the mailbox overflowed and someone checked on us. I had my writing to keep me busy; I worried what Don would do with his free time. He talked big about trout fishing, manicuring our lawn to look like a baseball park infield, and auditing classes at the college. I wondered how he'd cope without the daily interaction with a congregation, without his weekly routine of sermon preparation. I worried he'd be under my feet, giving his opinion about how I could change things. Would he expect us to keep the same divisions of labor? Would he be willing to reset our balance? I emptied my glass and decided to stop worrying. Don and I had managed to stay together this long. I expected we'd survive another summer on the lookout. And I expected we'd find things to do to keep us occupied when we came back home. We always did.

Don loaded our belongings from the Nebraska apartment into a U-Haul truck and pulled his Jeep on a trailer behind. He didn't need a map. He knew the route out I-80 to Twin Falls by heart. It was the same route he'd driven in 1970 and many times after that on our visits to Pennsylvania. Don unloaded the furniture and boxes into our garage. They'd sit there until we needed them for his next interim. He reviewed my list for the lookout and added things I hadn't thought of: a griddle for huckleberry pancakes, an Idaho and an American flag, a coffee thermos, and fun games to entertain us at night.

Closing our house this time wasn't as simple as turning my key in the front-door lock. We scheduled yard care and rerouted our mail. We reprogramed the digital thermostat and the irrigation control, adjusted the water heaters, plugged lamps into timers, and laid plastic sheets over the furniture. We emptied the refrigerator and filled coolers with food for the lookout. Don and I conducted our standard, full-house, double-check walk-through. I shut the garage door with the remote. No neighbors lived on the empty lots around us to watch the house. I activated the alarm system. We hadn't spent much time in our new home, but I'd grown attached. It troubled me to leave it again to go on the lookout.

Food, clothes, gadgets, and creature comforts filled every inch of my paprika-red, 1999 Dodge Durango with a black bra on its hood. I depressed the button on my new walkie-talkie and radioed Don to head 'em up. "Move 'em out" he replied. I followed behind his Jeep. My car was so full that I couldn't see out my back window. We turned right at the corner to start our 550-mile trek to Middle Sister Peak Lookout. I gave our home a hope-to-see-you-soon glance out the passenger window. I wished I had another Dalmatian for company. We stopped for the night in Moscow and shared dinner with our seminary friends, Jerry and Tammy.

The next day Don used a garden hose on the front lawn at Hoyt Flat to fill a dozen 5.8-gallon, plastic-lined cardboard containers with built-in plastic pour spouts. He loaded the containers onto the work crew chief's truck because neither of our cars had an extra inch of space to squeeze them in. Every road-blocking snowbank had melted weeks earlier. We went straight up to the lookout. For the third time Don and I followed a Forest Service pickup, white this time, to our mountaintop summer home. I was 38 years older than I'd been on Dunn Peak. I'd lived a sedentary life. I had a bad case of middle-age spread. I hoped I'd make it home alive.

I used to enjoy the open panoramas to neighboring ridges along Bluff Creek Road. Tall, spindly regrowth conifers had filled in the clear-cuts and shut out the views. We didn't pass a single logging truck. I'd requested my traditional rest stop at the Avery-Timber Creek intersection. I didn't recognize my bluebird corner. Knee-high trees that had hidden in the clear-cut's underbrush now towered more than forty feet tall. The crowded monoculture tree plantation blocked out any hope of spotting a bluebird, if any survived in that artificial environment.

Don at the Little Sister Lookout road sign

My bluebird corner with replanted trees

A brown metal sign at the intersection renamed the Avery-Timber Creek Road as Bluff Creek Saddle. The sign incorrectly identified Middle Sister Peak Lookout as Little Sister. The spring where Don had filled our water cans had been dismantled and had disappeared into the undergrowth. I worried how far we'd have to go to get water. The road to the lookout remained unchanged. But even in my Durango, the rocky climb felt rougher. Maybe it was my old bones. In 1972 Dunn Peak Lookout had been move-in ready. In 1973 Middle Sister Peak Lookout had been a dark, shuttered haven for pack rats. In 2010 we arrived to find a remodeling project still in progress.

I noticed a different sign posted at the bottom of the lookout's stairs. This one read:

Property of THE UNITED STATES. All persons are prohibited under penalty of the Law from committing trespass. REWARD for information leading to arrest and conviction of any person so charged. Particulars available from the Forest Supervisor.

I worried what had changed on the St. Joe to require such a threatening warning.

Don and the work crew chief each hauled one 48.5-pound box of water up the stairs. Don would have to drive 10 miles to refill the containers at Mammoth Springs campground. Paint cans and scraps of sawed lumber littered the catwalk. The taller railings, modified to comply with OSHA standards, smelled of fresh paint. The crew chief ushered us into the cab. I heaved a sigh of relief. The inside was clean and orderly. The stove and refrigerator were in place and running. Then the crew chief surprised us. He announced he and his crew would be back first thing in the morning to finish the railings and repair the shutters. He turned and left without a goodbye.

Don and I had been young Pennsylvania-preppy, wannabe forest dwellers our first summer as lookouts on Dunn Peak. Our second summer on Middle Sister Peak Lookout, we were senior citizens from south Idaho trying to recapture our youth. I think we'd changed more over the years than the lookout had. The bed was the same. The wooden dining table, the bench stowed underneath, and the small footstool looked familiar. The Osborne Firefinder had its up-to-date map. An eight-inch-long handheld radio had replaced the clunky shelf-top Motorola. There were two cabinets instead of one. Their tops were covered with green oil cloth. The stove looked new. A small propane refrigerator/freezer with exposed insulation looked like it had been ripped out of an RV. White, plastic mini-blinds hung on most windows. Two dilapidated office chairs rolled on four casters (not five as OSHA recommends). A simple wooden stool with Sister LO stenciled on top in red paint, a metal flip-top trash can, a pot rack attached to the ceiling, and a three-shelf metal and wood kitchen cart completed the furnishings. Outside, a solar panel and several antennae sat on the roof. A counterweight hung from the catwalk's trap door. We examined the view and heaved another sigh of relief. No fires had marred its beauty.

Don and I had twenty-seven moves under our belts. We'd organized everything we needed for our first night on the lookout, and for breakfast the next morning, at the back end of my Durango. We unloaded a cooler, food, dishes, pots and pans, the coffee maker, bedding, outhouse supplies, and suitcases into a huge pile at the foot of the stairs. Don and I were out of shape. We weren't acclimated to life at nearly seven thousand feet in elevation. We groaned at the memory of hauling our belongings up forty-two steps to the catwalk. Don remembered the pulley he'd used to lift the water cans. He looked to the catwalk and moaned. The pulley was gone. The wooden arm attached to the roof had been sawed off. Don devised a work-around. He dropped a rope through the railing. I loaded our things into a heavy-duty shopping bag we'd brought and tied the rope around the handles. Don hauled the bag thirty feet to the catwalk. In short order we'd lifted our necessities. It took four more days to unload our cars. It took ten days to arrange and rearrange everything before it found the place where it functioned best for our return to lookout living.

The next morning Don radioed his check-in to Coeur d'Alene instead of Avery. He had no competition for airtime. Middle Sister was the only staffed lookout on the forest. He still recorded air patrol's check-ins. This responsibility was one reason Middle Sister Peak Lookout had stayed open. Don conducted his first patrol around the catwalk. He hollered in through the window that the air looked clearer. He credited the EPA's air quality regulations. He scanned the 360-degree swath of terrain with his high-powered binoculars to reacquaint himself with the topography and the names of landmarks. He noticed that at least one old top railing had been reused, because it had flag holders screwed on. He ran to the car to grab our flags and hollered, "Three trucks driving in on the north fork, Nance. Put on more coffee." The crew chief invited himself onto the tower without a hello. He scrutinized the unfurled blue Idaho state flag as if it were a subversive banner. We took heart that he recognized the

Moving in

Settled in

American flag. Don walked past him toting a case of wine, not trusting such precious cargo to his jerry-rigged lift system. The chief gave the wine the same judgmental look he'd given the flag. Don and I whispered that the shotgun should stay in the car until he left.

The young men on the crew climbed the stairs without offering to carry any of our gear piled at the bottom and got to work. The crew chief's demeanor softened with a mug of freshly brewed French roast in his hand. He apologized that they hadn't finished their work before we arrived. The weather hadn't cooperated. The crew hammered and sawed and painted for two busy, noisy days. They finished the railings, repaired the shutters, and carried down their supplies. The chief walked into the cab to say goodbye. He handed Don a tub of caulk and a putty knife. He said he figured Don would have plenty of free time to finish caulking the windows. Soon we were alone, and it was quiet. Don and I wondered, once again, what this summer would bring.

Lookout living

21

SUMMERTIME ... AND
THE LIVIN' AIN'T EASY

Our first Sunday back on Middle Sister we listened to Garrison Keillor on our transistor. He reminisced about his grandparents' life on their farm in Lake Wobegon—no electricity, water from a pump, to bed at dusk, and up at dawn. Lookout life is much the same. No matter that Don and I had lived on an isolated fire lookout twice before, it still surprised us how quickly we missed the amenities of modern life.

A four-outlet power strip, connected to an electrical cord, connected to an AC/DC converter, attached to a twelve-volt storage battery charged by a solar panel on the roof, powered the refrigerator. Every night Don plugged his coffee grinder into the power strip, ground a measure of beans, and prepared the stove-top drip coffeemaker. Every morning he jumped out of bed, lit the propane burner under the coffeemaker with a match, and jumped back into his warm sleeping bag to wait. The coffee's bracing tang mingled with the chill, pine-scented air that had seeped into the lookout overnight. Cozy fires in Dunn Peak's wood stove had warmed us on cold mornings with temperatures in the thirties. The only way to stop shivering on Middle Sister was to turn the stove burners on full blast, pile on layers of clothes, and hug a steaming mug of coffee.

Daily chores were an imperative. If we wanted to eat, we had to cook. The closest place to grab a sandwich was the fly-fishing store in Avery, forty-seven miles one way. It was eighty-three miles to eat a hot dinner served by a waitress in St. Maries. For breakfast I fixed oatmeal and toast, huckleberry pancakes and bacon, or a ham and cheese omelet. A hearty breakfast lasted us, with snacks, until an early dinner. That way we had to wash dishes only twice a day. We hated washing dishes, but dirty dishes attracted ants. Don scraped the dishes with a rubber spatula. I wiped off any remaining food with a wet paper towel. We named this system "goop-ragging." A thorough goop-ragging meant we could wash all the glasses, plates, silverware, lids, pots, and pans, in that order, with one basin of soapy water. Don filled a pot with water and heated it to boiling. He divided the hot water between two plastic basins set on the table. I added dish soap to the first basin. Don added cold water one splash at a time until I could tolerate putting my hands in. We washed and rinsed the dishes, dried them, put them away, wiped the stove, table, and counters, and hung the towels outside to dry on a cotton clothesline. One evening after dinner we'd left a bag of garbage on the catwalk. I stepped out of the cab and a rat scurried along the wall and over the edge. After that, the garbage went into the cans in the cubicle immediately after the dishes were done. Another basin that we didn't use for dishes was our bathtub and washing machine. We swept the lookout with a broom and dustpan. Don dumped my porta-potty into the outhouse. He said he worried I might go home if I had to empty the potty myself.

The cardboard water boxes gave us problems from the start. With no lift system, Don carried up one 48.5-pound box at a time to replace an empty. The water inside the uninsulated boxes matched the outside temperature. It was unpleasant to drink hot water on a hot day. The boxes had been designed for field use; to be used and disposed. They hadn't been designed to be refilled, or to last all summer. At first Don set a box on top of the cabinet with the spout pointing over the edge. We got a clean-washed floor wiping up the leak from the first failed spout. To control the leaks, we set the boxes on the counter with the spouts pointing up. It took both of us to pour until a box was half empty. Don lifted a box, turned the spout down, and held on so he could flip it if it started to leak. I pushed in the spout's control button and held it until we filled a pot or a pitcher.

After we'd hauled all our belongings into the cab over the first few days, we stank. Our body odor motivated Don to pitch our spiffy two-room shower tent. He'd decided to put it under the lookout's stairs where the ground was flat and free of sharp rocks. He tied ropes from the tent to the lookout's supporting timbers so a heavy wind wouldn't loft it over the Bitterroot Mountains into Montana. Then he drove his Jeep to Mammoth Springs to refill the empty water boxes. I stayed in the tower to take air patrol's check-ins.

Staying warm on a cold morning

Huckleberry pancakes

The pipe from the campground's well rose as high as Don's thigh. The faucet was spring-loaded. He set an empty box on the ground to fill it. More water splashed around the box than went in. He lifted the box and balanced it against his stomach with one hand. He held the faucet open with the other. He ran water into the box until it was too heavy to hold, then put it on the ground. He ran water into the second box and poured it into the first until it was full. He ran water into the second box until it was too heavy to hold, then stacked it on top of the first box. He ran water into the third box and used it to fill the second. The stack of filled boxes grew close enough to the faucet so that Don could fill the box on top without holding it. Then he hefted 11 boxes, each filled with 48.5 pounds of water, into the back of the Jeep. He needed a better system.

Don also filled the black, plastic solar water-heater bags. Back at the lookout we laid them on the Jeep's hood. I put towels, soap, shampoo, and conditioner in the shower tent. We stripped to robes and flip-flops. We smiled in anticipation of a luxurious, hot shower. But the sun disappeared behind heavy clouds. We didn't know how much propane the remodeling crew had used, but we decided it was worth burning every molecule left in the tank to heat enough water for two showers.

Don grabbed two potholders and toted down the soup pot full of hot water. I carried an empty pot. He poured hot water into the empty pot, mixed in cold water from a box at the bottom of the stairs to a tolerable temperature, and poured the mix into the shower wand's pump bag. The lookout's rough side-support timber was a little less than three feet off the ground. Don easily clambered over. I handed him the shower bag and he carried it into the tent. I grabbed the timber, threw my right leg over, hefted myself onto the timber, and straightened up. My feet swung inches above the ground. I didn't have enough strength to swing my left leg over. Sharp splinters poked into my unprotected crotch. "Help, I'm stuck!" I hollered. Don charged to my rescue and carefully maneuvered me off my rough perch. Soothing hot water coursed over my shampooed head and soapy body, calming me with a brief but rejuvenating rinse. By the time I stepped out to dry off, Don had secured heavy plastic around the offending timber with duct tape. He'd laid a large flat steppingstone on each side of the timber so I could climb over with ease. I air-dried myself on Middle Sister's highest outcrop while Don showered.

Bath time

I had to laugh at how ridiculous I must have looked. I was a plump, saggy sixty-one year old who hadn't exercised in years. I sat naked on a beach towel decorated with dolphins and turtles swimming through swirly blue waves. Years earlier I'd spread this towel on soft, white-sand Hawaiian beaches. Now I'd folded it onto Middle Sister's hard, gray, granite summit to cushion my ample rear end. I combed my fingers through my hair to fluff it dry. I circled my arms around my doubled-up legs and rocked my head on my knees. I contemplated how in the hell two overweight, sedentary, set-in-their-ways hardheads would survive an entire summer squeezed together in a box with windows for walls that hadn't expanded one atom from the fourteen feet four inches by fourteen feet two inches it had measured thirty-seven years earlier. I had to hike uphill two city blocks from the outhouse, then climb thirty feet to the cab. I decided that by the end of the summer, I'd be thinner and fitter, filing for divorce, or dead from a heart attack.

Climbing the lookout's forty-two steep stairs had shown me that I wasn't as flexible as I used to be. The first day I struggled to make it to the third landing without a rest. I negotiated the final flight one step at a time like a tubby toddler. I placed both feet sideways to fit on the narrow step, used the handrail to help pull myself to the next step, then paused to catch my breath. My Achilles tendons were so tight that I also had to go down that steep flight one step at a time. But I made the effort and I improved. I promised myself a party when I could walk from the outhouse and climb to the catwalk without stopping to catch my breath. Three weeks later I shopped in St. Maries for my celebration. I could only buy as much refrigerated or frozen food that would fit in our two large coolers alongside a bag of ice. When the ice melted all the food left in the coolers needed to fit into the tiny refrigerator. I bought king crab legs, a lemon meringue pie, and a bottle of the store's best sauvignon blanc for my party. I also bought a large, insulated water cooler with a durable spout, and the widest heavy-duty funnel I could find to make it easier for Don to fill the water boxes.

A bizarre problem had exposed itself on our first night. A bright light, like a beacon from an airport control tower, revolved from behind West Sister and split the night. The light was below the lookout, so it didn't flash through the windows. The next morning Don pointed his high-powered binoculars in the light's direction. He spotted a large, brown, mushroom-shaped structure set on a square concrete base. Every forest worker and local visitor we asked about the complex said it had been rumored during construction that it was an Air Force listening station. Don and I decided to test the rumor. We'd heard that

Filling water cartons at Mammoth Springs campground

listening satellites were programmed to identify specific words. We salted our conversations with words like Moscow and Russia and the Air Force. We joked about being spied on.

One afternoon a plain gray sedan parked under the lookout. Two exceptionally fit men in their early thirties climbed out. Don talked with the men from the catwalk and decided they seemed okay. He invited them into the tower. The clean-shaven, buzz-cut duo sported aviator sunglasses, collared golf shirts tucked into belted blue jeans pressed with a crease, and mirror shined lace-up black shoes with thick rubber soles. When I'd worked for spacecraft integration, Air Force officers who came to meetings for classified IUS launches sometimes wore civilian clothes instead of their uniforms. They dressed exactly like these two men, and they wore the same shoes. I couldn't know for sure, but I suspected these men had come from the listening station to check us out.

The well-spoken visitors examined every detail inside the lookout. Instead of the usual questions about fires, they asked polite but probing questions about Don and me. We asked questions about them in return. They gave us vague answers. After about fifteen minutes the odd pair thanked us for the tour and headed for the door. But Don had one last question before he'd let them leave. "If you're headed back through Avery, would you do us a favor?" The men in shiny black shoes drove off, never to return, with three bags of our garbage in the trunk of their gray sedan. I wondered if they would search through the bags. Don and I never salted our conversations with provocative language again.

A Low fire danger rating gave us long afternoons with nothing to do but occupy ourselves with being "occupied." Don relaxed on the bed and scrutinized the sky beyond his feet for signs of smoke. I worked crossword puzzles at the table. He took long walks. I stretched out on the bed and read murder mysteries. We surveyed our food supply and negotiated our dinner menu. One night we decided on roast chicken with mushroom gravy, canned green beans, and instant mashed potatoes. The crew chief had told us that the oven burner ignited electrically. I plugged in the cord and turned the dial to 350 degrees. Blue flames rose with a familiar whoosh. I opened the door to put in the chicken. The oven was cold. Don concluded that the storage battery had enough power to ignite the burner, but not enough to sustain the on-off cycles to maintain the temperature. Don was so hungry for roast chicken that he decided to connect the oven to our generator. He tinkered for over an hour. He made more trips up and down the stairs than I could count. But he succeeded. Don sipped a well-earned glass of wine while the chicken roasted.

Staying occupied

After dinner and the dishes, Don arranged my broad-brimmed hat over the battery-powered lantern to tamp the glare. He poured wine and dealt the cards for a game of UNO. The formal, polite structure of cribbage no longer appealed to us. We wanted a fast-paced game that made us laugh. I wanted a game where I didn't have to count to fifteen on my fingers.

Dinner time

Sunset

A game of UNO

When the games were over, Don and I danced a tightly choreographed bedtime routine. The extra cabinet occupied more space, so my cot wouldn't fit next to the bed like it had. The only place it would fit, and not interfere with Don's morning routine, was in the narrow space between the Firefinder podium and the table. I hated being jammed in there, but I could sleep late, shielded from the bright morning sun. Don and I rolled the office chairs back from the table. We dragged out the bench and my cot from underneath. We shoved the bench back under the table. I unfolded my cot and inserted the crossbar for tension. Don lifted my bedding off the top of his bed. I arranged it on my cot to suit me. Don edged my cot into the gap from one end. I pulled from the other end, walking backwards. We moved carefully so my blanket didn't fall off my slick sleeping bag onto the floor. Don and I high-fived our flawless performance, changed into our pajamas, and exited onto the catwalk.

Don scanned his high-powered spotlight across the forest to assure no critters lurked about. He double-checked the bolted hatch. The OSHA-code railings were taller and the openings narrower, so he had to be more flexible when he relieved himself. On pleasant nights I lingered on my odor-free porta-potty's comfortable seat, overwhelmed by the beauty of the nighttime sky. Then I tiptoed inside.

Don falls asleep in the snap of two fingers. I sometimes lay awake for hours. If I shifted my head to quiet Don's snoring percussion, my blanket or pillow slid onto the floor. By the time I unzipped my sleeping bag, grabbed my bedding off the floor, laid it back on, and zipped the bag without snagging it or knocking everything back on the floor, I was wide awake again. I'd lay on my back and gaze out the windows into the endless black space studded with strobing stars, silvery planets, and swirling nebulas. I pondered the purpose of my infinitesimal presence in this ever-expanding cosmos. I rearranged my body, pajamas, and pillow until I achieved the perfect position without any annoying wrinkles, and hoped my wandering mind would submit to sleep. When my mother was in the hospital for cancer surgery, I discovered that I'd come by this quirk honestly. She'd fuss and fidget until the bed-maker nurse had smoothed every wrinkle from her gown and bedding. Then she'd be content and quiet for hours, lost in her thoughts. Knowing this, I straightened and tucked the satin sheets in her coffin so she could rest in peace.

One night at 3:10 AM, I screamed, "I've been shot!" The spring-loaded tension bar had exploded off my cot. It took almost an hour to pull out my cot, reset the bar, and put everything back in place. Every time the tension bar detonated after that, I spent the rest of the night on a saggy bed. Neither of us wanted to stand in the cold to fix it. I couldn't complain because I'd chosen that miserable cot myself.

The weather warmed and a familiar problem returned. The winged ants were back. But this summer their numbers were fewer. We could keep the windows open on the shady side of the tower and we could use the stairs without getting bombarded. And the exhaust pipe in the corner had been removed. Evening breezes still swept the dead males off the catwalk. But the trees west of the tower were taller and closer together and blocked the setting sun. There were no rainbow clouds this summer as they blew away.

Winged ants

Don and I had developed communication shortcuts over the years that served us well in our busy, social lifestyle—some as simple as a word or a glance. If a conversation edged toward a controversial topic, we'd exchange smiles or raised eyebrows. Smiles meant we'd enter the fray. Raised eyebrows said to keep our opinions to ourselves. At the start of our relationship, we'd agreed to call each other by name, not honey or dear. If one of us used that term it meant to change the subject, or it was time to leave.

After only a few days of living nose-to-nose in a box with glass walls, we found ourselves wrangling over who sat in the more comfortable chair, who chose classical music or classic rock on the transistor, or who took their afternoon nap first. We didn't have other people, or our valued elbow room, or our creature comforts to distract us. Our small grievances quickly grew large. We didn't relish being locked in stony silence or in a childish tug-of-war over who ruled the roost. We aired our frustrations over a glass of wine. We agreed to speak up when something bothered us. We agreed to not get angry when we heard the problem. We agreed to abide by our compromises. Neither of us wanted to regret coming back to Middle Sister Peak Lookout.

When I required time alone, but wanted to stay close to the tower, I'd walk across to the drop-off that faces East Sister. I called it my contemplation corner. There I'd stand and breathe. I'd look and listen. Once, sharp barks and menacing growls raged for minutes from the valley below, then suddenly fell quiet. I guessed that a coyote or wolf or feral dog had stood its ground against an enemy. The outcome remained a mystery. I'd scoot down the cliff on my rear end and sit on a smooth, sun-warmed rock. Insects I'd never seen before fed on red, yellow, white, or blue wildflowers that hugged the ground, or branched geometrically into sturdy low bushes, or swayed tall in the breeze on straight spiked stalks. A red-tailed hawk roller-coastered in thermals over my head. A hummingbird, more sound than substance, circled my hat for a landing. Glittery green with an iridescent red-striped throat, three and a half inches long, and weighing one-tenth of an ounce, Calliope hummingbirds are the smallest breeding bird in North America.

I'd use Don's high-powered binoculars to search for East Sister's resident mountain goats, barely visible as fuzzy, pink puffs against the gray, granite escarpment. I think the goats watched us, too, and noticed one evening that the lookout stood dark. We arrived back from town and our headlights illuminated two goats scrounging for treats under the tower. They bolted at our approach. I cursed that my camera sat zipped in my purse on the back seat.

Golden-mantled ground squirrels now lived under the rocks and roads around the lookout. One who burrowed near the lookout's corner post came out to pose for pictures every time I walked by. Not a single elk clattered across the shale under the lookout all summer. Instead, a lone mule deer buck with sprouting horns arrived regularly at cocktail hour. We named him Herb.

And because neither Don nor I could distinguish between the several does who sometimes joined Herb, we called them all Peaches. One of the Peaches developed a habit that unsettled me. If she was nearby when I walked to the outhouse, she'd follow me along the road, wait for me, and follow me back to the lookout like a pet dog. Having a wild creature so close made me nervous. We worried that the deer's familiarity around people might result in them falling easy prey to hunters. But no yelling or shooing chased them off.

My contemplation corner

Idaho hunters we knew hunted deer and elk to supplement their food supply. Don had hunted a few times with a borrowed rifle, but he couldn't bring himself to pull the trigger. A few out-of-state hunters dressed in gear fresh from a catalogue visited the lookout. They didn't ask a single question about fires. They'd come to scout the St. Joe's terrain. Don always answered their queries about game sightings with, "Nope, haven't seen a single mule deer or elk or mountain goat all summer."

A final problem arose before Don and I could enjoy our lookout life. One day the high sun angled in just right when I lifted the lid on the outhouse toilet seat. The light illuminated a pyramid of solid human waste that reached

Golden mantled ground squirrel

Herb the deer

to within a few inches of my seated rear end. I told Don we needed a honey-bucket truck to pump out the vault. That proved easier said than done. The ranger himself drove from Coeur d'Alene to inspect the outhouse. He concluded that all the liquids drained out through a crack in the concrete.

Before the crack could be repaired, a tanker truck needed to fill the vault with water to slurry the contents. Then the honey-bucket truck could pump it out. The ranger explained there were problems. The water tanker and the pump truck were so wide they might get damaged by rocks or trees sticking out along the narrow parts of the lookout road. The trucks were so heavy they could break off the road edge along a cliff and tumble over the side of the mountain. The ranger didn't know if they'd take the risk. And this was their busy season. He didn't know if they were even available. The ranger had brought water and dumped it into the vault to lower the pile. He suggested we do the same. He'd get back to us when he knew more.

Don poured precious water into the outhouse for almost three weeks. One day the sound of grinding gears rose to the lookout. It was music to our ears. Two Forest Service pickups guided a loaded water tanker as it struggled to pull itself up the narrow south fork to the outhouse. The honey-bucket truck and two more Forest Service pickups followed. A sizeable crowd of curious onlookers exited the pickups. I thought about the summer of 1973, when the St. Joe Forest had been locked down. It was obvious to me that the fire danger was Low this summer because so many firefighters had nothing more important to do than watch a honey-bucket truck pump out an outhouse vault, then eat their lunch at our open-air bistro with a view toward Montana.

Avery District firefighters lunching at Middle Sister Peak

22

I'VE LOOKED AT CLOUDS
FROM BOTH SIDES NOW

Like most human sisters, Middle, East, and West Sister Peaks display individual shape and character. Conical Middle Sister stands the tallest at 6,903 feet. High on her flanks, sheer drop-offs piled with sharp-edged boulders separate stands of conifers from open expanses of grassy alpine meadows. Her lower forests are interrupted by scattered, brown, clear-cut tracts, still barren in 2010, and still littered with rotting waste left behind by loggers who had hauled off her trees.

West Sister is a softly rounded symmetrical hump that rises 6,735 feet. Much of this peak sits exposed; her easy-to-reach forests logged off years before.

A sharp, stony backbone tops off East Sister, erect and challenging at 6,857 feet. Vertical granite cliffs break through her forests. A clearing shaped like a Valentine heart sits near the crest of her long ridge. To me East Sister exemplifies the beating heart of the St. Joe: a haven for wildlife and a treasure trove of serene beauty for people.

Subalpine firs, *Abies Lasiocarpa*, were my favorite trees on Middle Sister. The petite beauties, whose trunks grow less than one inch a year, dotted the ground near the lookout. Short branches spiked with emerald-green needles thrust out at ninety-degree angles from its light gray trunk. Clusters of ripening, dark purple pinecones stood erect on the branches and oozed tiny honey-colored balls of resin that glisten in the reflected morning sun like strings of Christmas lights. During our first summer on Middle Sister, Don had declared

Bear Grass, *Xerophyllum tenax*, his favorite wildflower. He was pleased to see that it still grew scattered across Middle Sister's steep meadows. Its showy white blooms resembled knitted caps on top of tall spindly spikes that rose from a ground-hugging cluster of grassy leaves.

Middle Sister Peak

East Sister Peak

West Sister Peak

Don and I alternated tower duty to set out alone on long walks. Or Don clipped the Forest Service radio to his belt and, switching the lead like peloton bikers, we broke through neglected overgrown trails. We spit out spider webs, wiped away blood dripping down our arms from mosquito or fly bites, and plodded forward to see what lay ahead. On each excursion we compared memories of what the St. Joe Forest had looked like thirty-seven years earlier. Sometimes I thought to myself how I had changed, too, how I'd adjusted to get through hard times inflicted on me by others, or by my own choices, or by fate.

Subalpine fir

Bear grass

For years Don had been involved in an affair that had started in Indiana. It took me a long time to recognize the signs. He'd rush out after a phone call at all hours. He'd come home with his blazer smelling of perfume and with makeup rubbed off on his shoulder. Almost every week he had meetings that lasted until ten o'clock. He went out of town alone to conferences. Once he moved into a motel, miles from home. He moved us around the country chasing after his obsession. He'd break off the relationship for months, even for a year or more. Other times he was the one who got dumped. The gut-wrenching breakups threw him into dark moods. He'd swear it was over and he would never go back. But he always did. I had to deal with my jealousy and hurt. How does a woman compete when her husband's mistress is the church?

When we lived in Maryland, I realized that our process of shouting and door slamming no longer functioned to resolve our disagreements. I'd retreat into myself to avoid the confrontations and the pain that came with them. I carried a sack inside my gut where I shoved every real or perceived unresolved issue to avoid dealing with it. As I filled the sack, the tension in my gut grew until it exploded. Every stored grievance poured out of my mouth like a torrent of whitewater raging over boulders through a narrow canyon. Don retreated from me for self-protection. I fell into a dark despair. It scared me. I had to find a way out. Something in my head told me to put my feelings on paper instead of holding them inside. I grabbed a spiral notebook and a pen. My words tumbled onto the page, almost illegible. My anger calmed as I wrote. After I inked the final period, I read the pain embodied in my words. I laid my hand across the page in grief and remorse. Sometimes quiet tears slipped down my cheeks, sometimes I sobbed and wailed. Writing helped me to vent my emotions rather than hold them inside. It helped me to deal with one issue at a time. It helped me to find a path out of my despair.

I admit there were times when I rated the men around me as possible candidates for my next husband. But none of them lit a fire in me like Don did. And none of them made the grade to cover the cost Don and I would pay for the exchange. I knew in my heart I was only looking. On our hikes on Middle Sister that summer, Don steadied me if I stumbled. If he got thirsty I handed him water. It was, as if having to depend on each other to survive in the isolated forest, we were learning to take care of each other again. I felt like we'd reaffirmed our vows to love, honor, and be faithful.

On one of his solo excursions, Don noticed an odd-looking structure, a thick sawed-off debarked tree stump surrounded by a rock pile. He said it reminded him of a memorial or a grave marker. He said the view from the spot was so stunning he understood why someone might want to spend eternity there. We inquired about the marker's origin, but no one could give us an answer until the ranger himself visited. He told us that the first lookouts on the St. Joe Forest had used telephones for communication. When the Forest Service switched to radios, they tore out the telephone lines and sawed down the poles. The ranger agreed that the stump and rock pile was a memorial—to an old technology no longer in use. Don liked his story better.

Telephone systems in national forests were an outgrowth of the Weeks Act. The massive devastation of the Great Fires of 1910 had influenced President Taft to sign the act into law on March 1, 1911. Congress gained authority to use receipts from national forests to purchase private lands near the headwaters of navigable streams and to permanently maintain the lands as national forests for their protection and the protection of the nation's water supply. Section 2 of the act provided for cooperative firefighting between the National Forest Service and the states. These cooperative efforts erected fire lookout towers across the nation and improved communication in remote areas. The Forest Service had begun constructing telephone lines in Wyoming in 1906. By 1939 Montana's Flathead Forest contained 1,675 miles of line. The concurrent emergence of short-wave and FM radio communication began to overtake the telephone systems. The Forest Service officially converted to FM radios in 1946. A few telephone lines remained in use through the mid-1950s because of uncertain radio reception in some remote areas.

Telephone pole stump

At times moisture-laden air currents raced up from the St. Joe's warm valleys and condensed into clouds in the cool mountain heights. Some days the clouds floated like wisps and fractured the sun's rays into long, arching rainbows. Other days the clouds formed thick blankets that lay heavy along the river and its streams. On those mornings Don and I looked over a white ocean laid out below us. Mountain tops poked through like dark isolated islands.

One afternoon the valley between Middle Sister and East Sister filled with clouds as the sun lowered behind the lookout. Don yelled from the catwalk for me to grab my camera and run out before it disappeared. The lookout's shadow was reflected on the cloud. A halo surrounded the shadow. It was wondrous. Don waved his arms. We laughed as the shadow did the same. The phenomenon is called a Brocken Spectre. It was described by observers in 1780 when the sun cast shadows of objects onto the misty mountainside of the Brocken, a peak in Germany's Hartz Mountains.

On clear moonless nights on Middle Sister, rocks and stones cast crisp shadows onto the ground from the starlight alone. On clear nights with a full moon, we regretted we hadn't brought sleep masks to dim the brightness. One night, light from a full moon woke me. I rubbed my eyes in doubt. I even pinched my arm to prove to myself that I was awake. A carnation pink moon shimmered outside the windows.

In August Don and I hunted for ripe, purple huckleberries. We hung buckets we'd made with a string and a plastic cup around our necks. Huckleberry bushes rarely grow next to the road for easy picking. It's a challenge to balance on a steep hillside and bend over to pick the best berries that grow under the bush's leaves. It's also a challenge to slide down the hill and not dump out your hard-won treasure. The bears left us alone that summer because they had an abundance of places to pick berries. Avery locals picked berries on the old clear-cuts. One day Don hollered that two cougars were searching the road for lunch leftovers the pickers had thrown out. The big cats disappeared into the brush before I could spot them.

After our first stormy night on Dunn Peak, I'd gained confidence that a wildly swaying lookout wouldn't blow over in howling winds. Middle Sister's fifty-six-year-old, worn, splintered support timbers still made me worry about her ability to withstand a severe windstorm. But the first time the lookout's timbers shook and the cab rocked that summer it was a calm, sunny day.

"What was that?" Don and I cried out in confused unison. I swung my head in the direction of the thunderous *ka-thunk*. A giant pair of bird feet with long, pointed talons gripped the edge of the shutter above the door. A long,

Clouds below Middle Sister

brown and white striped tail hung between them. A huge bird had tackled the lookout. I grabbed my camera. Those monstrous feet held on for only a few moments. The lookout shuddered again when the bird released its grip and flew off. The only big bird with a brown and white striped tail listed in my Idaho bird book was the osprey, an eagle-like bird that was two feet tall with a wingspan up to five and a half feet. I wish I'd seen it coming in for the attack.

A "Brocken Spectre" of Middle Sister Peak Lookout

Rainbows

Huckleberries

An osprey stops by

The second time the lookout shook and swayed that summer, the Coeur d'Alene dispatcher had alerted Don that a storm packing high winds was predicted to stall on top of Middle Sister. She attempted to cheer us with the fact that no lightning was associated with the squall. Don and I hugged and kissed and exchanged I love you's before we climbed into bed, just in case the tower blew over. The storm slammed into the lookout as suddenly and as powerfully as the osprey had. Thick clouds rolled in, and an unrelenting wind howled. The lookout creaked and rocked. I feared her old timbers would snap and plummet us onto the rocky summit in the pitch blackness. I crunched into a protective curl on my cot and prayed that we'd survive the night. I'd watched battle scenes in war movies and had tried without success to imagine the fear the soldiers experienced in the trenches, knowing their next breath could be their last. That night I feared for my own next breath.

I told Don we should go to the car to be safe. He was nervous, too, but he said if the lookout fell over, it would hit the car. We'd be done for whether we were in the cab or on the ground. I reluctantly agreed with his logic. I was surprised when the sun woke us, safe and sound. Don radioed a celebratory morning check-in. "Coeur d'Alene, I'm pleased to report that Middle Sister Peak Lookout is still on Middle Sister Peak. Middle Sister clear."

"Glad to hear you're still attached. Coeur d'Alene clear," the dispatcher replied with a chuckle.

Local Idaho and Washington media covered Avery's upcoming events on August 21, 2010, to recognize the one-hundredth anniversary of the Big Burn of the Great Fires of 1910. The reports generated a lot of vehicle traffic to our lookout. Robot-voiced global positioning systems precisely guided air-conditioned, four-wheel-drive sport utility vehicles to the lookout. Most of our visitors were eager to learn about the 1910 fires, the surrounding geography, and life on a Forest Service lookout. Visitors who drove up on ATVs, with children or dogs riding on the back, made for good company. Our longtime friends arrived with a gourmet lunch to share. A gaggle of bubbly girl scouts brightened our day. The great-grandmother who braved the climb to the top earned our admiration. And we found pleasure sharing stories with other lookouts, especially those who had staffed towers on the St. Joe. But as my dear mother had taught me, there's good and bad in any group.

Abandoned logging roads crisscrossed Middle Sister Peak's clear-cuts. Their washed-out ruts made them the domain of dirt bikes and ATVs with high clearance. Don used his binoculars to focus on the four ATVs as the drivers and one passenger parked and dismounted at the intersection of our main road with an old logging road. The crack of rifle fire shook us to our bones. Don marched into the cab and told me the men were shooting at targets across the valley. He pulled the bench next to the Firefinder, stepped up, opened the ceiling hatch, and carefully angled out the shotgun. I laid the gun on the bed. Don went back on the catwalk and wished out loud that the ATV riders would leave the mountain. Long minutes later the gunfire ceased. Don yelled that the ATVs were headed to the lookout. He came inside, loaded the shotgun, and laid it on the table, just in case there was trouble.

I opened the door and the windows facing the south fork and the parking area to better hear any conversation. Don drove the Jeep behind the trees and locked both cars and the hatch. He put on a ball cap to shade his eyes. He tucked in his shirt. He explained he wanted to look professional. He told me to stay inside. He hoped the ATV riders would think he was alone.

The four ATVs roared up the south fork in a cloud of dust. I sneaked a look as they parked facing East Sister. Large caliber rifles with scopes laid stretched across each handlebar. Each ATV, except the one toting the passenger, had an ice cooler strapped on its back. The drivers wore camouflage and military-style boots. Each had a large pistol holstered on his hip. The teenaged passenger wore jeans and cowboy boots. He packed a pistol, too. The men walked to my contemplation corner, hollered obscenities at the view, and waved their arms in emphasis. Beer sloshed out of the cans in their hands. They threw their empty cans over the cliff, turned to pull more beers from the coolers, and noticed Don on the catwalk. I turned away from the window without a sound and sat at the table out of their view.

Don welcomed the visitors in calm, even tones. One man focused on my Durango's Idaho license plate. He slurred, "Where's 2T? Where're you from?" Standard Idaho license plate designators on cars begin with a number and a letter that identify the county where the car is registered. Don said he lived in Idaho, in Twin Falls. The man asked Don what he was doing way up here from the south. He asked Don if he worked for the "gov'ment." Don said he was a volunteer fire lookout. He didn't work for the Forest Service. But, Don calmly emphasized, the lookout was Forest Service property.

A different voice, more distant, joined the conversation. "Me and the guys are checkin' the huntin'. You seen any deer or elk? Hey, kid. Don't go up them stairs. That tower belongs to the feds. I'm not afraid of Mr. Volunteer there. I got my weapon right here. I learned to use it in Afghanistan. But we don't want trouble with the feds."

I didn't need the speaker to confirm that someone was climbing the stairs. The tower vibrated with each heavy footfall. I lifted the shotgun off the table and laid it across my lap. Its weight helped to stop my legs from shaking from the adrenaline pumping through my system. I'd had one afternoon's practice at a shooting range. But I sat ready to defend my husband and myself with a borrowed weapon against drinking, heavily armed, ex-paramilitary men suspicious of the federal government.

Don attempted to build comradery. He told the men that he'd served in the Navy during Vietnam. He asked the speaker if he'd been with the Army in Afghanistan.

"Nawh, I was a contractor," he said. "Made lots more money than them gov'ment grunts. I told you to get off that tower, boy."

"Okay, I'm comin'," the younger voice confirmed.

I stared to breathe again, but the shotgun stayed on my lap.

The conversation turned back to hunting and calmed for a while. I heard the men crunch their cans, throw them down the mountain, and grab more beers from the coolers. Don suggested they slow their drinking. The Afghanistan contractor's voice challenged Don to come off the tower and tell him what to do. Don said he was going inside. He told the men to enjoy the rest of their day. He walked into the cab with his index finger over his lips, as if I needed a reminder to stay quiet. He looked out the window. The men high-fived and chorused, "We sure showed him." They mounted their ATVs and roared out the south fork waving a beer can or their middle finger in salute.

Don grabbed the shotgun off my lap and laid it on the bed. I tried to stand but my legs were like rubber. We debated what to do if they came back. Rifle fire cracked close to the lookout and made the decision for us. We feared the men could accidentally shoot someone driving up the road. Don radioed for help. Knowing that the police were on the way gave us little comfort. Anything could happen in the hours it would take for them to arrive. Don and I were still on our own.

The rifle fire ceased. We held our breath waiting to discover which direction the men would take. Don saw three ATVs heading off the mountain. We worried where the fourth one was. We paced and watched for twenty long minutes until we saw the last ATV drive off.

A Forest Service police officer and a forest ranger were the next people to arrive at Middle Sister Peak Lookout. They'd met the Shoshone County sheriff's deputy at Dismal Lake. They'd found the men asleep in their tents. Their story matched ours. The ranger assured us the men wouldn't cause us any more problems. It didn't occur to us to ask why. It took us days to decompress. It took us weeks to process how living on a lookout had changed. For us, some things had changed for the worse. The safe haven Don had sought as a boy no longer existed on Middle Sister Peak Lookout, perched on a busy road.

23

AUGUST 2010

Clear Idaho-blue skies the first two weeks in August, no rain, increased wind, and rising temperatures elevated concerns on the St. Joe Forest that we could face another fire season like the historic calamity exactly one hundred years before. Despite the dangerous conditions, the fire crew tempted fate. They wanted overtime. They begged Don to find some fires. The very next day a dry lightning strike ignited flames close to our lookout. The fire crew extinguished the easy to reach, small blaze during regular working hours with no overtime.

The young men on Avery's fire crew respected Don. They'd likely heard how he'd earned his lookout stripes during the fiery summer of 1973. But the same couldn't be said for air patrol. They seemed to regard Don as no more than a scribe to record their check-in locations, and an inexperienced volunteer to boot. Air patrol's role had been reduced to flying only when the fire danger was High or above, following a thunderstorm, or when a smoke had been spotted. Don and I saw their plane only twice that summer when it angled through our viewing area on the way to a smoke in another district. Our brief conversations with the pilot never became more familiar than the anonymous, "Middle Sister, air patrol," and, "Air patrol, Middle Sister."

Don spotted a narrow spiral of smoke rising in the five miles between the lookout and the St. Joe River. The smoke disappeared and came back three times, then disappeared altogether. Don had observed the spiral for just a few short minutes. He struggled to accurately plot the smoke's township, range, and section. He decided to radio in his best estimate of the coordinates, rather than wait for the smoke to reappear. Air patrol was already flying. They headed toward the location. A fire crew on patrol was right behind.

"Middle Sister, this is air patrol. We're over the fire. Your coordinates are off by a mile," the anonymous pilot radioed out to the forest with a discernable smirk in his voice.

"I'll double-check," Don responded, "but I think my reading is correct."

Smoke plume close to Middle Sister Peak Lookout

The challenge bounced back and forth over the airwaves until a third voice interrupted. "Middle Sister, this is fire control. We're at the fire. Your readings are right on, Don. Thanks for the good directions." Air patrol didn't respond.

Days later the fire crew drove to the lookout to present Don with a congratulatory cold beer. They said none of them could figure out how he'd zeroed in on that smoke. They said he shouldn't have been able to see it at all from the lookout. They said they'd given him a new name, Eagle Eye Don. Don hoisted his beer in salute and said, "Take that air patrol."

The first large smoke Don spotted that summer burned across the St. Joe's border in the Clearwater National Forest, more than twenty miles south of the lookout. The lightning-caused wildfire posed no danger to people or resources. It met the Forest Service's criteria to let it burn. There was nothing for Don to do but watch and report information if requested.

In 1972 and 1973 the Forest Service had operated under the 10 AM policy, which suppressed fires at all costs. Don and I understood the importance of the revised policy to let wildfires burn to maintain a healthy forest ecosystem. But we knew from experience that given certain conditions, a fire can quickly grow beyond control. We knew that fire professionals monitored the fire on the Clearwater, but it still made us nervous to watch the smoke on the horizon grow larger every day. It felt odd to know that no effort was being made to put the fire out. Cool night air pushed down the wildfire's smoke. It infiltrated north along the valleys and reached our lookout. Just as I began to worry that we'd be surrounded by smoke, the wildfire burned itself out.

Rain showers arrived on the St. Joe and lowered the fire danger below High. Don and I received permission to come off Middle Sister Peak Lookout to attend the Big Burn centennial celebration in Avery. Forest Service personnel dressed in sharply creased uniforms passed out Smokey Bear stickers to kids munching on free hot dogs. Local authors gave seminars on the Big Burn's history. The ranger dedicated a centennial memorial plaque affixed to a boulder. A young Western White pine stood behind. Don and I chatted with lookout acquaintances we'd known since our days on Dunn Peak. Everyone concurred we were grateful for the weather this year instead of the conditions that had prevailed in 1910.

I mulled over the day's events on the drive back to the lookout. I wondered if great fires could burn again. I wondered if indicators in today's economy and politics mirrored the risk factors from 1910. Were climate warning signs already in place? Were Forest Service policies, technologies, and budgets adequate to control raging wildfires? Would more dedicated firefighters lose their lives battling ferocious blazes? A counselor once advised me that I worried too much about things that would never happen. Sadly, in the coming years, headlines again proclaimed that wildfires in the west had turned from damaging to deadly. Brave firefighters and residents in the path of uncontrolled blazes again became victims.

Following passage of the Wilderness Act in 1964, the National Park Service had recognized fire as a natural ecological process. The NPS implemented its policy for "Prescribed Natural Fires" in 1968. Fires ignited by lightning or lava that posed little risk in national parks were permitted to burn for research or to benefit resources. The NPS also lit prescribed fires to reduce hazardous fuels, minimize the spread of diseases and insect pests, remove unwanted species that threatened a native ecosystem, provide forage for game, improve habitat for endangered species, recycle soil nutrients, promote plant growth, and hopefully reduce the number of extreme wildfires. The NPS policy was to light prescribed fires after careful planning and under controlled conditions that considered weather, the safety of the public and the fire staff, and the objectives of the burn.

Fire on the Clearwater National Forest viewed from Middle Sister Peak Lookout

The Forest Service had begun to introduce prescribed fires in 1974. They officially abandoned the 10 AM policy in 1978. Their "Let it Burn" policy allowed naturally caused fires to burn in designated wilderness areas to meet management objectives.

In 1978 the lightning-ignited Ouzel fire in Colorado's Rocky Mountain National Park had been monitored for more than one month. Strong winds drove the blaze toward the community of Allenspark outside the park's boundary. About five hundred firefighters were required to keep the wildfire inside the park. A review board concluded that the park's fire plan had not been properly implemented.

In 1988, nine major natural and human-caused fires burning in and around Yellowstone National Park combined to develop perilous conditions that required all the fires to be suppressed. At the same time the Canyon Creek fire in the Bob Marshall Wilderness threatened Augusta, Montana, before it too was suppressed. Prescribed natural fire programs in national parks and wilderness areas were suspended. Federal reports said that while some parks had inadequate fire management plans, the natural fire policy was sound.

On July 6, 1994, fourteen firefighters died on Storm King Mountain in Colorado's South Canyon fire. They were unable to outrun wind-driven flames one hundred feet in height. Another comprehensive review of federal wildland fire policies emphasized that the first priority of all federal wildland fire programs was firefighter and public safety.

In 2000 a prescribed fire on New Mexico's Bandelier National Monument burned more than 48,000 acres in the Santa Fe National Forest and on the Department of Energy's Los Alamos National Laboratory. The fire destroyed 255 homes in the town of Los Alamos. Causation again landed on improper implementation of the prescribed burn, plus inadequate contingency resources to suppress the fire. Another review group was convened. Two documents, one revised in 2001 and the other in 2009, named just two kinds of fires: wildfire (unplanned fire) and prescribed fire (planned fire). The documents stated that the primary responsibility for protecting private property and rural communities lay with individual property owners and local governments.

Wildfires in 2012 burned nearly ten million acres across the west. The Forest Service revised its protocols again. Wildfires would be aggressively attacked where public safety and pre-identified assets were at greatest risk and the fire could be successfully controlled in size. The service would still manage other fires as an essential ecological process and a natural change agent, considering safety first. The Forest Service announced that the decision to attack all fires that summer, while not a direct reversal of prescribed burning, did represent a departure from the practice of natural restoration. The announcement acknowledged that working within short-term fiscal restraints almost always required tough choices, such as trade-offs.

In 2013 Arizona experienced an historic drought. The state baked under triple-digit temperatures. The 20-person, elite Granite Mountain Hotshot crew had joined about 200 other firefighters to battle an uncontrolled wildfire near the tiny mountain town of Yarnell. Fifty mile per hour gusts expanded the blaze from 200 to 2,000 acres in a few hours. The wind changed direction and pushed the wildfire in the direction of the hotshots. They followed protocol and pulled foil-lined, heat-resistant tarps from their backpacks, laid face down, and covered themselves to trap cool, breathable air as the firestorm raced over them. But the tarps failed against the raging inferno and 19 hotshots died. Only the crewman moving their truck survived. From 2007 to 2016 a total of 170 wildland firefighters died during operations, 28 by entrapment.

On August 20, 2014, 104 years to the day after the start of the Big Burn, the Department of Agriculture and the Office of Management and Budget released a joint report. The report highlighted that expenses for wildland firefighting had grown from 16 percent of the Forest Service's overall budget in 1995 to 42 percent in 2014. In years when the service's base appropriation wasn't sufficient to cover the costs of fighting wildland fires, it had the authority to transfer, or "borrow," funds from non-fire activities to cover the fire suppression deficit. From 2000 to 2012, $2.7 billion had been transferred to pay for fighting wildfires. The funds came from programs whose budgets had already been cut over the previous 20 years. The shift in funds delayed or cancelled projects that would have improved the health and resilience of forests to mitigate fire potential. Congress restored only $2.3 billion of the transferred money in subsequent appropriations.

In 2018 a national disaster was declared when more than 58,000 wildfires burned more than 8.8 million acres. In California alone, 97 civilians, 1 utility worker, and 6 firefighters were reported to have lost their lives to the flames. The Omnibus Spending Package approved by Congress in 2018 made $2.25 billion available for wildfire suppression starting in fiscal year 2020. The budget would increase by $100 million each year for the bill's eight-year duration. But the fire suppression account would be funded only at the fiscal year 2015 amount of $1.011 billion. If the funding cap was exceeded, the Secretary of Agriculture must submit a report to Congress documenting aspects of the fire season, such as decision-making and cost drivers, which led to the expenditures.

In 2021 U.S. Forest Service Chief Randy Moore announced that the year's fire season posed a national crisis. More than 22,000 personnel battled more than 70 large fires burning across the nation. Chief Moore put a hold on the Service's mission to groom forest lands, at times by letting wildfires clear them. Instead, the agency would use its strained resources to help prevent small blazes from growing into uncontrollable conflagrations. A later agency statement read, "There is a misconception out there that the Forest Service has a 'let it burn' policy. We do not. Every fire has a suppression strategy ... we will continue to aggressively engage all wildfires while prioritizing the safety of our firefighters and surrounding communities."

In April 2022 two prescribed fires on the Santa Fe National Forest in New Mexico escaped and merged to become the Calf Canyon/Hermits Peak Fire, the largest and most destructive wildfire recorded in New Mexico. The blaze burned more than 340,000 acres and destroyed 903 structures. No fatalities occurred. A Forest Service report released in June stated that most, but not all, of the approved fire plan was followed. Following a four-month suspension on prescribed burns, Chief Moore required that seven recommendations be implemented nationwide to ensure that prescribed fire plans are updated with the most recent science, that key factors and conditions are evaluated the day of the fire, and that decision-makers are engaged in real time to determine whether a prescribed fire should be implemented.

The National Interagency Fire Center (NIFC), located in Boise, Idaho, reported Forest Service and Department of Interior total federal fire suppression costs for 2021 at $4.4 billion dollars, the most expensive year on record to that date and compared to the ten-year average cost of $2.4 billion.

In 1911 Forester Greeley concluded his official District One report on the 1910 fires with words that still ring true. "An analysis of the conditions leading to this tremendous destruction of government property, with a view to future betterment, is called for. The situation may be put in a nutshell. The present organization, equipment, and resources of the Forest Service ... are utterly inadequate to meet such an emergency as the climactic conditions of last summer brought upon us."

Before all the fires in District One had been extinguished, Forester Greeley had advocated to his superiors in Washington, DC, that any man who had died fighting the fires—employee or temporary—should be properly buried at government expense. He also pressed his superiors that injured firefighters should not be required to meet their own medical and hospital costs. The Agriculture Department's solicitor had told Greeley that government funds could not be used for those purposes, because nothing in Forest Service regulations or in budget allocations addressed caring for or burying firefighters. Greeley suggested that his employees subscribe to have $1.00 deducted from their pay to help cover firefighters' medical costs. The workers raised $1,700. The American Red Cross Society donated an additional $1,000. But Greeley estimated that up to $3,000 more would be needed.

Greeley himself paid to ship home many of the dead temporary firefighters whose bodies had been claimed by friends or relatives. The bodies of unclaimed Butte copper miners and other firefighters lay in temporary graves for two years after the 1910 fires. The Forest Service contracted a local undertaker to disinter fifty-three bodies near Setzer Creek and rebury them in Woodlawn Cemetery at a cost of $60.15 per corpse. Some firefighters killed at Placer Creek were interred in Wallace's Nine Mile Cemetery. The youngest firefighter, 16-year-old Val Nicholson, is buried there with his father, who reportedly died of a broken heart two weeks after his son's death.

For years after the Big Burn, St. Joe Ranger Edward Crockett Pulaski personally tended the firefighters' graves at his own expense. Not until 1921 did Greeley, then US Forester, allocate $500 to mark the graves and improve the plot. Pulaski spent $445 to install grass and a permanent granite memorial. Greeley didn't allocate further monies to maintain the graves.

When Don and I had first visited the firefighters' graves at the top of Woodlawn Cemetery, a plain wooden sign marked the circle of headstones. An American flag waved next to the memorial marker. Visitors' footsteps had trampled the path between the gravestones into a rutted track. We read the firefighters' names out loud, then scraped off some of the thick moss that encrusted the stones. We made a promise to return to the graves more often to pay our respects, to let the firefighters know they weren't forgotten.

In preparation for the Big Burn's centennial commemoration, the Forest Service had the firefighters' gravestones cleaned, a rock path laid to line the circle, and a new plaque and flag installed on the memorial. An arc of sentinel conifers casts shadows of remembrance over the gravesite.

That night on Middle Sister Peak Lookout our candlelight conversation turned toward the future. Don posed a question to me in a tone that implied he'd already decided his answer. "Tell me truthfully, Nance, do you want to come back to the lookout?"

"I don't feel safe anymore. Those ATVers hated you because you worked for the government. They scared me."

"Me too," Don agreed. "I'm glad we came back to Middle Sister, but the romance is gone. I'm done being a lookout, forever."

We felt sad, but we had no doubt this was the right choice for us. We promised to enjoy every minute on Middle Sister until it was time to go home.

One August morning we woke to a low-lying, thick, black blanket of smoke to the west. Our first summer on Middle Sister I'd had no allergic reaction to smoke from the wildfires. In Maryland, whenever Don had burned leaves or trimmings from the fifty-seven trees in our yard, I left for the mall. I got congested and coughed when I inhaled the smoke. This summer I'd hoped my allergy was to smoke from hardwoods, not from conifers. But this smoke caused every sinus in my head to clog up. The air warmed, the smoke rose and spread, and my breathing grew worse. Coeur d'Alene radioed that the fire was from Forest Service land in conditions that made it difficult to contain. It could be days before it was under control. No rain was forecast to knock down the fire or clear the air. My breathing worsened. I hated leaving Don, but I needed to get to clean air.

Once decided, my departure from Middle Sister Peak Lookout progressed quickly. Don suggested I only take my clothes and toiletries. He'd need the food and utensils. Then he decided he wouldn't use the soup pot or the baking pans. And he'd survive with paper plates and plastic utensils. He wouldn't eat my Cheerios or granola bars. I should take all the food he didn't like, and the grill, my cot, my sleeping bag, and my porta-potty. He thought he could squeeze everything else into the Jeep. That evening a fire ignited on the east side of Snow Peak and sealed my departure.

The next morning, after goodbye hugs and kisses, I drove my Durango away from Middle Sister Peak. Don stood on the south fork and waved goodbye. When he was out of sight in my rearview mirror, I didn't look back again. I parked at Hoyt Flat, ran inside, and bade everyone in the office farewell. "You're leaving? Today?" they wondered at my unannounced departure.

Woodlawn Cemetery, St. Maries, Idaho, 1994

Woodlawn Cemetery, 2010

Woodlawn Cemetery, 2010

"Yes. I'm sad to leave, but I have to go. Can't handle that smoke with my allergies. Don will stay until the fire season is over."

Just like that, I wrapped up my lookout life. I'd never again experience the joys, amazement, and challenges of life in a fire tower in the middle of a clean, green forest. I'd never again fear for my safety locked inside a forest primed to erupt into wildfire. I'd never again be a member of the team responsible for managing wildfire in our national forests. I'd never again inhabit the high world. It was time to think about my future, to get serious about writing.

On my way home I stopped to do research. I read microfiche newspaper articles at the Spokane Library on the 1910 fires. I stopped at DeBorgia and Haugan, Montana, towns burned in 1910 but still on the map. I toured the Savenac Nursery, now on the National Register of Historic Places. Home again, I parked my Durango in our garage and unpacked. I could be alone for weeks. The house was dusty, the fridge was empty, and weeds ran rampant in my flower gardens. I'd be busy until Don came home.

Leaving the lookout when I did, I missed the danger and excitement of the closest fire that summer. It burned within a mile of Middle Sister Peak Lookout. Don called in the coordinates, then drove to where he could see the base of the fire. He updated Coeur d'Alene on the fire's size and spread. He snapped photos of the growing smoke spiral, the helicopter dropping water, and the smokejumpers' parachutes. The fire was controlled by dark. Don settled in. It could be weeks until the fire season ended.

In less than a week, the 2010 fire season on the St. Joe Forest ended in August snows, like the summer of 1973 and the fires in 1910. The unseasonal cold and precipitation knocked down the fire danger. Low clouds socked in the lookout for days, and sloppy, wet snowflakes pelted the windows. Don radioed, "Coeur d'Alene dispatch, this is Middle Sister. I'm freezing and I can't see anything past the top of this mountain. My summer's over and I'm going home." The first week in September, with permission granted, Don loaded all our belongings remaining in the lookout into and onto his Jeep.

Fire on Snow Peak viewed from Middle Sister

Don completed his final task as a Middle Sister Peak Lookout with little ceremony. He sat on the toilet seat and added "& 2010" to our names he'd carved into the outhouse wall in 1973. He thought the two guys from the fire crew would lock the tower behind him, but Coeur d'Alene still wanted a presence in the lookout. Don shook their hands, wished them well, and drove off Middle Sister Peak. At the end of Bluff Creek Road, he turned right toward St. Regis, Montana and headed for home. He didn't stop at Hoyt Flat to say goodbye and he didn't look back.

After the summer of 2010 on Middle Sister, Don accepted three more calls to serve interim ministries. We locked our home and moved to Massachusetts, Michigan, and Maine. Between Michigan and Maine, we rehomed an adult Pumi, a breed of Hungarian herding dog. Every day she makes us laugh. Every day she makes us play.

Smoke plume

Helicopter water drop

Smokejumper drop

September snow on Middle Sister Peak

An editor I'd met in Massachusetts urged me to put my book on the 1910 weather disasters aside. She said I should write about our lookout experiences while I could still remember what had happened. I took her advice. I sat in parsonages at desks borrowed from parishioners and wrote about our lookout life. All told, researching and writing both books has occupied my spare time for more than fifteen years.

We're home in Idaho. Don and I did our best to not succumb to COVID-19. We were isolated and locked down again. But this time our isolation was by choice. We didn't go to church. We didn't go out to eat. We learned to shop online for groceries. When we did venture out, we wore masks. Our experiences living on lookouts helped us cope. We occupied ourselves with being occupied. Don "unretired" four times. In 2022 he became the interim minister at First Presbyterian Church in Twin Falls.

Don and I are thankful every day to have a home with elbow room and a yard with flowers, fruit trees, and a garden that require upkeep. We cook with tomatoes, peppers, and herbs from our garden. I bake with cherries, peaches, nectarines, and plums from our trees. If one works, the other works. Don mows the lawn, I tend the flower beds. He manages our finances, I write. We play Frisbee with our dog. Mother Nature provides our entertainment. Swainson's hawks hover and dive for voles, house finches swoop in for drinks at the birdbath, California quails parade across our lawn, and calliope hummingbirds dart in front of our faces for two seconds to say hello. Evenings, over a glass of wine, Don and I make plans for tomorrow. In July 2023 we celebrated our fifty-third anniversary. Don calls it a good start. We have each other to depend on—'til death do us part.

SOURCES

PREFACE

Stan Cohen and Don Miller, *The Big Burn, The Northwest's Fire of 1910.* Pictorial Histories Publishing Company. Missoula, Montana. 1978.

Sandra A. Crowell and David O. Asleson, *Up the Swiftwater, A Pictorial History of the Colorful Upper St. Joe River Country.* Museum of North Idaho. Coeur d'Alene, Idaho. 1995.

Ruby El Hult, *Northwest Disaster: Avalanche and Fire.* Binfords and Mort Publishers. Portland, Oregon. 1960.

Ray Kresek, *Fire Lookouts of the Northwest.* Ye Galleon Press. Fairfield, Washington. 1984.

CHAPTER 1

Arthur M. Borak, "The Chicago, Milwaukee, and St. Paul Railroad: Recent History of the Last Transcontinental." *Journal of Economic and Business History.* Vol. III, November 1930.

Thomas E. Burg, "History of the WI&M Railway." *Washington, Idaho & Montana Railway History Preservation Group, Inc.* https://www.wimry.org/.

Rodney A. Clark, "The Milwaukee Electrification—A Proud Era Passes." *The Milwaukee Road Magazine.* (July–August 1973): 1–12. http://milwaukeeroadarchives.com/MilwaukeeRoadMagazine/1973JulyAugust.pdf.

Jacqueline Harvey, "National Forests in Idaho—Idaho State University," 1999. https://digitalatlas.cose.isu.cdu/geog/forestry/foresmn.htm.

Henry M. Hyde, "The War with the Mountains." *The Technical World Magazine*, Vol. XII (December 1909): 349–51. Michael Sol Collection.

Ben Long, "Gold, Trees Lured Settlers to Harvard, Princeton," *Moscow-Pullman Daily News,* May 17, 1988.

"A Visit to Potlatch Evokes Memories of the Past." *Palouse Living,* May 17, 1988.

"Avery Milwaukee Railroad Station," The Idaho Heritage Trust. https://www.idahoheritage.org/assets/popups/north/n_averyrr.html.

"Big Game Hunting," USDA Forest Service, Idaho Panhandle National Forests. https://www.fs.usda.gov/activity/ipnf/recreation/hunting.

Coeur d'Alene Nat. Forest 1910, Idaho, Library of Congress. Prints and Photographs Online Catalog, Call Number LC-F81-3356 [P&P].

Historic Avery Ranger Station, St. Joe Ranger District. Avery, Idaho.

Idaho—Wallace, i.e., Wallace destroyed by forest fires, 1915, Library of Congress. Prints and Photographs Online Catalog, Call Number LOT 12352-8.

Idaho Wilderness Areas—List & Map, Mountain Journey, July 31, 2018. http://mountainjourney.com/idaho-wilderness-areas-list-map/.

Lumber Mill and Town, Potlatch Lumber Company Photograph Collection, Digital Initiatives, University of Idaho Library. https://digital.lib.uidaho.edu/digital/iiif/plcphotos/1546/full/max/0/default.jpg.

"St. Paul After Orient Trade," *Railway World*, January 15, 1909, 43–44. https://milwaukeeroadarchives.com/Construction/Railway%20Age/1909%20January%2015,%20St%20Paul%20After%20Oriental%20Traffic.%20St.%20Paul%20Merger%20Financed%20%20The_Railway_world%20--%20part%20owner%20of%20Japanese%20Steamships.pdf.

"The Extension of the Chicago, Milwaukee & St. Paul Railway to the Pacific Coast," *Scientific American*, February 20, 1909, 151–52, 156.

"The Milwaukee Road Mainline—Forum," *Trains Magazine—Online Community Form nanaimo73*, August 28, 2005. https://cs.trains.com/trn/f/507/t/44086.aspx.

United States Department of Justice Wilderness Act of 1964, updated May 12, 2015. https://www.justice.gov/enrd/wilderness-act-1964.

"Why are logs kept or stored wet before being milled?" Yahoo Answers. (Site shut down May 4, 2021.)

CHAPTER 2

Leon F. Neuenschwander, et al., "White Pine in the American West: A Vanishing Species—Can We Save It?" Department of Agriculture Forest Service. General Technical Report RMRS-GTR-35 (August 1999). https://www.fs.usda.gov/research/treesearch/4549

St. Joe Idaho Fire 1910, National Photo Company—Library of Congress. Prints and Photographs Online Catalog, Coeur d'Alene National Forest Idaho. Call No. LC=581-3356[P&P]. Reproduction No. LC-DIG-npcc-20068. https://tile.loc.gov/storage-services/service/pnp/npcc/20000/20068r.jpg.

Wallace, Idaho Destroyed by Forest Fires, 1910, National Photo Company—Library of Congress. Prints and Photographs Online Catalog, Call No. LOT 12352-8. Reproduction No. LC-USZ-100916. https://www.loc.gov/pictures/item/90715594/.

CHAPTER 3

Harry Grace, et al., "Fireman's Guide, Fire Handbook, California Region," Chapter III, U.S. Department of Agriculture Forest Service. May 9, 1956: 136–148. https:// babel.hathitrust.org/cgi/pt?id=umn.319510003935100&view=1up&seq=5.

Ray Kresek, "Osborne Facts and History," Forest Fire Lookout Association. https:// www.firelookout.org/osborne-facts.html.

Andrew J. Larson, "Introduction to the Article by Elers Koch: The Passing of the Lolo Trail," *Fire Ecology*. Vol. 12, April 2016: 1–6. https://fireecology.springeropen. com/articles/10.4996/fireecology.1201001.

Art Halverson on Baptiste Lookout, Hungry Horse Ranger District. Flathead National Forest Est. 1915–1920's. US Forest Service—Flathead National Forest. https://www. facebook.com/discovertheflathead/posts/214711947509575.

"Township and Range System," Lab 7—Topographic Maps, University of Texas, Arlington. https://www.uta.edu/paleomap/geol1435/township.htm.

CHAPTER 4

Global Ministries. Reformed Church in Hungary. https://www.globalministries.org/ reformed_church_in_hungary_1.

Lassie, "Tinderbox," Season 11, Episode 27. Aired March 21, 1965. https://www.bing. com/videos/search?q=lassie+tinder+box&docid=608047303447939083&mid=B 96FB56F12FD578E473DB96FB56F12FD578E473D&view=detail&FORM =VIRE.

"The History of Dyslexia," Learning Disabilities Resource Foundation. https://www. ldrfa.org/the-history-of-dyslexia/.

CHAPTER 5

Denny Hatch, "About the First Bank of Troy, Idaho." *Target Marketing Magazine*, July 1, 2003. https://www.adweek.com/performance-marketing/about-first-bank-troy-idaho-28882/.

CHAPTER 6

Edward A. Beals, District Editor. *Climatological Data for District No. 12, Columbia Valley*, *Monthly Weather Review*, December 1909–September 1910 (NOAA Central Library Data Imaging Project). https://library.oarcloud.noaa.gov/docs.lib/htdocs/ rescue/mwr/038/mwr-038-04-0640.pdf

Stan Cohen and Don Miller, *The Big Burn, The Northwest's Fire of 1910*. Pictorial Histories Publishing Company. Missoula, Montana. 1978.

Sandra A. Crowell and David O. Asleson, *Up the Swiftwater, A Pictorial History of the Colorful Upper St. Joe River Country*. Museum of North Idaho. Coeur d'Alene, Idaho. 1995.

Ruby El Hult, *Northwest Disaster: Avalanche and Fire*. Binfords and Mort Publishers. Portland, Oregon. 1960.

Larry S. Bradshaw, et al., *The 1978 National Fire-Danger Rating System: Technical Documentation*. USDA Forest Service, Intermountain Forest and Range Experiment Station, Ogden, Utah. General Technical Report INT-169. July 1983. https://www.sdge. com/sites/default/files/regulatory/Bradshaw%20et%20al.%201983_The%20 1978%20National%20Fire-Danger%20Rating%20System.pdf.

Arnold I. Finklin and William C. Fischer, *Weather Station Handbook—an Interagency Guide for Wildland Managers. Part 2A. Manual Weather Stations: Measurements; Instruments*. National Wildlife Coordinating Group. March 1990. http://www.novalynx.com/ manuals/nfes-2140-part2a.pdf (Accessed September 7, 2020).

Roscoe Haines, Acting Forest Supervisor. *Coeur d'Alene—Fire*. U.S. Department of Agriculture Forest Service. January 5, 1911. https://www.fs.usda.gov/Internet/ FSE_DOCUMENTS/stelprdb5194249.pdf.

JG–Park Ranger (Yosemite Valley). *Bear Series, Part One: A Bear's Sense of Smell*. Yosemite Ranger Notes. Yosemite National Park. U.S. National Park Service. https://www. nps.gov/yose/blogs/bear-series-part-one-a-bears-sense-of-smell.htm.

Rex Kamstra, *Dunn Peak Lookout*. Forest Fire Lookout Page. http://www.firelookout. com/id/dunnpk.html.

"Bears: Facts." Science Trek: Idaho Public Television. https://sciencetrek.org/ sciencetrek/topics/bears/facts.cfm.

"Black Bear Sizes." Idaho Fish and Game. Questions. https://idfg.idaho.gov/question/ black-bear-sizes.

"Losses by Forest Fires. The Fires of 1910." Annual Reports of the Department of Agriculture for the Year Ending June 30, 1911. http://1910fire.com/Fire%20 Stories/1911%20U.S.D.A.%20Report/main.htm.

"North Idaho Interagency Fire Danger Operating Plan." USDA Forest Service, State of Idaho Department of lands, Coeur d'Alene tribe, Bureau of Land Management. June 2015. https://vdocuments.mx/north-idaho-interagency-fire-danger-operating -plan-this-north-idaho-interagency.html?page=1.

Forest Service, U.S. Department of Agriculture, undated. http://fs.usda.gov/Internet/ FSE_DOCUMENTS/fsm9_021350.pdf.

"Savenac Historic Tree Nursery," Superior Ranger District, Lolo National Forest, U.S. Forest Service. https://www.fs.usda.gov/Internet/FSE_DOCUMENTS/ fsm9_021348.pdf.

"Understanding Fire Danger." U.S. National Park Service. https://www.nps.gov/ articles/understanding-fire-danger.htm.

USDA Forest Service. National Fire Danger Rating System. Francis Marion and Sumter National Forests. https://www.fs.usda.gov/detail/scnfs/home/?cid=f seprd634957.

Gary Weber, Director, Montana/Idaho North Chapter of Forest Fire Lookout Association. Email on Dunn Peak name sent to author, May 15, 2009.

Stephan Matz, Idaho Panhandle NF Heritage Manager. Email on Dunn Peak name change sent to author, May 18, 2009.

Butte Miners Detraining at Avery, Idaho, August 1910. Photo FI-1-42. The Museum of North Idaho.

Pat Grogin, Camp Cook, Avery, Idaho, August 1910. Photo FI-1-1. The Museum of North Idaho.

U.S. Forest Ranger Debit, U.S. Army Soldiers and Forest Guard, Avery, Idaho. August 1910. Photo FI-1-22. The Museum of North Idaho.

The Butte Miner. Numerous Articles. Butte Miner Company, Publisher. Butte-Silverbow Public Archives, Butte, Montana. July–September 1910.

Spokane Daily Chronicle. Numerous Articles. Chronicle Publishing Company. Spokane, Washington. May–September 1910.

Spokesman Review. Numerous Articles. Cowles Publishing Company. Spokane, Washington. July–September 1910.

Smokey Bear Licensing. Single Use, Non-Exclusive, Non-Transferable Permission Letter to Grantee Nancy Hammond. U.S. Forest Service. October 26, 2009.

"95.9 Records of Forest Service Regional Offices, 1870–1982." [Online version] Records of the Forest Service (Record Group 95) 1870–1998. National Archives of the United States. https://www.archives.gov/research/guide-fed-records/groups/095.html#95.9.1.

Wikipedia, "Great Fire of 1910." https://en.wikipedia.org/wiki/Great_Fire_of_1910.

CHAPTER 8

Stephen G. Michaud, *The Only Living Witness: The True Story of Ted Bundy.* Authorlink Press. July 1999. https://www.amazon.com/Only-Living-Witness-Serial-Killer/dp/1928704115?ref_=ast_author_dp.

"Running Out of Worries?" *TIME Magazine.* Vol. 103. No. March 4, 1974. http://content.time.com/time/magazine/article/0,9171,944756,00.html.

"Daylight Fireball of August 10, 1972." Internet Archive Wayback Machine. http://web.archive.org/web/20050120051405/www.maa.agleia.de/Comet/Other/1972.html.

Yi Chen et al., "Nesting Sites of the Carpenter Ant, *Camponotus vicinus* (Mayr) (Hymenoptera: Formicidae) in Northern Idaho." *Environmental Entomology* Vol. 31, Issue 6 (Dec 2002), 1037–42. https://doi.org/10.1603/0046-225X-31.6.1037.

CHAPTER 11

Rex Kamstra, *"Middle Sister Peak Lookout,"* Forest Fire Lookout Page. http://www.firelookout.com/id/middlesister.html.

Ray Kresek, *Fire Lookouts of the Northwest,* Ye Galleon Press. Fairfield, Washington. 1984.

A Database of Paleoecological Records from Neotoma Middens in Western North America, USGS/ NOAA North American Midden Database (version 4, June 2016). https:// geochange.er.usgs.gov/midden.

Wikipedia, "Bushy-tailed Woodrat." https://en.wikipedia.org/wiki/Bushy-tailed_woodrat.

Middle Sister Peak Lookout. National Historic Lookout Register. http://nhlr.org/ lookouts/us/id/middle-sister-peak-lookout/ (Accessed March 7, 2008 and October 30, 2019).

Pacific Northwest Fire lookout Tower Sites, Definitions. https://www.firelookout.com/lktpix. html.

CHAPTER 12

Stephan Wilkinson, "Firebombers! Flying on the Edge to Fight Fires." HistoryNet. com. *HistoryNet LLC. Aviation History.* March 2018. https://www.historynet.com/ firebombers.htm.

"Common Terms—National Fire Danger Rating System." Geographic Area Coordinating Centers. National Interagency Fire Center. https://gacc.nifc.gov/rmcc/predictive/ fuels_fire-danger/drgloss.htm.

NFDRS System Inputs and Outputs, PMS-437, Fire Danger Section, Primary System Components and Indices. https://www.nwcg.gov/publications/pms437/fire-danger/nfdrs-system-inputs-outputs.

Pocket Cards Burning Index. National Wildfire Coordinating Group. Fire Environment Committee, Fire Danger Subcommittee. https://famtest.nwcg.gov/fam-web/ pocketcards/bi.htm.

"Borate or Bentonite Fire Retardant Powder." The National Museum of Forest Service History. http://forestservicemuseum.pastperfectonline.com/webobject/ A93D09F1-9D23-4F47-8A17-550326570119.

CHAPTER 13

Bill Hawes, "The Sunshine Mine Fire: A Rescuer Remembers," *Mining History Journal,* Vol. 13, 2006. http://mininghistoryassociation.org/Journal/MHJ-v13-2006-Hawes.pdf.

Stanley M. Jarrett, et al., *Final Report of Major Mine Fire Disaster, Sunshine Mine, Sunshine Mining Company, Kellogg, Shoshone County, Idaho* (USDI, Bureau of Mines. May 2, 1972). http://cholla.mmto.org/mines/sunshine_report.pdf.

Mining Safety and Health Administration: *Mining Disasters—An Exhibition,* 1972 Sunshine Mining Company Mining Disaster, Kellogg, Idaho.

"Sunshine Mining Company, May 2, 1972–91 Killed," *Mine Accidents and Disasters,* United States Mine Rescue Association. https://usminedisasters.miningquiz.com/ saxsewell/sunshine.htm.

Alicia Warren, "Remembering Sunshine," *Times-News.* Twin Falls, Idaho. Lee Enterprises. April 11, 2010.

CHAPTER 15

Dane Vanhoozer, *9/13/17–The "10 a.m. Policy," US Forest Service and Wildfire Suppression,* Stevens Historical Research Associates. September 13, 2017. https://www.shraboise.com/2017/09/91317-10-m-policy-u-s-forest-service-wildfire-suppression/.

Hotshots: firefighting special forces, CBS Interactive Inc. 2020. https://www.cbsnews.com/pictures/hotshots-americas-most-badass-firefighters/16.

Idaho Panhandle Interagency Hotshot Crew History 1967-Present, Hotshot Crew History in America, November 2013, National Interagency Hotshot Crew Steering Committee, US Department of Agriculture Forest Service. https://gacc.nifc.gov/swcc/dc/nmsdc/documents/Crews/NMSDC_Hotshot_Crew_History_2013.pdf.

Missoula Smokejumpers, (US Department of Agriculture Forest Service). https://www.fs.usda.gov/science-technology/fire/smokejumpers/missoula.

National Smokejumper Training Guide, History of Smokejumping—Unit 1, Chapter 1, US Department of Agriculture Forest Service, 2016. https://www.fs.usda.gov/sites/default/files/media_wysiwyg/nsjtg_2016_-_combined_units_1-3signed.pdf.

80 Years of Wildland Firefighting, ArcGis StoryMaps. Esri, March 18, 2020. https://storymaps.arcgis.com/stories/381fcd4a36584aa28f9d836247d9a939.

CHAPTER 16

Dennis W Baird, Editor, *The Early Years of the Bitterroot Reserve: Major Frank Fenn Reports to Congress.* Northwest Historical Manuscript Series. University of Idaho Library, 1999. https://sbw.lib.uidaho.edu/Pages/02-complete.pdf.

Andrew Glass, "President Lincoln creates Yosemite Park, June 30, 1864," *Politico.* Politico LLC. 2018. U.S. Library of Congress. https://www.politico.com/story/2016/06/president-lincoln-creates-yosemite-park-june-30-1864-224818.

Russel T. Graham and Theresa Benavidez Jain, *Past, Present, and Future Role of Silviculture in Forest Management,* USDA Forest Service Proceedings, 2004. https://www.fs.usda.gov/research/treesearch/7207.

Rick McClure, "Washington's 'Awful Conflagration'—The Yacolt Fire of 1902," *Fire Management Today,* Winter 2005, Vol. 65, No 1. https://www.frames.gov/catalog/42957.

Gifford Pinchot, *Forest Reserves in Idaho, 1905.* Forest Service Bulletin No. 67 (Washington: Government Printing Office, U.S. Archives, U.S. Department of Agriculture).

Ted Widmer, "The Civil War's Environmental Impact," *The New York Times,* November 15, 2014. https://opinionator.blogs.nytimes.com/2014/11/15/the-civil-wars-environmental-impact.

Gerald Williams, *Chiefs of the U.S. Forest Service.* US Forest Service History. https://foresthistory.org/research-explore/us-forest-service-history/people/chiefs.

"An act to repeal timber culture laws, and for other purposes," Proceedings March 3, 1891. *Annals of Congress.* House of Representatives, 51st Congress, 2nd Session. Chapter 561. Pages 1095–103. https://web.archive.org/web/20190714162221/http:/legisworks.org:80/congress/51/session-2/chap-561.pdf.

Wikipedia, "Forest Reserve Act of 1891." https://en.wikipedia.org/wiki/Forest-Reserve-Act-of-1891.

"The Early Forest Service Organization Era (1905–1909)," U.S. Department of Agriculture Forest Service. Last updated June 9, 2008. http://npshistory.com/publications/usfs/fs-650/sec2.htm.

"The USDA Forest Service—The First Century." United States Department of Agriculture Forest Service. https://www.fs.usda.gov/sites/default/files/media/2015/06/The_USDA_Forest_Service_TheFirstCentury.pdf.

"U.S. Forest Service," United States History. Online Highways. Alicia Spooner, Editor. http://www.u-s-history.com/pages/h1602.html.

"Yale School of the Environment, History." https://environment.yale.edu/about/history.

CHAPTER 18

"History of the Disciples—Christian Church Disciples of Christ." https://disciples.org/our-identity/history-of-the-disciples.

CHAPTER 19

Santosh Valvi and Stewart J. Kellie, "Ewing Sarcoma: Focus on Medical Management," *Journal of Bone and Soft Tissue Tumors,* Vol 1, Issue 1. May–August 2015. http://www.jbstjournal.com/ewing-sarcoma-focus-on-medical-management.

"Idaho Panhandle National Forests—About the Forest," U.S. Department of Agriculture Forest Service. https://www.fs.usda.gov/main/ipnf/about-forest.

CHAPTER 22

R.C. Davis, Editor, "Weeks Act," *Encyclopedia of American Forest and Conservation History, Vol. Two.* New York: Macmillan, 1983.

Wikipedia, "Brocken Spectre." https://en.wikipedia.org/wiki/Brocken_spectre.

"Communications. Trails of the Past: Historical Overview of the Flathead National Forest, Montana, 1800-1960." *Forest History.* https://foresthistory.org/wp-content/uploads/2017/01/TRAILS-OF-THE-PAST.pdf.

CHAPTER 23

Anita Chabria and Lila Seidman, "Forest Service changes 'let-it-burn' policy following criticism from western politicians," *Los Angeles Times,* August 4, 2021. https://www.latimes.com/california/story/2021-08-04/forest-service-modifies-let-it-burn-policy.

Bill Gabbert. "US Forest Service to Resume Prescribed Fires," *Wildfire Today*. September 15, 2022. https://wildfiretoday.com/tag/report.

M. Johnson, "Wildland Fire: What is a Prescribed Fire?" U.S. National Park Service. Last updated March 19, 2020. https://www.nps.gov/articles/what-is-a-prescribed-fire.htm.

George Lobsenz, "'Let it burn' forest fire policy suspended for 1989," *UPI Archives*. May 9, 1989. https://www.upi.com/Archives/1989/05/19/Let-it-burn-forest-fire-policy-suspended-for-1989/8133611553600/ (Accessed Nov. 9, 2022).

Dennis O'Brien, "1910 Graves Nine Mile Cemetery," Email to author, October 30, 2017.

"Federal Firefighting Cost (Suppression Only) 1985–2021," National Interagency Fire Center, 2022. https://nifc.gov/fire-information/statistics/suppression-costs.

"Wildland Fire, Summary and Statistics Annual Report, 2021," National Interagency Coordination Center. https://www.nifc.gov/sites/default/files/NICC/2-Predictive%20Services/Intelligence/Annual%20Reports/2021/annual_report_0.pdf.

"NWCG Report on Wildland Firefighter Fatalities in the United States: 2007–2016," PMS 841, National Wildfire Coordinating Group, December 2017. https://www.nwcg.gov/sites/files/publications/pms841.pdf.

"Ouzel Fire, 1978," Fire History—Rocky Mountain National Park. U.S. National Park Service. Last updated September 27, 2019. https://www.nps.gov/romo/learn/fire-history.htm.

"Point Zone Protection," National Glossary of Wildland Fire, PMS 205. National Wildfire Coordinating Group. https://www.nwcg.gov/term/glossary/pointzone-protection.

"South Canyon Fire," We Will Never Forget, South Canyon Fire Committee. Glenwood Springs, CO. https://www.southcanyonfire.com/about.

"Secretary Perdue Applauds Fire Funding Fix in Omnibus," U.S. Department of Agriculture Press Release No. 0064.18. Washington, D.C. March 23, 2018. https://www.usda.gov/media/press-releases/2018/03/23/secretary-perdue-applauds-fire-funding-fix-omnibus.

"Understanding the Information Provided in the National Incident Management Situation Report," Predictive Services. National Interagency Coordination Center. National Interagency Fire Center. Updated January 9, 2017. https://www.predictiveservices.nifc.gov/intelligence/Reading_the_Situation_Report.pdf#:~:text=Understanding%20the%20Information%20Provided%20in%20the%20National%20Incident,during%20weekly%20reporting%29.%20It%20also%20reports%20non-fire%20incidents.

"Wildland Fire Policy, 2009," National Interagency Fire Center External Affairs. *Wildfire Today—Wildfire News and Opinion*. March 26, 2009. https://wildfiretoday.com/2009/04/02/wildland-fire-policy-2009.

"Wildland Fire Use," U.S. Fish and Wildlife Service: Fire Management. Last updated October 4, 2009. https://www.fws.gov/fire/what_we_do/wildland_fire_use. shtml.

Wikipedia, "2018 California Wildfires." https://en.wikipedia.org/wiki/2018_ California_wildfires.

NANCY SULE HAMMOND

BIOGRAPHY

Nancy Sule Hammond lived in U.S. Forest Service fire lookouts in the 1970s and in 2010. She also worked in system safety to prepare Space Shuttle payloads for flight, wrote and assessed worker health and safety programs, is married to a minister, and the mother of two sons. This true story of Nancy and her husband Don's determination to fulfill their dreams is her first published book.